SFX Libr

000620

G000047570

LRC
St. Francis Xavier College
Halwood Rd
London SW12 8EN

Continuum Renaissance Drama

Series Editors: Andrew Hiscock, University of Wales Bangor, UK and
Lisa Hopkins, Sheffield Hallam University, UK

Continuum Renaissance Drama offers practical and accessible introductions to the critical and performative contexts of key Elizabethan and Jacobean plays. Each guide introduces the text's critical and performance history but also provides students with an invaluable insight into the landscape of current scholarly research through a keynote essay on the state of the art and newly commissioned essays of fresh research from different critical perspectives.

Current titles:

A Midsummer Night's Dream, ed. Regina Buccola
Doctor Faustus, ed. Sarah Munson Deats
'Tis Pity She's a Whore, ed. Lisa Hopkins
Women Beware Women, ed. Andrew Hiscock

Forthcoming titles:

1 Henry IV, ed. Stephen Longstaffe
Duchess of Malfi, ed. Christina Luckyj
King Lear, ed. Andrew Hiscock and Lisa Hopkins

FHANu
ORM COL LGE
MALWOOD ROAD SW1
13/9/12 LIBRARY 12.74
620 55 / 322 JON

VOLPONE

A Critical Guide

Edited by Matthew Steggle

continuum

Continuum International Publishing Group

The Tower Building   80 Maiden Lane
11 York Road   Suite 704
London SE1 7NX   New York, NY 10038

www.continuumbooks.com

© Matthew Steggle and contributors 2011

All rights reserved. No part of this publication may be reproduced or
transmitted in any form or by any means, electronic or mechanical,
including photocopying, recording, or any information storage or
retrieval system, without prior permission in writing from the publishers.

British Library Cataloguing-in-Publication Data
A catalogue record for this book is available from the British Library.

ISBN: 978-0-8264-2495-2 (Hardback)
        978-0-8264-1153-2 (Paperback)

Library of Congress Cataloging-in-Publication Data
A catalog record for this book is available from the Library of Congress.

Typeset by Newgen Imaging Systems Pvt Ltd, Chennai, India
Printed and bound in India by Replika Press Pvt Ltd

Contents

Series Introduction

The drama of Shakespeare and his contemporaries has remained at the very heart of English curricula internationally and the pedagogic needs surrounding this body of literature have grown increasingly complex as more sophisticated resources become available to scholars, tutors and students. This series aims to offer a clear picture of the critical and performative contexts of a range of chosen texts. In addition, each volume furnishes readers with invaluable insights into the landscape of current scholarly research as well as including new pieces of research by leading critics.

This series is designed to respond to the clearly identified needs of scholars, tutors and students for volumes which will bridge the gap between accounts of previous critical developments and performance history and an acquaintance with new research initiatives related to the chosen plays. Thus, our ambition is to offer innovative and challenging Guides which will provide practical, accessible and thought-provoking analyses of Renaissance drama. Each volume is organised according to a progressive reading strategy involving introductory discussion, critical review and cutting-edge scholarly debate. It has been an enormous pleasure to work with so many dedicated scholars of Renaissance drama and we are sure that this series will encourage to you read 400-year old playtexts with fresh eyes.

Andrew Hiscock and Lisa Hopkins

Timeline

1572: Birth of Ben Jonson in London. Death of his father. Jonson's mother later remarries Robert Brett, a bricklayer.

1580s: Jonson attends Westminster School, studying under the scholar William Camden.

1589: Jonson apprenticed as a bricklayer.

Early 1590s: Jonson serves as a soldier in the Low Countries, killing a man in single combat.

1594: Jonson marries Anne Lewis, whom he later described as 'a shrew yet honest'. Jonson becomes involved in theatre, as an actor and a writer.

1597: *The Isle of Dogs*, a (now-lost) comedy co-written by Jonson and the satirist Thomas Nashe, is performed. The authorities order it to be banned and arrest all of those involved.

1598: *Every Man in His Humour* performed, Jonson's first major success and an early example of 'humours comedy'.

Jonson kills his fellow-actor Gabriel Spencer in a duel. Jonson is sentenced to death for murder, and escapes the gallows only by pleading 'benefit of clergy' and being branded on the thumb. Jonson converts to Catholicism while in prison.

1599: *Every Man Out of his Humour* performed, and printed the following year.

1600: *Cynthia's Revels* performed.

1601: *Poetaster* performed. *Poetaster* contains personal satire on Thomas Dekker and John Marston, and is part of the 'War of the Theatres'.

1602: Jonson is paid by Henslowe for writing extra scenes for Kyd's *Spanish Tragedy*.

1603: Jonson's tragedy *Sejanus* performed, leading to accusations against Jonson of 'Popery and treason'.

The Entertainment at Althorpe performed, marking the start of Jonson's career as a writer of courtly entertainments and masques.

Jonson's son Benjamin dies of plague, commemorated in the poem 'On my first son'.

1605: Performance of *The Masque of Blackness* at court, a masque written by Jonson, with Inigo Jones as designer, for James I's wife Queen Anne. Jonson continues for many years thereafter to provide masques and entertainments for the court.

Jonson, George Chapman, and John Marston collaborate on *Eastward Ho!* Jonson is arrested on account of the play's satire against the Scots.

Oct 9 (approximately): Jonson dines with Robert Catesby.

Nov 4: Discovery of the Gunpowder Plot, whose conspirators include Robert Catesby.

Nov 7: Privy Council requests Jonson to make contact with an (unnamed) priest in connection with the investigation of the Gunpowder Plot. The following day Jonson replies that he is unable to find him.

1606: *Volpone* performed. The first performance is usually ascribed to February or March 1606.

1607: *Volpone* printed in quarto. According to its title-page, the comedy has been performed at the universities of Oxford and Cambridge by the time of its printing.

1609: *The Entertainment at Britain's Burse* performed.

Epicoene performed.

1610: *The Alchemist* performed.

Jonson renounces Catholicism and returns to the Anglican faith.

1611: Jonson's tragedy *Catiline* performed.

1612–13: Jonson travels in France, acting as a tutor to the son of Sir Walter Ralegh.

1614: First performance of *Bartholomew Fair*, at the Hope Theatre, also used for bear-baiting.

1616: *Volpone* is among the plays printed in Jonson's Folio *Workes*.

The Devil is an Ass performed.

1618: Jonson walks to Scotland and back. En route, he visits William Drummond of Hawthornden, and Drummond records in detail their conversations.

1623: Jonson's library largely destroyed in a fire (commemorated in his poem *An Execration upon Vulcan*).

1624: *Volpone* performed at court.

1625: Death of King James, and accession of Charles. Jonson still engaged as a court masque-writer, but starts to become a more marginalized figure.

1629: Jonson suffers a stroke.

The New Inn performed. It fails on the stage. Jonson writes the *Ode to Himself*, condemning the audience for being unworthy of the play.

1630: *Volpone* performed again at court.

1631: Final breakdown of Jonson's stormy relationship with Inigo Jones, chief designer for his masques.

1632: *The Magnetic Lady* performed.

1633: *A Tale of a Tub* performed.

1634: *Love's Welcome to Bolsover* performed, a masque written for his last and most loyal patron, William Cavendish.

1637: Death of Ben Jonson at Westminster.

1638: *Volpone* performed again at court.

1640: Posthumous publication of a new and expanded *Works*.

1665: *Volpone* seen by Samuel Pepys in one of its numerous Restoration revivals.

1700–1710: Fifty-eight performances of *Volpone* in London recorded in this decade, and numerous ones thereafter.

1771: Debut of George Colman's adaptation of *Volpone* in London.

1785: Last recorded performance of Colman's adaptation, or of any version of *Volpone* for the next 136 years.

1921: The Phoenix Society perform the play at the Lyric Theatre, Hammersmith.

1926: First performance of Stefan Zweig's adaptation of the play.

1938: Opening of a production of *Volpone* starring Donald Wolfit at the Westminster Theatre, the first of many productions starring Wolfit over the next twenty-one years.

1964: Opening of Tyrone Guthrie's influential production of the play in Minneapolis.

1976: *Sly Fox*, Larry Gelbart's adaptation of the play, opens on Broadway.

1995: *Volpone* produced at the National Theatre, starring Michael Gambon and Simon Russell Beale.

2004: Operatic version of *Volpone* premiered at the Wolf Trap, Virginia.

Introduction

This volume aims to explore the detail and complexity of Ben Jonson's *Volpone*, one of the finest plays of Shakespeare's leading contemporary rival.

In fact, much of *Volpone*'s significance is bound up with the fact that it is not written by Shakespeare. While 'Shakespeare', broadly defined, has penetrated deeply into all aspects of Western culture and education, the rest of the theatrical world from which Shakespeare's plays come and in which they participate is much less well known. *Volpone,* along with Marlowe's *Doctor Faustus*, is particularly prominent in many people's imaginations of early modern theatre as a whole. As the best-known and most-taught plays of Shakespeare's two major contemporaries, *Volpone* and *Doctor Faustus* are the first (and perhaps only) tastes that many people have of non-Shakespearean Renaissance drama.

Volpone and *Doctor Faustus* are similar, too, in that neither is entirely typical of the *oeuvre* of the writer that they represent. *Doctor Faustus* is more obviously theological than political, whereas most of the rest of the Marlowe canon could fairly be described as more obviously political than theological; and this very fact has made it perhaps the most easily teachable of Marlowe's works to an audience not grounded in Elizabethan politics. In a similar way, the very qualities that make *Volpone* particularly teachable also make it something of an oddity in the Ben Jonson canon. Set as it is in a brilliantly sketched, jewel-like Venice, it omits the mess, complexity and specificity of the contemporary London that Jonson loved and that forms the basis for the three other great comedies, *Epicoene, The Alchemist* and *Bartholomew Fair*. It omits, too, much of Jonson's characteristic interest in money and wealth. This seems a strange thing to say of a play in which riches are so obviously centre stage from the opening tableau –

Good morning to the day; and next, my gold:
Open the shrine, that I may see my Saint.

(1.1.1–2)

And yet Jonson's other plays are far more fascinated with the *detail* of wealth and poverty, with what Robert Miola, writing about *Every Man In His Humour*, calls each 'precisely calibrated instance of impecuniousness'.[1] In that play, for instance, we hear about the prices of individual items; the problems of managing tavern expenses; how one character pawns his stockings in order to raise the money to arrest another for a debt to him. But in *Volpone*, none of the main characters are poor in this sense. In *Every Man In His Humour* and most other Jonson plays, money is interesting because it has a double nature: it is simultaneously the tool required for the competitive display necessary to exercise social power, and also the tool required to keep starvation at arm's length. That doubleness is what makes it slippery and fascinating. But in *Volpone*, where no-one seems in danger of actually going hungry, money has a rather different value. Instead, riches in *Volpone* become something more abstract and symbolic, an aspect of the personified Goods of the morality play tradition rather than part of the complicated daily struggle to survive and thrive. Like the stylized location, this aspect of *Volpone* makes it no weaker as a play compared to Jonson's others, merely different, and it certainly makes it easier to teach. But it still makes it somewhat untypical of Jonson as a whole.

One further aspect of this deviance should be mentioned: the question of character and sympathy. Jonson is often said to write in a 'humours' tradition in which characters are constructed, rather one-dimensionally, around a single character trait or obsession. This, so the theory goes: permits a quasi-scientific examination of that character trait; leaves little room for subtlety or sympathy in the character so created; and tends to lead to the character's punishment. *Volpone* appears to be an almost textbook example of this – austere in its development and elaboration of the obsessions of Volpone, Corvino, Sir Pol and the rest. Moreover, it brings all of these humours to a courtroom, and subjects them to correction, shame and punishment. To some readers, even early ones, this has seemed so bitter and punitive as to make the play more of a moral tract than a pleasure, and to make the play almost anti-theatrical: as 'H. Ramsay' commented at Jonson's death, intending it as high praise, 'His *lines* did relish mirth, but so severe | That as they tickled, they did wound the ear'.[2] By contrast, in the morally compromised world of *The Alchemist*, or of *Bartholomew Fair*, where even reformers are shown to be not free from human weakness, things are rarely so tidy or so schematic. Generalizations about Jonson based primarily on *Volpone* will, necessarily, miss the things that make *Volpone* itself a strange and difficult play within the Jonson canon. There are more complexities in *Volpone* than originally meet the eye, as can be seen by a look at some of the past and current reactions to Jonson's play.

This volume begins with Sam Thompson's overview of *Volpone*'s critical history. One of the keynotes of Thompson's chapter – as of many of those that follow – is the energy of this text, right from the opening description of it bowling over one critic 'like a playful lion, with sheer, gorgeous strength'. Through the critical history of the play until the end of the last century, Thompson traces the hugely different reactions that this text has provoked. Complimenting Thompson's chapter – and, at many points, connecting with it – is Rebecca Yearling's stage history of the play, the most performed Renaissance play outside the work of Shakespeare, in spite of its long period of neglect through the nineteenth century. The contributions of Thompson and Yearling prepare the ground for Robert C. Evans's magisterial map of the current state of the art in *Volpone* studies, a map interesting for the extent to which the possibilities of new scholarly tools – most obviously, those of a digital nature – encroach upon the space which might, in accounts written twenty years ago, have been given over to the opportunities of new critical theories. These are, as Evans says, exciting times to be a scholar.

Evans's chapter, in turn, sets the stage for the four New Directions chapters, each of which represents a new contribution to debate about the play, and each of which comes from a different critical position. The first two presented here offer two radically different approaches, in their voice, their reference points and their critical procedures, and yet they share a common concern with *Volpone* and performance, Volpone and theatricality. Both, in different ways, take aim at the critical construct of Jonson as an 'antitheatrical' writer, but they do so in entirely different ways and to different ends, and it is a sign of the diversity of Jonson studies as it is currently practised that they coexist in the same volume. First, James P. Bednarz's piece 'Jonson's Literary Theatre: *Volpone* in performance and print (1606–7)' takes a fresh look at the usual assumption that Jonson used print publication as a way of distancing himself from the corruption of performance. On the contrary, argues Bednarz, the early performances of *Volpone* in the university towns of Oxford and Cambridge are mentioned prominently in the first quarto of the play (and Bednarz offers, too, a careful sifting of the historical evidence concerning those two early performances). Not merely, he suggests, do Jonson and his commendatory poets use reference to the Oxford and Cambridge connection to validate the play's intellectual credentials, but the fact that these plays did well in performance there is equally important. This reflects, argues Bednarz, the fact that

> For Jonson, a 'poet-playwright' would have been a walking contradiction, since a great dramatist was a 'poet' and a bad one was a

'playwright' or 'poetaster' . . . he perceived a vital connection between theatrical and what we now call 'literary' culture.[3]

Almost entirely at odds with Bednarz's approach is that taken by Rick Bowers, in his chapter '"Live free, . . . Rob Churches, . . . Lend me your Dwarf": What's Funny about *Volpone*?' The intellectual co-ordinates for this work are provided by a postmodern reading of Bakhtin, a reading explored at greater length in Bowers's earlier book in this area, *Radical Comedy in Early Modern England*.[4] Bowers looks in different places for his evidence: from recent performance history, to different critical traditions. It gives him an entirely different prose style, and it brings him to different conclusions:

> People don't usually leave a performance of *Volpone* feeling morally instructed. Instead, they feel theatrically exhausted, piqued, and delighted [. . .] Great comedies such as *Volpone* insist on their own confusions.

Fortunately, one does not have to decide that one approach is right and the other wrong. A reader of *Volpone* – even an experienced one – will find in each of these two chapters new stuff to stir the imagination: whether it be Bednarz's reconstruction of the precarious realities of touring performance in Cambridge – down to such prosaic details as having to take out the glass windows, in case they got damaged – or Bowers's richly detailed reading of the moment where Volpone, having got Celia where he wants her, veers off into boasts about his own past as an actor.

In a sense, Chapter 6 and Chapter 7 in this section – those of Frances Teague and Stella Achilleos – also form a pair with one another, both, in different ways, approaching the question of what used to be called the historical context of the play. Teague's interest is in the play's relationship to two of the most archetypical sorts of history: Jonson's own biographical experience, which included at least three spells in prison; and high politics as it has been conventionally defined, in the specific form of the Gunpowder Plot and its aftermath. Jonson's links to radical Catholicism have attracted a good deal of attention in recent years, and Teague's chapter is in productive dialogue with other work on *Volpone* and the Gunpowder Plot, notably that of Richard Dutton. And yet this is not a return to old-style historicism: her concerns are grounded in recent theoretical and imaginative work on the nature of captivity. Teague traces, through the play, the themes of imprisonment, surveillance and power, adroitly relating them to both historical and biographical anchoring points. Surprising, and particularly striking, is the resulting reading of Celia and Volpone as fellow prisoners: 'a prisoner', she comments, 'has no privacy'.

While Teague's chapter starts from the most concrete of historical points – biography and high politics – Achilleos deals with a cultural history: early modern attitudes to age and ageing, in a discussion which 'aims to bring Jonson's play into dialogue with his culture's assumptions about senescence'. As Achilleos describes, ageing – that long-taboo topic which our culture is itself now having to engage with harder than before – is one of the central themes of the play, focused upon Corbaccio, the old man who hopes to become young again. In Achilleos's analysis, resemblances start to appear between *Volpone* and the near-contemporary *King Lear*: and Jonson's wide classical reading, so often treated as a dead-end, becomes part of a dialogue about the whole nexus of old age, desire and power. In the final contribution to the volume, Matthew C. Hansen compiles a list of 'Resources for teaching and studying *Volpone*': particularly useful scholarly articles, out-of-the-way books now available in online forms, ideas not just for essays but for a number of other forms of project.

To close this introduction, one might consider a particularly interesting moment from *Volpone*. Towards the end of the play, Corbaccio, the elderly man who chases after legacies although close to death himself, believes he has outlived Volpone, and comes to Mosca to collect – as he thinks – his winnings in the form of Volpone's entire inheritance. Mosca's response to him is crushing:

> Stop your mouth,
> Or I shall draw the only tooth is left.
> Are not you he, that filthy covetous wretch,
> With the three legs, that, here, in hope of prey,
> Have, any time this three years, snuff'd about,
> With your most grovelling nose; and would have hired
> Me to the poisoning of my patron, sir?
> Are not you he that have to-day in court
> Profess'd the disinheriting of your son?
> Perjured yourself? Go home, and die, and stink.
>
> (5.3.66–75)

Anyone who knows *Volpone* will have their own favourite passage in the play. For some, it is Volpone's whole performance as a travelling mountebank, lively on the page and frequently hilarious in performance, featuring that memorable word 'turdy-facy-nasty-paty-lousy-fartical'. Others are struck by the lusciously, ludicrously decadent pleasures that Volpone offers to the horrified Celia. In a straw poll of this book's contributors, many mentioned their enjoyment of the 'Lend me your dwarf' exchange, analysed and celebrated by Bowers in his chapter in this volume. But for me, a really breathtaking moment in the play is this one.

Partly it is a matter of the stage effect: Corbaccio's scenes are always the most physically engaging of those featuring the three gulls, and this one, like the others, provides room for stage business as Mosca circles the old man, perhaps kicking away his stick, or, in some productions, grabbing hold of his ear trumpet. The language too is a thing of beauty. The phrase 'with the three legs', while perfectly comprehensible in its own right on stage, also activates in four words the whole classical inter-text of the Riddle of the Sphinx, according to which man walks on four legs in his infancy, two in his maturity, and three in his dotage: an entire history of man which bears on the issues of ageing and mortality that, as Achilleos argues in this volume, run through the play, and in doing so demonstrates the extent to which 'literature' and performance are, for Jonson, as Bednarz argues, overlapping categories. In the next line 'snuffed' is a particularly vivid word, recalling earlier references to the scent of carrion in the play. Corbaccio is like Death in Milton's as yet unwritten *Paradise Lost* ('with delight he snuffed the smell | Of mortal change on earth') – and at the same time, like a feeble old man breathing heavily.[5] It is an elegant double insult.

Mosca's ire builds through a series of enjambement effects and a series of accusations to that final, killing tricolon, 'Go home, and die, and stink' which, of course, is utterly illogical. You can command someone to kill themselves, but you cannot really command them to die: and you certainly cannot command them to decompose. The joke, if joke there is in such a splendidly bleak line, is an almost Beckettian one about the inability of human will truly to compete with those processes of mortality that Volpone has spent the play faking.

And that, for me, is the really interesting thing about this speech: the tension between the crisp, masterly language and the complexities and tensions of its implications. It is what Mosca reveals for the first time about himself and Volpone – the fact that the scam has been going for three years, confining them both to the imprisonment described by Teague; the fact that the only word he can come up with, even now, for his supposedly dead master is the awkward 'patron' (although this itself is a word pregnant with meaning for Jonson, as Robert C. Evans has explored).[6] There is even the sense that the righteous anger he is simulating is mixed up, too, with outrage at Corbaccio which is real (and therefore, potentially troubling, to a conman). The attempted murder, it seems, is not even the weightiest crime on Mosca's list. Worse still is the breaking of a parental bond, a crime that neither Mosca nor

Volpone, both childless, could ever commit. Worse even than that is the betrayal of one's own self in a lie. Mosca appeals, in this speech, to senses of personal integrity and family bonds which he himself has long since forfeited, and does he do so in a spirit of tranquil cynicism, or with some confused sense that it still ought to matter? That last explosion of frustration, and the complexities it leaves hanging in the air like the scent of decay, suggest that this speech does provide interiority and complexity of just the sort that it is often taught that Jonson does not engage in.

As the chapters in this volume show, I hope, *Volpone* has many pleasures to offer, and many that still await exploration.

Notes

1   Ben Jonson. *Every Man In His Humour*, ed. Robert Miola (Manchester: Manchester UP, 2000), Introduction 22.

2   Ben Jonson, *Ben Jonson* ed. C. H. Herford, P. Simpson, and E. Simpson (Oxford: Clarendon Press, 1925–52), 11.453, 472.

3   The groundwork for this approach is partly laid in Bednarz's own earlier book, *Shakespeare and the Poets' War* (New York: Columbia UP, 2001), which sees the plays of early Jonson, in particular, in terms of an emerging dialogue, with Shakespeare and others, about the nature of literariness and theatre.

4   Rick Bowers, *Radical Comedy in Early Modern England* (Aldershot: Ashgate, 2008).

5   John Milton, *Paradise Lost*, ed. A. Fowler, 2nd edition (London: Longman, 1998), 10.272–3.

6   Robert C. Evans, *Ben Jonson and the Poetics of Patronage* (Lewisburg: Bucknell UP, 1989).

CHAPTER ONE

The Critical Backstory

Sam Thompson

Over four hundred years, criticism of *Volpone* has reached many
extremes. The play has been seen as the greatest masterpiece of the best
writer of his time, but also as the laborious contrivance of a pedant. For
critics, it has been an effective means of teaching its audience to behave
better, or a cynical denial that art can make any difference in the world;
a feast of theatrical energy and pleasure, or a bitter condemnation of
theatre's falsity; the finest model of neoclassical comedy in English, or a
strange creation that fits into no recognizable tradition.[1] Donne and
Dryden praised it effusively, as did Eliot and Yeats, while Coleridge and
Hazlitt read it with a mixture of admiration and dislike. Samuel Pepys
called it 'a most excellent play – the best I think I ever saw'.[2] James Joyce
echoed its first scene in the opening pages of *Ulysses*.[3] Seventeenth-
century critics rated it above Shakespeare's plays, and some in the
twentieth century have agreed: Joan Littlewood, who directed *Volpone*
in 1955, called it 'the greatest comedy ever written', adding 'I did so many
of those Shakespeares because we had to but I don't like his comedies
compared with Ben Jonson'.[4] In a review of Tyrone Guthrie's production
in 1968, Ronald Bryden wrote that '*Volpone* bowls me over, like a playful
lion, with sheer, gorgeous strength. Intoxicated, I come away sharing
momentarily the seventeenth-century judgment that Shakespeare had a
nice touch with landscape and human emotions, but Jonson is what one
really means by art'.[5]

The first critic of *Volpone* was Ben Jonson. The first printed
edition, the 1607 quarto, was a literary manifesto as well as a playtext: it
positioned the play within a carefully-designed critical apparatus,
presenting it not as disposable theatrical entertainment but as a substantial literary work drawing deeply on classical traditions to create an

innovative form of English comedy. Earlier in his career, Jonson had rejected classical models (*Every Man Out of his Humour* dismissed ancient 'laws of comedy' as 'too nice observations'),[6] but *Volpone*'s Prologue invokes Horace and Aristotle, promising to 'mix profit with your pleasure' (8) and to observe the 'laws of Time, Place, Persons' (31).[7] The quarto was dedicated to the universities of Oxford and Cambridge 'for their love and acceptance shown to his poem in the presentation', advertising that the play had been performed with conspicuous success in the university towns: Jonson was keen to associate his learned drama with scholarly, judicious audiences.[8] In calling the play a 'poem' he represented himself as a literary dramatist, and further literary value was added by the quarto's English and Latin commendatory verses, which made the case for *Volpone* as a breakthrough in neoclassicism. Edmund Bolton's contribution describes Jonson as 'an explorer translating the ancient literary monuments of the Greeks and of the Roman theatre'.[9] Francis Beaumont adds that *Volpone* preserves classical formal decorum, 'the rules of time, of place, | And other rites, delivered with the grace | Of comick style', better than any English play before it. John Donne goes further, claiming that Jonson sets an example for lawmakers: 'If counsellors in the law[s] of men and God would dare follow and emulate what you have dared here in your art, Poet, O, we all should have the wisdom needed for salvation'.[10] For Donne, Jonson's fidelity to the classics produces formal artistic excellence, but it also has practical moral value. The play will live on and 'raise a new race from our wickedness'.[11]

Above all, it is in the quarto's dedicatory Epistle to the universities that Jonson sets out his manifesto. Contemporary literature is corrupt, he says, and the popular theatre is artistically bankrupt, but by returning to classical literary values he aims to 'raise the despised head of poetry again and, stripping her out of those rotten and base rags wherewith the times have adulterated her form, restore her to her primitive habit, feature, and majesty' (118–21). He claims an important office for the poet as a public moralist, a teacher of 'good disciplines' and 'great virtues' and insists on 'the impossibility of any man's being the good poet without first being a good man' (20–23). Accordingly he has 'laboured ... to reduce not only the ancient forms, but manners of the scene – the easiness, the propriety, the innocence and, last, the doctrine which is the principal end of poesy: to inform men in the best reason of living' (96–100). This somewhat opaque passage is the theoretical heart of the Epistle. By emulating the artistic forms and conventions of classical drama, Jonson asserts, he has produced a comedy which fulfils the highest purpose of literature, which is to teach its audience the right way to live.

We might detect some irony in Jonson's Olympian professions of social responsibility and moral spotlessness, given his turbulent career in the years leading up to *Volpone*. He wrote the play and its Epistle in the aftermath of 'a whole sequence of traumas and confrontations with authority', including being prosecuted for his writing, imprisoned, branded and peripherally entangled with the Gunpowder Plot.[12] Because he had found the literary life so perilous, he had a vehement interest in justifying himself and his work, and this fuels the Epistle's argument for a stable set of formal and moral rules for English literature. The Epistle would prove to be an influential document in the history of criticism: Richard Dutton points out that, by taking such a strong position, Jonson 'branded himself to posterity as a keeper of the laws', becoming a figure of solid neoclassical authority with which later writers could negotiate or argue.[13] Jonson's prominence as a theorist would at times overshadow his own practice as a dramatist. He himself acknowledged that in one respect *Volpone* did not adhere to his 'laws': the final punishments imposed on Volpone and Mosca could be seen as breaking generic decorum, because they are too harsh for a comedy. Jonson asks 'the learned and charitable critic' (102) to give him the benefit of the doubt on this point, insisting that he could easily have obeyed 'the strict rigour of comic law' (100), but has chosen not to do so in order to emphasize the morality of the play's conclusion: 'my special aim being to put the snaffle in their mouths that cry out we never punish vice in our interludes &c., I took the more liberty' (105–7). Finding it necessary to choose between moral purpose and formal perfection, he has decided that the former is more important. In calling attention to this dilemma, and in pointing out a mismatch between Jonson's theory of comedy and his practice, the Epistle established the framework for much of the discussion of *Volpone* that followed over four centuries.

Volpone's gallery of charlatans and fools immediately gained a place in cultural consciousness. The first published allusion to the play came as early as 1606,[14] and through the seventeenth century its characters appeared in various contexts as archetypal, almost folkloric figures. In *The Anatomy of Melancholy*, Robert Burton, discussing men who try to seduce women with magnificent promises, recalls how 'old Volpone courted Cælia in the Comedy'.[15] Restoration playwrights invoked Jonson's satiric types to colour their own characters. In John Wilson's *The Projectors*, the self-deluded Sir Gudgeon Credulous is described as 'So brave a Sir *Poll*',[16] and William Congreve's *The Way of the World* cites Mosca as the archetypal treacherous servant: 'I wou'd not tempt my Servant to betray me by trusting him too far,' says Mirabell, 'he might like *Mosca* in the *Fox*, stand upon Terms; so I made him sure beforehand'.[17] In Aphra Behn's *Sir Patient Fancy*, as Wittmore opens what he believes is a basket of gold, he echoes Volpone's first lines: 'Good morrow to the day, and next the Gold, open the Shrine, that I may see my Saint – hail the Worlds Soul'.[18] The quotation evokes grandiose cupidity, but it is deflated when in the basket Wittmore discovers not treasure, but Sir Credulous Easy (another descendant of Sir Politic).[19] Specific allusions like these help to show audiences' familiarity with Jonson's works,[20] but they also register the general debt owed by Restoration comedy to Jonson's style of satirical characterization: to link Sir Gudgeon Credulous explicitly to Sir Politic Would-Be is to place Jonson's play at the beginning of a stage tradition of foolish knights whose names diagnose their characters. (Peregrine notices Sir Politic's theatrical potential: 'O, this knight, | Were he well known, would be a precious thing | To fit our English stage' (II.1.56–8).) Sir Politic also carried the influence of *Volpone* into foreign literatures: Saint-Evremond's play *Sir Politick Would-Be* (subtitled 'Comédie à la manière des Anglois') involves characters based on the knight and his wife.[21] The debt to Jonson is similarly blatant in Thomas Killigrew's play *Thomaso, or The Wanderer*, in which a mountebank, addressing a crowd that includes a young woman called Celia, reels off large sections of the sales-pitch Volpone delivers in the guise of Scoto of Mantua.[22] Aphra Behn draws on the same scene in *The Rover, Part Two*, departing further from Jonson's text but retaining more of his performative vigour.[23] Other debts are more diffuse. Mary Pix's play *The Deceiver Deceived* (1698) features a miserly Venetian merchant who fakes blindness much as Volpone fakes sickness, but is outwitted by his wife and daughter; Susanna Centlivre's *The Basset Table* (1705) echoes the tortoise scene.[24] The general regard for *Volpone* is suggested by Thomas Rawlins's *Tunbridge-Wells*, which features a gentleman who 'beat a modish Fop for discharging a Volley of crittical non sence upon *Ben Johnsons* Fox'.[25]

Outside the theatres, the play was a satirical toolkit. The preface to George Wither's allegorical poem *Faire-Virtue* explains that the author has chosen not to clarify the meaning of certain obscure passages, in defiance of gossipmongers: 'he would purposely leave somewhat remaining doubtful, to see what Sir Politic Would-be and his companions could pick out of it'.[26] Sir Politic proves useful, too, when the clergyman and poet Jasper Mayne wants to ridicule a rival preacher: 'I see a piece of *Ben Johnson's* best *Comedy*, the *Fox*, presented to me; that is, *you*, a *Politique Would-be* the *second*, sheltring your self under a *capacious Tortoise-shell*'.[27] The same tactic is used by Barten Holyday, who lampoons the Catholic church by observing that '*Paul* the Third and *Morone* (they so compact) | At *Rome* and *Trent*, *Volpone* and *Mosca* act';[28] and by Andrew Marvell, who describes certain misguided clerics as 'the "Politic Would-be's" of the clergy'.[29] By the eighteenth century the play was a standard reference-point for satirical observations of avarice and deceit, especially in politicians.[30] 'Volpone' was the nickname of Sidney Godolphin, lord high treasurer under Queen Anne, and the most striking instance of the satirical efficacy of Jonson's characters came in 1709, when Godolphin had the clergyman Henry Sacheverell impeached for delivering an inflammatory sermon in which he used the insult. The ensuing political incident contributed to the fall of the Whig government in 1710.[31] Subsequently, the play remained a ready source of offensive name-tags. In a 1743 pamphlet denouncing the business practices of two theatre managers, William Rufus Chetwood alleged that 'a solemn League and Covenant was entered into between *Volpone* and *Mosca*, to exclude all [actors] who had any merit, and only keep in such who were not of Consequence enough to grumble'.[32]

In alluding to *Volpone* polemically, these writers were not only appropriating the play to their own ends, but were also endorsing Jonson's theory of drama. *Volpone*, they implied, was continuing to perform precisely the function its author had intended, exposing folly and vice to healing laughter. In the same way, the values of Jonson's Epistle underpinned most seventeenth-century critical judgments of *Volpone*. Jonson appears as a character in Sir John Suckling's poem 'A Sessions of the Poets', in which Apollo is judging a contest for the bays. 'Good old Ben' drunkenly insists he deserves the prize:

[He bade] them remember how he had purg'd the Stage
Of errors, that had lasted many an Age,
And he hopes they did think the silent Woman,
The Fox, and the Alchymist out done by no man.[33]

The tone is comic, and Jonson is mocked for his arrogance, but his claims of merit are not gainsaid. Later in the century, various critical treatises repeated an approving formula framed obediently in Jonson's own terms: *Volpone* is a work for learned, judicious readers as well as for theatre audiences; it emulates ancient comedy admirably, and shows he was 'the *first Reformer* of the *English* Stage'.[34] In 1691, the 1607 quarto's account of *Volpone* could still be cited without qualification: 'its value is sufficiently manifested by the verses of Mr. Beaumont, and Dr. Donne'.[35]

Such comments are as much statements of a literary theory as responses to the play: for these critics *Volpone* is significant as a model of neoclassical principles, and Jonson stands for an older, better dramatic practice, technically and morally. Consequently, praising him is often a way of finding fault with later writers, actors and audiences. A commendatory verse prefixed to Richard Brome's play *The Antipodes* (1640) imagines Jonson's ghost has been driven into exile by the decline of comedy and the ignorance of critics; the solution is to read his work again, and recognize that his virtues live on in 'his' Brome's writings.[36] In the same year, a verse prefixed to Samuel Harding's *Sicily and Naples* suggests that if the play's detractors were confronted with *Volpone*, their inadequacies as critics would be instantly exposed: 'Poore fooles! I pitty them; how would they looke, | If at the barre BEN JOHNSON were their booke? | His *Fox* would on these *geese* revenge thee'.[37] At the turn of the century, Jeremy Collier defined 'the Nature of Comedy' by citing the Epistle,[38] and another critic placed Jonson with Moliere as 'the surest Standards to judge of Comedy'.[39] The moral usefulness of *Volpone* was in no doubt: discussing a 1712 production at Drury Lane, Richard Steele suggested that 'When we come to characters directly comical, it is not to be imagined what Effect a well regulated Stage would have upon Men's Manners', and that the actor who played Corbaccio 'must have given all who saw him a thorough Detestation of aged Avarice'.[40] For Steele, this production had the power to reform its audience's conduct in exactly the way proposed by Jonson's theory of comedy.

Dryden, who calls Jonson 'the greatest man of the last age' and 'the most learned and judicious Writer which any Theater ever had', was the first critic to engage in detail with the claims of the Epistle.[41] According to the *Essay of Dramatic Poesy*, Jonson's greatness was due to his emulation of the classics, but *Volpone* falls short of classical per-fection because 'the unity of design seems not exactly observ'd in it'. There are 'two actions in the play', in that the final act does not follow inevitably from what has gone before: Volpone could bring his schemes to a flawless conclusion after the first trial scene, but instead he invites disaster with the reckless decision to fake his death, go out in disguise and put his fate entirely in Mosca's hands. In a sense, Dryden touches on the same crux that had troubled Jonson: why disrupt a perfect comic structure in order to bring about harsh punishments for the tricksters? Like Jonson, Dryden finally allows the formal imperfection because it furthers a moral purpose: 'by it the Poet gain'd the end he aym'd at, the punishment of Vice, and the reward of Virtue'. In passing, however, Dryden recognizes a different justification, based not in didacticism but in the peculiarity of Volpone as a character. His rash-ness does not fit with 'his character as a crafty or covetous person', but does make sense if we notice he is also a 'voluptuary': rather than con-demning the fifth act as faulty, Dryden implies, we might revise our own judgments.[42] Nevertheless, his critique of *Volpone* in the *Essay* and elsewhere is framed predominantly in terms of neoclassical rules. He judges Jonson by the standards of the Epistle, preferring *Epicoene* 'before all other Plays' because it observes the unities best,[43] and finding that Jonson lets himself down when he descends from comic decorum into farce: 'When in the Fox I see the Tortois hist, | I lose the Author of the Alchymist'.[44]

Ironically, then, the authority accorded to Jonson's theory of comedy meant that his plays themselves came in for censure. On occasion, the task of identifying flaws in *Volpone* is carried out with grovelling apologies: 'I beg Ben's pardon for this presumption'.[45] For John Dennis, the Prologue shows 'it was the Opinion of the greatest of all our Comick Poets, That the Rules were absolutely necessary to Perfection',[46] but the play deviates from those rules: the plot is 'unreasonable'; the play makes fun of Corbaccio's deafness, which is 'contrary to the end of Comedy Instruction' because deafness is a blameless misfortune, not a moral defect which can be cured by mockery; the Politic Would-Bes have nothing to do with the main plot, and are therefore 'Excrescencies'; and Volpone's sudden shift from cunning to recklessness in the last act is an offence against the rules of dramaturgy and also, because it is improbable, against nature.[47] Within the neoclassical orthodoxy, then, a recognition was growing that the critical theories for which Jonson stood seldom corresponded with what he actually did as a dramatist. Margaret Cavendish, writing with the agenda of a playwright rather than a critic, had earlier pointed out that Jonson could be interpreted as an authority not for neoclassical decorum but for its violation: in the preface to her collected *Plays* of 1662 she noted that *Volpone* and *The Alchemist* break the unity of time, justifying her decision to 'follow not the Ancient Custome' in her own work.[48]

As the eighteenth century continued, the tone of criticism began to change. Critics still professed admiration, but it was accompanied by little enthusiasm or sympathy. The habit of listing minor imperfections grew into a suspicion that the play was more profoundly flawed. In 1753, Richard Hurd judged that *Volpone*'s subject-matter is 'fitted for the entertainment of all times', but the play is marred by Jonson's indelicacy: 'his wit is too frequently caustic; his raillery coarse; and his humour excessive'.[49] The gathering critical chill was felt also in the theatres, where from 1754 *Volpone* lay dormant for seventeen seasons. For its revival at Covent Garden in 1771, the play was altered to minimize its well-known structural faults[50] and expurgate its blasphemies and obscenities.[51] In 1783, after a further revival of the 1771 production, a reviewer reported that the changes, notably the omission of Sir Politic and his wife, 'manifestly improve the Stage effect of the piece very considerably'.[52] Even so, the play now appeared obsolete, and it would not be produced again for a hundred and thirty-six years. In 1784 Thomas Davies judged *Volpone* 'truly admirable', but made it sound unreadable: 'there is not much to be censured, except the language, which is so pedantic and stuck so full of Latinity, that few, except the

learned, can perfectly understand it'. It might also soon be unperform-
able. Jonson's characters 'were so difficult, and their manners so distant,
from those of all other authors' that acting them was a special tradition,
'a kind of stage learning', which had died out, so that the secret of
delivering unusual lines like Mosca's 'Think, think, think, think, think,
think, think, sir' (II.vi.59) was 'absolutely lost to the stage'.[53]

This shift in critical sensibility saw Jonson's reputation plummet as
Shakespeare's rose. Jonson's scholarly craftsmanship, formerly the
bedrock of his pre-eminence, appeared staid by comparison with
Shakespeare's inspirational style: 'It requires an almost painful Attention
to mark the Propriety and Accuracy of Johnson, and your Satisfaction
arises from Reflection and Comparison; But the Fire and Invention of
Shakespear in an Instant are shot into your Soul'.[54] David Erskine Baker
admitted it was hard to imagine a 'more highly finished' play than
Volpone, but found it cold, laboured, uninteresting, and lacking the
imaginative qualities of 'the unequalled Shakespeare'.[55] A reviewer of
Volpone's 1771 revival was puzzled that some had tried to place Jonson
on an equal footing with 'the immortal Shakespear', and declared that
Shakespeare greatly excels Jonson, and all other authors, in 'knowledge
of human Nature'.[56] The contrast between a learned Jonson and a
Shakespeare attuned to 'Nature' was not new, but now Shakespeare's
qualities were admired above all, and Jonson's former virtues became
impediments: his plays are 'written with such labour and art, that Nature
sometimes seems to lie buried under them'.[57] By 1798, the idea that Jonson had ever been preferred was frankly incomprehensible to Nathan
Drake, who was 'astonished at the miserable taste of our ancestors, for of
Jonson, the celebrated but pedantic Jonson, if we except two or three of
his comedies, there is little commendatory to be said'. Even those few
comedies 'are of a kind by no means generally relished or understood,
nor would they now, nor probably will they hereafter, have any popularity on the stage'.[58]

In 1800, Charles Dibdin encapsulated the reversal of critical fortunes.
Why, he asked, has *Volpone* 'never greatly succeeded' although it is seen as
Jonson's best play, and is based on a 'meritorious principle'?[59] The answer
is that 'Quaint, dry, studied correctness, unsupported by quickness, spirit,
and fire, can never satisfy'.[60] The Jonson-Shakespeare antithesis silently
underpins this conclusion: Jonson's supposed lack of Shakespearean
virtues leaves him dessicated, with no positive qualities at all. As the
nineteenth century proceeded, *Volpone* found itself in an inhospitable
critical landscape, stranded by the rejection of neoclassical values
that was one aspect of Romanticism.[61] The Romantics' temperamental
incompatibility with Jonson shows in Coleridge's view that *Volpone* is
'admirable, indeed, but yet more wonderful than admirable', but is in the

end a failure, painful to sit through and lacking 'pleasurable interest', because 'there is no goodness of heart in any of the prominent characters'. The desire for good and likeable characters represents critical assumptions very different from Jonson's own; tellingly, Coleridge compares *Volpone*'s characters with those found in novels, and suggests the play might have been a 'delightful comedy' if Jonson had centred the action on Celia and Bonario and made them lovers.[62] The same thought had already occurred to Ludwig Tieck, who had done precisely that in his German adaptation of 1793, producing a conventional sentimental drama.[63]

Although the Romantic era saw Jonson's critical fortunes at their lowest, some readers continued to respond to his work.[64] Crucially, the ground for his later rehabilitation was laid with William Gifford's 1816 edition of the collected works, which attacked the critical clichés that had grown up around Jonson and introduced the possibility of an assessment on fresh terms, although this was not to bear fruit until the twentieth century. In his defence of *Volpone*, Gifford takes issue with a 1788 essay by Richard Cumberland, which rates *Volpone* as close to dramatic 'perfection', but repeats the commonplace indictment of Volpone's behaviour in the last act as absurd, inconsistent and fatal to the unity of the plot.[65] Gifford argues that, far from being 'a violation of nature' as Cumberland claims, Volpone's reckless decision 'forms the great moral of the play'. By having his gleeful antihero overreach and destroy himself, Jonson achieves a triumph of artifice and naturalism alike, 'consistent with himself and with the invariable experience of mankind'.[66] Gifford is foregrounding the insight that Dryden had glimpsed: for all Jonson's emphasis on the 'laws' of comic drama, *Volpone* follows its own complex comic logic, and tends to confound expectations based on inflexible critical theory.

Cumberland himself was alert to *Volpone*'s idiosyncrasy, calling it 'a drama of so peculiar a species, that it cannot be dragged into a comparison with the production of any other modern poet whatsoever'. Bardolatry was not a useful critical framework either: *Volpone*'s 'construction is so dissimilar from any thing of Shakespear's writing, that it would be going greatly out of our way, and a very gross abuse of criticism to attempt to settle the relative degrees of merit'.[67] This idea that *Volpone* was singularly strange would flourish in the twentieth century, but in one respect it had been seeded by Jonson himself, in the Prologue's boast that 'five weeks fully penned it' (16): here is *Volpone* as a play born in a blaze of inspiration, overturning Jonson's reputation for slowness. For Jonson the roles of labouring scholar and inspired poet were not antithetical but interdependent, and the inspiration claimed in the Prologue is 'the kind of breakthrough to brilliance which humanist poets quite consciously hoped for', 'a hard-won access of *furor poeticus*' achieved through long apprenticeship.[68] In a letter written to Jonson near the end of his life, James Howell represented him as a poet frequently inspired with such divine madness: 'you were mad when you writ your Fox, and madder when you writ your Alchymist, you were mad when you writ Catilin, and stark mad when you writ Sejanus . . . The madness I mean is that divine fury, that heating and heightning Spirit which Ovid speaks of'.[69] But the idea of an exceptional inspiration colours the language of later critics in relation to *Volpone* in particular. William Hazlitt sees the play as a passionate achievement: 'It is prolix and improbable, but intense and powerful. It is written *con amore*'. Nor is Jonson the detached 'good man' of the Epistle, morally distant from his cast of characters: 'It is made up of cheats and dupes, and the author is at home among them'. Hazlitt does not ultimately find *Volpone* to his taste ('the whole is worked up too mechanically, and our credulity overstretched at last revolts into scepticism') but nor does he dismiss it outright.[70] Jonson's is an alien and perhaps unpalatable form of drama, but it is potent nevertheless. Even where the view of Jonson as a dry pedant holds some sway, *Volpone* may be seen as an inspired exception: as an 1830 review of Gifford's edition puts it, the play 'is one continued and lofty flight – here are no frosty passages, and none of those prolixities that abound in his ordinary compositions'.[71]

Despite Gifford's advocacy, criticism of *Volpone* lay fallow for much of the nineteenth century (though in 1874 Emile Zola wrote a loose stage adaptation, *Les Héritiers Rabourdin*).[72] It was not until the late 1880s that studies by J. A. Symonds[73] and Algernon Charles Swinburne signalled the beginnings of a critical renaissance. In a review of Symonds, Oscar Wilde sketched a sympathetic portrait of a Jonson who broke down dichotomies between vernacular and classical, life and literature and nature and culture:

> In Jonson's comedies London slang and learned scholarship go hand in hand. Literature was as living a thing to him as life itself. He used his classical lore not merely to give form to his verse, but to give flesh and blood to the persons of his plays. He could build up a breathing creature out of quotations. He made the poets of Greece and Rome terribly modern, and introduced them to the oddest company. His very culture is an element in his coarseness [. . .] Jonson's characters are true to nature [. . .] all creatures of flesh and blood.[74]

Swinburne called *Volpone* a 'triumphant and transcendent masterpiece', and dismissed the allegations of a structural flaw, declaring that Volpone's self-destruction is not 'a sacrifice of art to morality' but 'a masterstroke of character', in keeping with Volpone's 'haughty audacity of caprice'. Swinburne conjured a different play from that of either the neoclassical or the Romantic critics, because unlike the former his primary interest was in character, and unlike the latter he found Jonson's characters exciting. They were no longer puppets illustrating a moralistic thesis, but entities possessed of grotesque individuality and driven by amoral energy: 'the serious fervour and passionate intensity of their resolute and resourceful wickedness give somewhat of a lurid and distorted dignity to the display of their doings and sufferings'.[75] In emphasizing the perception that *Volpone* is not the working-out of a formula but a drama with its own quiddity, Swinburne was sounding in advance a keynote of twentieth-century criticism.

T. S. Eliot struck that note more forcefully in a 1919 essay which set out radically to 'remodel the image of Jonson'. Jonson, he argued, had been damned with a false reputation for worthy dullness, but if we were to read enough to achieve 'intelligent saturation in his work as a whole', we would discover that while he looks at first like a satirist, only concerned with criticizing the world around him, his writing actually 'projects a new world into a new orbit'; he 'escapes the formulae'. For Eliot, *Volpone* was the play in which Jonson 'found his genius', revealing himself as Marlowe's 'legitimate heir' and writing with a 'bold, even shocking and terrifying directness' to create drama with 'a unity of inspiration that radiates into plot and personages alike'.[76] This Jonson is a modernist:

> Of all the dramatists of his time, Jonson is probably the one whom the present age would find the most sympathetic, if it knew him. There is a brutality, a lack of sentiment, a polished surface, a handling of large bold designs in brilliant colours [. . .] if we had a contemporary Shakespeare and a contemporary Jonson, it would be the Jonson who would arouse the enthusiasm of the intelligentsia! Though he is saturated in literature, he never sacrifices the theatrical qualities – theatrical in the most favourable sense – to literature or to the study of character. His work is a titanic show.[77]

Six years later this revitalized Jonson was in evidence in C. H. Herford's introduction to *Volpone*. Herford noted the play's differences from the observational realism of *Every Man in His Humour* and its similarities with the tale of 'two able villains' told in *Sejanus*, and found a play *sui generis*, obeying neither the comic conventions of the early modern theatre nor the classical laws of comedy. It is a sinister, 'even repellent' vision of inhumanity, but is vivified by something like Eliot's 'unity of inspiration': 'for all its strangeness, it attains, in the grip of Jonson's mind, an amazing imaginative veracity'. For Herford, too, Jonson was modern-minded: eighteenth-century critics had misunderstood Volpone's self-destruction because they assumed characters should always behave rationally, but 'the Elizabethans retained no such illusion'. Perhaps, Herford implied, the twentieth century was more attuned to Jonson than intervening periods had been.[78]

This sense that Jonson had rediscovered his audience was justified over the decades that followed. A 1985 study of his fortunes on the twentieth-century stage concluded that his satirical aggression and unsympathetic mode of characterization, anathema in the nineteenth century, had proved resonant in the twentieth, and that a culture which admired the work of Bernard Shaw, Evelyn Waugh, Edward Albee, Eugene Ionesco, Ezra Pound and Kurt Vonnegut was bound to rate Jonson highly.[79] The gulf between nineteenth- and twentieth-century attitudes is exemplified in the responses of two poets: whereas Coleridge had wished for Celia and Bonario to live happily ever after, Yeats was thrilled by Jonson's refusal to allow it, observing that 'the two young people who have gone through so much suffering together leave in the end for their fathers' houses with no hint of marriage, and this excites us because it makes us share in Jonson's cold implacability'.[80]

No longer constrained by neoclassical admiration or stifled by Romantic dislike, twentieth-century critics were able to develop new modes of analysis, notably by locating the play in its cultural and historical circumstances. L. C. Knights signalled a heightened contextual awareness when he stressed that Jonson's drama 'presupposes an active relationship with a particular audience'. With a bow to Eliot, Knights acknowledges Jonson as a creator of unique dramatic worlds, but insists that these worlds are in close communication with actuality: 'The comedy of *Volpone* is universal, but it would be perverse not to relate it to the acquisitiveness of a particular time and place'.[81] In this spirit, critics explored a proliferation of historical and literary contexts, uncovering the breadth of Jonson's classical, medieval and contemporary source-material, and finding in it evidence not of laboriousness, but of creativity: 'the various hints from his studies came together in a lightning flash of illumination that fused them into a new and brilliant whole'.[82] Helen Ostovich's introduction to her 1997 edition, for instance, calls the play a 'potent blend of Aristophanic and revels comedy' and points out its debt to *commedia dell'arte*, its topical satire of the businessman Thomas Sutton and its accurate depiction of early modern Venice, as well as its sources in 'Jonson's vast reading in classical literature'.[83] English late medieval morality plays are a major influence on structure and theme: with its satire of avarice, its Vice figures, its darkening tone and its stern punishments, *Volpone* might be called a

'Jacobean *Everyman*'.[84] The play's animal imagery indicates an extensive root system in popular culture and folklore, drawing on classical and medieval beast fables, fox lore and bestiary traditions, and especially on the mock-heroic beast epic *Reynard the Fox*,[85] in which, amongst other misdeeds, the trickster Reynard feigns death, impersonates a doctor, commits a rape, is put on trial and escapes justice. R. B. Parker comments that the Reynard tradition, like *Volpone*, is 'a tug-of-war between an anarchic identification with the fox and a satiric condemnation of the evils he represents'.[86] Increased awareness of the beast-fable scheme also influenced twentieth-century staging, notably in Guthrie's 1968 production.[87]

Beast fable was traditionally 'a form of coded political satire', and early Jacobean politics forms another source for the play.[88] Julie Sanders (who faults most *Volpone* criticism for being 'a politics-free zone') argues for a close relation between theatricality and politics, reading Jonson's Venice as a space in which 'contemporary political debate over republicanism' is enacted through 'experimentation with dramatic conventions'.[89] Richard Dutton, too, decries the 'singularly ahistorical and apolitical' nature of much criticism, suggesting that *Volpone* is 'in important ways "about" Robert Cecil, the most problematic of all Jonson's patrons', and that the play enacts a daring intervention in the political aftermath of the Gunpowder Plot.[90]

Edmund Wilson's 1947 essay 'Morose Ben Jonson' introduced a psychoanalytical strand to criticism. Wilson judged Jonson harshly – he was crude, mechanical, often arid and sometimes incompetent – but read these failings as symptoms of a troubled personality, effectively translating the Epistle's equation of 'good poet' and 'good man' into a modern vocabulary, pathological rather than ethical. Jonson was a clear case of the Freudian 'anal erotic', burdened with all the pedantry, avarice, irascibility, vindictiveness and neurotic fear of failure that characterize the type. Unlike the free-flowing Shakespeare, he wrote in spite of his own obstructed nature, and *Volpone* is such a 'strange play' because it so nakedly represents its author's obsessive hoarding and withholding.[91] Other critics have followed suit, diagnosing Jonson's 'abiding melancholy' and 'the depressions of *tedium vitae*'.[92] W. Speed Hill argues that *Volpone* must be understood in relation to Jonson's account of his life: the play is not the moral lesson that its manifesto implies, Jonson's claim to be 'a good man' masks a checkered biography and life and art alike show 'a conflict between intention and impulse'.[93] David Riggs sees Volpone as Jonson's self-portrait, especially in the mountebank scene: 'The creative process, as Jonson envisions it here, foreshadows the modern, psychological concept of sublimation. [. . .] Jonson could identify with his villain-hero because his own instinctual drives had taken him down the very path that leads Volpone to ruin'.[94] The idea that Jonson calls for a psychoanalytic approach has also been echoed from across the disciplinary boundary. A 2008 article in the psychoanalytic journal *American Imago* takes him as a case study, concluding that his characters 'are pawns in a highly personalized game played by Jonson to satisfy his inner needs'.[95]

Elsewhere, critics have combined the psychoanalytic accent with the study of cultural contexts, to explore the psychopathology of Jonson's social and professional circumstances. John Gordon Sweeney reads Jonson's theatre as a site of barely-controlled hostility between author and spectator, and *Volpone* as an aggressive 'attempt to come to terms with an audience'.[96] Bruce Thomas Boehrer argues Jonson was caught in a 'schizophrenic' predicament by his need to flatter authority but simultaneously critique it, and that he lived in anxious complicity with his social superiors' self-indulgence in 'the kinds of gluttonous excess that disfigures characters like Volpone': 'Jonson as courtier finally cannot help participating in the same patterns of consumption and display that Jonson as moral critic denounces'.[97] According to Richard Barbour, Jonson's theatricality is modelled on eroticized delay: 'Volpone's great fear – which he enacts daily for his clients, as if to master it – is to be immobilized, impotent, void of desire: to be postcoital, spent', and his tactics for postponing this fate form the structure of the play. His 'richly autoerotic' attempt to seduce Celia 'parodies the exhibitionism of the playhouse, which evades genital fulfillments'.[98] Joseph Loewenstein views Jonson's promotion of 'possessive authorship' in psychologised terms, suggesting that, like his obsessions with eating and consuming, his assertion of 'the bibliographic ego' offers a way of achieving a stable selfhood.[99]

Two essay collections represented other new critical directions at the end of the twentieth century. *Re-Presenting Ben Jonson*, edited by Martin Butler, addresses 'the future of Jonson editing' by asking how the Herford and Simpson edition, still 'the necessary point of reference for all work on Jonson', might best be superseded.[100] *Refashioning Ben Jonson: Gender, Politics and the Jonsonian Canon*, edited by Julie Sanders, Kate Chedgzoy and Susan Wiseman, sets out to 'reconfigure the Jonsonian canon' by subjecting Jonson to 'an historicized and self-consciously post-New Historicism reading', attending to neglected issues of gender and sexuality, and analyzing how Jonson has been constructed by modern academic criticism.[101] A central aim of both volumes is to rectify a situation in which a few core Jonson texts, including *Volpone*, are widely studied as 'isolated monoliths' while a large periphery is ignored.[102] Consequently, both collections paradoxically contribute to *Volpone* criticism by paying as little attention to the play as possible.

Refashioning contains an essay on the Epistle, but this too is a displacement of *Volpone* itself, attempting 'to detach [the Epistle] from the direct concerns of the play and apply it to the micropolitical context of the moment in which Jonson authored that preface'.[103] Perhaps, then, the critical future of *Volpone* is to relinquish ground within Jonson studies to more marginal works. In advocating this, these editors are nevertheless promoting a fuller appreciation of the play, by furthering Eliot's programme of 'intelligent saturation in his work as a whole'.

The critical sophistications of the twentieth century have not supplanted the Epistle's central question of the relation between artistic form and moral purpose: new critical tools have given fresh life to the old debates. Whereas neoclassicists condemned the double plot, more recent critics have vindicated it by finding unity in thematic patterning: Barish and others have argued the subplot is integral to the play's moral vision, which emerges from the structure of parallels and contrasts in which English folly mimics Italian vice.[104] Other critics have reassessed whether *Volpone* adheres to 'comic law' or belongs to a hybrid genre of its own.[105] Much analysis has focused on whether the play really does 'punish vice' as Jonson claimed, with some critics maintaining that *Volpone* is an ironic moral lesson, teaching virtue by staging a world consumed by evil,[106] but others voicing the suspicion that this dramatic world escapes Jonson's moral purposes entirely, due to the appealing vitality of the villains. In such readings, the play is a struggle between Jonson's antitheatrical conviction that 'all role-playing is evil'[107] and the pleasure created in performance by Volpone's virtuosic brio.[108] Ian Donaldson notes that Volpone is animated not by any fixed goal, but by 'continual self-projection into feigned and alien identity [. . .] the infinite and exhilarating play of possibility'.[109] At least temporarily, Volpone and Mosca evade interpretation in moral terms, as their carnivalesque energy tugs against the condemnation they inspire.[110]

The emphasis on theatricality offers further perspectives on Volpone's downfall. Alexander Leggatt argues his histrionic energy masks an emptiness: 'life is ultimately blank, ending in a death that is not fulfilment but annihilation, and the urge for pleasure before the final silence is a little desperate'. In the end he 'consciously and deliberately' ruins himself to achieve an aesthetic effect: 'Material punishment does not matter to Volpone, for he has succeeded as an artist, and put Mosca, the rival artist, in his place'.[111] Stephen Greenblatt sees Volpone, with his outward masks and his inner vacuum, as a prototype of the modern self: in the moment of emptiness at the beginning of Act Five, we perceive 'those vast spaces that opened up on both a physical and psychological plane in the Renaissance', and as we witness Volpone compulsively performing himself into existence 'we feel ourselves present at the very fountainhead of modern consciousness'.[112] Ultimately, the collapse of Volpone's vertiginous selfhood marks the play as a satire of theatrical fakery in all its forms. Scoto's sales-pitch is Jonson's 'brilliant and bitter parody' of early modern defences of the stage:

> is this not derisive laughter at those sixteenth and seventeenth century apologists for the drama who never tire of telling us that our tuppenny admission is the best investment we could ever make, that plays cure all moral hernias? Is this not the disturbing self-mockery of the man who in the Dedicatory Epistle to *Volpone* – an epistle addressed to those greatest of gulls, the universities of Oxford and Cambridge – wrote with a straight face of the 'impossibility of any mans being the good Poet, without first being a good man'?

Much as Jonson wanted to believe in such notions, Greenblatt suggests, he was aware of their resemblance to a mountebank's patter.[113] According to James Hirsh, the play reveals a 'corrosive cynicism' about Jonson's declared intentions, intimating that a writer purporting to mend the world's folly is either 'a naïve fool' or 'a con artist, a mountebank selling a phony elixir'.[114]

It might seem that, assailed by Volpone's devilish theatricality on one hand, and undermined by Jonson's ambivalent antitheatricality on the other, the Epistle's hope to 'inform men in the best reason of living' has little credibility left. But critics continue to engage with the play in moral terms, and often note the stringency with which it tests its audience. If the Epistle's theories cannot provide a map, it is up to the audience to negotiate the 'labyrinth' (V.x.42) as best we can: 'While we as spectators are allowed to see more clearly than the characters within the play, it is essential to Jonson's purposes that we cannot see everything'.[115] The conclusion requires an act of judgment from the spectator, not least in committing to the applause that, according to Volpone's epilogue, will pardon him from his due punishment.[116] In this way the play is structured so that a meaningful response necessarily has a moral dimension. In a 1968 essay, William Empson argued that 'the pietistic strain in Eng. Lit. [...] regularly produces crippled or perverted moral judgements', and reported the experience of reading students' exam answers on *Volpone*:

> What the children write down is a good deal hotter and cruder than most of the stuff in the textbooks, but it is the same grand muddle which appeared so novel and charming about half a century ago. They write: 'Volpone is a miser. The play does nothing

but denounce misers, and he is the worst one, because he worships his gold. All the characters are loathsome except the young couple, and they are subnormal because they talk in a conventional poetic style; but Volpone is the most loathsome, as he blasphemes. Jonson had a theory about plays, that they ought to make you sick of being wicked, and the reason why his plays are so good is that they make you so sick. They are written in poetry which is meant to excite contempt and nausea, and that is why it is such good poetry. Good people enjoy these plays very much, though they are in pain all the time, aching for the tortures to begin.'[117]

He is pointing out that a moral reading of *Volpone* is quite different from a moralistic one. The students he describes have been taught to parrot a formulaic interpretation instead of bringing their own imaginative sympathies and powers of judgment to Jonson's drama. The critic of *Volpone* – who, today as in Empson's day, is likely to be a student at school or university – must do otherwise. If we notice the epilogue in which Volpone asks for our pardon, and consider his request seriously, we can begin to understand the play.

Notes

1   Throughout this essay I am indebted to several studies and anthologies which chart the responses of readers and theatre audiences to Jonson's work. Seventeenth-century allusions to Jonson are collected in *The Jonson Allusion-Book: A Collection of Allusions to Ben Jonson from 1597 to 1700*, ed. Jesse Franklin Bradley and Joseph Quincy Adams (New Haven: Yale University Press, 1922), and in Gerald Eades Bentley, *Shakespeare & Jonson: their reputations in the seventeenth century compared* (Chicago: University of Chicago Press, 1945). Jonson's fortunes in the eighteenth century, both in criticism and in the theatre repertoire, are traced in Robert Gale Noyes, *Ben Jonson on the English Stage, 1660–1776* (Cambridge, Mass: Harvard University Press, 1935). Samples of important Jonson criticism from his time to 1798 are collected in *Ben Jonson: The Critical Heritage*, ed. D. H. Craig (London: Routledge, 1990). For the critical history of *Volpone* in particular, the most useful and accessible single volume is *Volpone: A Casebook*, ed. Jonas Barish (London: Macmillan, 1972), which prints a selection of key texts from 1662 to 1968. For surveys of twentieth-century scholarship, see Robert C. Evans, *Ben Jonson's Major Plays: Summaries of Modern Monographs* (West Cornwall, CT: Locust Hill Press, 2000), Walter D. Lehrman, Dolores J. Sarafinski, and Elizabeth Savage, *The Plays of Ben Jonson: a reference guide* (Boston: G.K. Hall, 1980), *The New Intellectuals: A Survey and bibliography of recent studies in English Renaissance drama*, ed. Terence P. Logan and Denzell S. Smith (Lincoln: University of Nebraska Press, 1977).
2   Samuel Pepys, *The Diary of Samuel Pepys*, ed. Robert Latham and William Matthews, 11 Vols (London: G. Bell, 1970–1983), vi, 10.
3   Richard Cave, Elizabeth Schafer, and Brian Woolland, *Ben Jonson and Theatre: Performance, Practice and Theory* (London: Routledge, 1999), 135 n1.
4   Ibid., 160.

5   Ronald Bryden, 'View-halloo Volpone,' *The Observer*, 21 January 1968.
6   Ben Jonson, *Every Man Out Of His Humour*, ed. Helen Ostovich (Manchester: Manchester University Press, 2001), Induction, 231–9.
7   References to *Volpone* are to Ben Jonson, *Volpone, or The Fox*, ed. Brian Parker (Manchester: Manchester University Press, 1999).
8   Ibid., 8.
9   Translation from the Latin from *Critical Heritage*, ed. Craig, 95.
10 These counsellors are presumably 'civil lawyers and canon lawyers.' David Kovacs, 'Donne's Latin Poem on Jonson's *Volpone*: Some Observations and a Textual Conjecture,' *International Journal of the Classical Tradition* 12, no. 4 (2006): 566. Kovacs wonders whether Donne is 'suggesting that it would behoove his contemporaries to return not only to the old authors but also to the Old Religion.'
11 Translation from the Latin from Jonson, *Volpone*, ed. Parker, 72.
12 Richard Dutton, *Licensing, Censorship and Authorship in early Modern England: Buggeswords* (Basingstoke: Palgrave, 2000), 121. The relevant section is also published as Richard Dutton, 'The Lone Wolf: Jonson's Epistle to *Volpone*,' in *Refashioning Ben Jonson*, ed. Julie Sanders, Kate Chedgzoy, and Susan Wiseman (Houndmills: Macmillan, 1998).
13 Dutton, *Buggeswords*, 121.
14 Arthur Freeman, 'The Earliest Allusion to Volpone,' *Notes and Queries* 14 (1967).
15 Robert Burton, *The Anatomy of Melancholy*, ed. Floyd Dell and Paul Jordan-Smith (London: Routledge, 1931), 713. Compare *Volpone*, III.vii.201–215.
16 John Wilson, *The Projectors, a comedy* (London, 1665), Sig. I1v. Wilson also refers to 'grave Sir Poll' in the Prologue to *The Cheats*. John Wilson, *The Cheats, a comedy* (London, 1664), Sig. A4r.
17 William Congreve, *The Way of the World* (London, 1700), Sig. D4v-E1r.
18 Aphra Behn, *Sir Patient Fancy: A Comedy* (London, 1678), Sig. M4v.
19 C. B. Graham, 'An Echo of Jonson in Aphra Behn's *Sir Patient Fancy*,' *Modern Language Notes* 53, no. 4 (1938).
20 C. B. Graham, 'Jonson Allusions in Restoration Comedy,' *The Review of English Studies* 15, no. 58 (1939): 200.
21 Jeffrey Barnouw, 'Britain and European Literature and Thought,' in *The Cambridge History of English Literature, 1660–1780*, ed. John J. Richetti (Cambridge: Cambridge University Press, 2005), 429.
22 Thomas Killigrew, *Comedies and tragedies* (London, 1664), Sig. Yy4v.
23 Carolyn D. Williams, '"This Play will be mine A[rse]": Aphra Behn's Jonsonian Negotiations,' in *Jonsonians: Living Traditions*, ed. Brian Woolland (Aldershot: Ashgate, 2003), 103–5.
24 Alison Findlay, 'Daughters of Ben,' Ibid., ed. Brian Woolland, 117–19.
25 Thomas Rawlins, *Tunbridge-Wells, or, A Day's Courtship* (London, 1678), Sig. C1v.
26 George Wither, *Faire-virtue, the mistresse of Phil'arete* (London, 1622), Sig. A4r.
27 Jasper Mayne, *A late printed sermon against false prophets, vindicated by letter, from the causeless aspersions of Mr. Francis Cheynell* (London, 1647), Sig. C4r-C4v.
28 Barten Holyday, *A survey of the world in ten books* (Oxford, 1661), Sig. H4r.
29 *The Rehearsal Transprosed*, in *Andrew Marvell*, Oxford Authors, ed. Frank Kermode and Keith Walker (Oxford: Oxford University Press, 1990), 242.
30 Noyes, *Ben Jonson on the English Stage, 1660–1776*, 67–68.
31 Robert G. Noyes, 'Volpone; or, The Fox – The Evolution of a Nickname,' *Harvard Studies and Notes in Philology and Literature* 16 (1934); Roy A. Sundstrom, 'Godolphin, Sidney, first earl of Godolphin (1645–1712), politician,' www.oxforddnb.com, accessed 6th December 2009.

32   William Rufus Chetwood, *The Dramatic Congress: A short state of the stage under the present management* (London, 1743), Sig. B4r.

33   John Suckling, *Fragmenta Aurea* (London: Humphrey Moseley, 1646), Sig. A4r. Suckling echoes a popular anonymous jingle: 'The Fox, the Alchemist, and Silent Woman, / Done by Ben Jonson, and outdone by no man'. Bentley, *Shakespeare & Jonson: their reputations in the seventeenth century compared*, 2, 273.

34   Thomas Pope Blount, *De Re Poetica* (London, 1694), P2r. See also Edward Phillips, *Theatrum Poetarum, or, A Compleat Collection of the Poets* (London, 1675), Sig. Aa10r; Gerard Langbaine and Charles Gildon, *The Lives and Characters of the English Dramatick Poets* (London, 1699), Sig. G1r.

35   Gerard Langbaine, *An Account of the English Dramatick Poets* (Oxford, 1691), Sig. T5v.

36   Richard Brome, *The Antipodes* (London, 1640), Sig. A3r.

37   Samuel Harding, *Sicily and Naples, or, The fatall union: A tragoedy* (Oxford, 1640), Sig. A3v.

38   Jeremy Collier, *A Defence of The Short View of the Profaneness and Immorality of the English Stage* (London, 1699), Sig. I7r.

39   William Burnaby, writing in 1701. Cited in *Critical Heritage*, ed. Craig, 353–54.

40   Joseph Addison and Richard Steele, *The Spectator*, ed. G. Gregory Smith, 4 vols. (London: J. M. Dent, 1907), iii, 200.

41   John Dryden, *Of Dramatick Poesie, An Essay* (London, 1668), Sig. C3v, H1r.

42   Ibid., Sig. G1r-v.

43   Dryden, 'A Defence of An Essay of Dramatique Poesy' (1668), cited in *Critical Heritage*, ed. Craig, 262.

44   Nicolas Boileau, *The Art of Poetry*, trans. William Soame and revised by John Dryden (London, 1683), Sig. D4v. The lines cited are Dryden's: *Critical Heritage*, ed. Craig, 315.

45   Anonymous, 'A Comparison Between the Two Stages' (1702), cited in *Critical Heritage*, ed. Craig, 353.

46   John Dennis, *The Characters and Conduct of Sir John Edgar* (London, 1720), letter ii, 28.

47   John Dennis, John Dryden, and William Wycherley, *Letters Upon Several Occasions* (London, 1696), Sig. F4r-F5r, G2v-G3r.

48   Margaret Cavendish, *Playes* (London, 1662), Sig. A4r-v. Cavendish's unfinished beast-fable drama *A Piece of a Play* (1668) owes much to *Volpone*. Richard Dutton, '*Volpone* and Beast Fable: Early Modern Analogic Reading,' *The Huntington Library Quarterly* 67, no. 3 (2004): 347; Alison Findlay, 'Daughters of Ben,' in *Jonsonians: Living Traditions*, ed. Brian Woolland (Aldershot: Ashgate, 2003), 114.

49   Richard Hurd, 'A Dissertation Concerning the Provinces of the several Species of the Drama,' in *Ars Poetica, Q. Horatii Flacci Epistolae ad Pisones, et Augustum: With an English Commentary and Notes* (London: 1753), i, 278–79.

50   Noyes, *Ben Jonson on the English Stage, 1660–1776*, 92–97.

51   David McPherson, 'Rough Beast into Tame Fox: The Adaptations of *Volpone*,' in *Ben Jonson: Quadricentennial Essays*, ed. Mary O. Thomas (Atlanta, Ga.: Georgia State University, 1973), 78–80.

52   Anonymous review in *The Morning Chronicle*, 13 September 1783.

53   Thomas Davies, *Dramatic Miscellanies*, 3 Vols (London, 1783–1784), ii, Sig. G1r-v, Sig. F8r.

54   Corbyn Morris, *An Essay Towards Fixing the True Standards of Wit, Humour, Raillery, Satire, and Ridicule* (London, 1744), 36.

55   David Erskine Baker, *The Companion to the Play-house* (London, 1764), i, Sig. Z6v-2A1r.

56   Anonymous, 'Covent-Garden Theatre, Nov 26. The Fox: A Comedy, by Ben Jonson,' *The theatrical review; or, New companion to the play-house* 1772, i, 226–32.

57   Letter from 'Horatio' to *The Gentleman's Magazine* (1772), cited in *Critical Heritage*, ed. Craig, 530.

58   Nathan Drake, *Literary Hours Or Sketches Critical and Narrative* (Sudbury, 1798), 449–50.

59   The claim that *Volpone* 'never greatly succeeded' contradicts the evidence. Jonas A. Barish, 'Introduction,' in *Jonson, Volpone: A Casebook* ed. Jonas A. Barish (London: Macmillan, 1972), 16.

60   Charles Dibdin, *A Complete History of the English Stage*, 5 vols. (London, 1800), iii, 293–94.

61   Paul H. Fry, 'Classical Standards,' in *The Cambridge History of Literary Criticism, Volume Five: Romanticism*, ed. Marshall Brown (Cambridge: Cambridge University Press, 2000), 7.

62   Samuel Taylor Coleridge, *Coleridge's Miscellaneous Criticism* (London: Constable, 1936), 55.

63   *Herr Von Fuchs: Ein Lustspiel in drei Aufzugen nach dem Volpone des Ben. Jonson*, in Ludwig Tieck, *Ludwig Tieck's Schriften*, vol. XII (Berlin, 1829), 1–154. Coleridge's comments may be indebted to Tieck's adaptation: McPherson, "Rough Beast into Tame Fox," 81.

64   Tom Lockwood, *Ben Jonson in the Romantic Age* (Oxford: Oxford University Press, 2005), passim.

65   Richard Cumberland, *The Observer*, 5 Vols (London, 1786–90), iv, 151–56.

66   Ben Jonson, *The Works of Ben Jonson*, ed. William Gifford, 9 Vols (London, 1816), iii, 331.

67   Cumberland, *The Observer*, iv, 155.

68   Douglas Duncan, *Ben Jonson and the Lucianic Tradition* (Cambridge: Cambridge University Press, 1979), 144.

69   James Howell, *Epistolae Ho-Elianae. Familiar Letters Domestic and Forren* (London, 1650), Sig. Kk5v.

70   William Hazlitt, *Lectures on the English Comic Writers* (London, 1819), 82–83.

71   Anonymous, 'The Works of Ben Jonson,' *The Southern Review* VI (1830): 109.

72   George W. Whiting, '*Volpone, Herr Von Fuchs*, and *Les Heritiers Rabourdin*,' *PMLA* 46, no. 2 (1931); Eileen E. Pryme, 'Zola's Plays in England, 1870–1900,' *French Studies* 12, no. 1 (1959).

73   J. A. Symonds, *Ben Jonson* (London: Longmans Green, 1886).

74   Oscar Wilde, *Pall Mall Gazette*, September 20 1886.

75   Algernon Charles Swinburne, *A Study of Ben Jonson* (London: Chatto and Windus, 1889), 35–36, 42.

76   T. S. Eliot, *Selected Essays* (London: Faber and Faber, 1951), 148–59.

77   Ibid., 159–60.

78   *Ben Jonson*, ed. C. H. Herford and Percy Simpson, Vol. 2 (Oxford: Clarendon Press, 1925), 49–65.

79   Ejner J. Jensen, *Ben Jonson's Comedies on the Modern Stage* (Ann Arbor, Mich: UMI Research Press, 1985), 124.

80   W. B. Yeats, *On The Boiler* (Dublin, 1939), 32–33, cited in Ian Donaldson, 'Volpone,' *Essays in Criticism* 22 (1972). The comparison between Coleridge's and Yeats's responses is drawn by McPherson, 'Rough Beast into Tame Fox', 81.

81   L. C. Knights, *Drama and Society in the Age of Jonson* (London: Chatto and Windus, 1937), 186–206.

82   Kay, *Literary Life*, 89.

83   Ben Jonson, *Four Comedies*, ed. Helen Ostovich (Harlow: Longman, 1997), 8–9, 60.
     On the debt to Aristophanes, see also P. H. Davison, 'Volpone and the Old Comedy,'
     Modern Language Quarterly 24 (1963); Coburn Gum, *The Aristophanic Comedies of
     Ben Jonson* (The Hague; New York: Mouton, Humanities, 1969); B. A. Park, 'Volpone
     and Old Comedy,' *English Language Notes* 19, no. 2 (1981); David C. McPherson,
     Shakespeare, Jonson, and the Myth of Venice (Newark: University of Delaware Press,
     1990), 91–116. See also Jonson, *Volpone,* ed. Parker, 10–12, 299–311. On the classical
     sources generally, see George A. E. Parfitt, 'Some Notes on the Classical Borrowings
     in *Volpone,' English Studies: A Journal of English Language and Literature* 55 (1974):
     131. On Sutton, see Robert C. Evans, *Jonson and the Contexts of His Time* (London
     and Toronto: Associated University Presses, 1994), 45–61; Matthew Steggle, *Wars of
     the Theatres: the poetics of personation in the age of Jonson* (Victoria, B. C.: English
     Literary Studies, University of Victoria, 1998), 101–02. On the representation of
     Venice, see R. B. Parker, 'Jonson's Venice,' in *Theatre of the English and Italian
     Renaissance,* ed. J. R. Mulryne and Margaret Shewring (Basingstoke: Macmillan,
     1991), 95–112; Leo Salingar, 'The Idea of Venice in Shakespeare and Ben Jonson,' in
     Shakespeare's Italy: Functions of Italian Locations in Renaissance Drama, ed. Michele
     Marrapodi, et al. (Manchester: Manchester University Press, 1993); Jonathan Bate,
     'The Elizabethans in Italy,' in *Travel and Drama in Shakespeare's Time,* ed. Jean-Pierre
     Maquerlot and Michele Willems (Cambridge University Press, Cambridge, England,
     1996).
84   Rainer Pineas, 'The Morality Vice in *Volpone,' Discourse* 5 (1962); Alan C. Dessen,
     Jonson's Moral Comedy (Evanston: Northwestern University Press, 1971), 75–104;
     Irena Janicka, *The Popular Theatrical Tradition and Ben Jonson* (Lodz: Uniwersytet
     Lodzki, 1972), 179–88; Gerard H. Cox, III, 'Celia, Bonario, and Jonson's Indebtedness
     to the Medieval Cycles,' *Etudes Anglaises* 25 (1972); Robert Potter, *The English
     Morality Play: Origins, History and Influence of a Dramatic Tradition* (London and
     Boston: Routledge and Kegan Paul, 1975), 144–52.
85   Translated into English by William Caxton in 1481. For a modern translation,
     see D. D. R. Owen, *The Romance of Reynard the Fox* (Oxford: Oxford University
     Press, 1994).
86   Jonson, *Volpone,* ed. Parker, 18.
87   Robert Shaughnessy, 'Twentieth-Century Fox: Volpone's Metamorphosis,' *Theatre
     Research International* 27, no. 1 (2002).
88   Dutton, '*Volpone* and Beast Fable', 347.
89   Julie Sanders, *Ben Jonson's Theatrical Republics* (Basingstoke: Macmillan, 1998),
     34–46.
90   Dutton, '*Volpone* and Beast Fable,' 349; Richard Dutton, *Ben Jonson, Volpone and the
     Gunpowder Plot* (Cambridge: Cambridge University Press, 2008), 4 and passim. On
     the influence of the Gunpowder Plot, see also James Tulip, 'Comedy as Equivocation:
     An Approach to the Reference of *Volpone,' Southern Review: Literary and Interdisci-
     plinary Essays* 5 (1972); William W. E. Slights, 'The Play of Conspiracies in *Volpone,'
     Texas Studies in Literature and Language* 27, no. 4 (1985); William W. E. Slights, *Ben
     Jonson and the Art of Secrecy* (Toronto: University of Toronto Press, 1994), 57–77.
91   Edmund Wilson, *The Triple Thinkers: Twelve Essays on Literary Subjects* (New York:
     Farrar, Straus and Giroux, 1976), 217–21.
92   William Kerrigan, 'Ben Jonson Full of Shame and Scorn,' in *Ben Jonson: Quadricen-
     tennial Essays,* ed. Mary O. Thomas, *Studies in the Literary Imagination,* 6 (Atlanta,
     Ga.: Georgia State University, 1973).
93   W. Speed Hill, 'Biography, Autobiography, and *Volpone,' Studies in English Literature,
     1500–1900* 12, no. 2 (1972).
94   Riggs, *Jonson,* 138–39.

95 George Mandelbaum, 'On Ben Jonson's Comedies,' *American Imago* 65, no. 2 (2008).

96 John Gordon Sweeney, *Jonson and the Psychology of Public Theater: To coin the spirit, spend the soul* (Princeton: Princeton University Press, 1985), 71.

97 Bruce Thomas Boehrer, *The Fury of Men's Gullets: Ben Jonson and the digestive canal* (Philadelphia: University of Pennsylvania Press, 1997), 94–111.

98 Richard Barbour, "When I Acted Young Antinous': Boy Actors and the Erotics of Jonsonian Theater,' *PMLA* 110, no. 5 (1995): 1010–11.

99 Joseph Loewenstein, *Ben Jonson and Possessive Authorship* (Cambridge: Cambridge University Press, 2002), 117–19.

100 *Re-Presenting Ben Jonson*, ed. Martin Butler (Houndmills: Macmillan, 1999), 1.

101 Kate Chedgzoy, Julie Sanders, and Susan Wiseman, 'Introduction: Refashioning Ben Jonson,' in *Refashioning Ben Jonson: Gender, Politics and the Jonsonian Canon*, ed. Julie Sanders, Kate Chedgzoy, and Susan Wiseman (Houndmills: Macmillan, 1998), 1–3.

102 *Re-Presenting Ben Jonson*, ed. Butler, 4.

103 Chedgzoy, Sanders, and Wiseman, 'Introduction: Refashioning Ben Jonson,' 3.

104 Jonas A. Barish, 'The Double Plot in *Volpone*,' *Modern Philology* 51, no. 2 (1953); Judd Arnold, 'The Double Plot in Volpone: A Note on Jonsonian Dramatic Structure,' *Seventeenth-Century News* 23, no. 4 (1965); Dorothy E. Litt, 'Unity of Theme in *Volpone*,' *Bulletin of the New York Public Library* 73 (1969); John Creaser, 'Vindication of Sir Politic Would-Be,' *English Studies* 57 (1976); Alexander Leggatt, '*Volpone*: The Double Plot Revisited,' in *New Perspectives on Ben Jonson*, ed. James Hirsh (Madison, NJ: Fairleigh Dickinson University Press, 1997), 103; Jonson, *Volpone*, ed. Parker, 37–41; David Bevington, 'The Major Comedies,' in *The Cambridge Companion to Ben Jonson*, ed. Richard Harp and Stanley Stewart (Cambridge: Cambridge University Press, 2000), 77–78.

105 G. Gregory Smith, *Ben Jonson* (London: Macmillan, 1919), 111; Helena Watts Baum, *The Satiric and the Didactic in Ben Jonson's Comedy* (Chapel Hill: University of North Carolina Press, 1947), 165–82; Freda L. Townsend, *Apologie for Batholomew Fayre: The Art of Jonson's Comedies* (New York, NY, 1947), 58–62; Ralph Nash, 'The Comic Intent of *Volpone*,' *Studies in Philology* 44 (1947); Knoll, *Ben Jonson's Plays: An Introduction*, 79–104; Joyce Miller, '*Volpone*: A Study of Dramatic Ambiguity,' in *Studies in English Language and Literature*, ed. Alice Shalvi and A. A. Mendilow, *Scripta Hierosolymitana: Publications of the Hebrew University Number: 17* (Hebrew Univ., Jerusalem Pagination: 35–95, 1966); Robert N. Watson, *Ben Jonson's Parodic Strategy: Literary Imperialism in the Comedies* (Cambridge, Massachusetts and London: Harvard University Press, 1987), 80–97; Rosalind Miles, *Ben Jonson: His Craft and Art* (London: Routledge, 1990), 104–11.

106 D. J. Enright, 'Poetic Satire and Satire in Verse: A Consideration of Jonson and Massinger,' *Scrutiny* 18 (1952); Edward B. Partridge, *The Broken Compass: A Study of the Major Comedies of Ben Jonson* (London: Chatto and Windus, 1958), 63–113; Dessen, *Jonson's Moral Comedy*, 75–104; Charles A. Hallett, '*Volpone* as the Source of the Sickroom Scheme in Middleton's *Mad World*,' *Notes and Queries* 18 (1971), 24–25; A. K. Nardo, 'The Transmigration of Folly: Volpone's Innocent Grotesques,' *English Studies* 58 (1977); George Parfitt, *Ben Jonson: Public Poet and Private Man* (New York: Barnes and Noble, 1977), 58–60, 88–91.

107 Peter Hyland, *Disguise and Role-Playing in Ben Jonson's Drama* (Salzburg: Institut fur Englische Sprache & Literatur, 1977), 88.

108 C. G. Thayer, *Ben Jonson: Studies in the Plays* (Norman: University of Oklahoma Press, 1963), 50–66; J. A. Bryant, *The Compassionate Satirist: Ben Jonson and his Imperfect World* (Athens, Georgia: University of Georgia Press, 1972), 65–69;

L. A. Beaurline, 'Volpone and the Power of Gorgeous Speech', *Studies in the Literary Imagination* 6 (1973); Robert Wescott, 'Volpone? Or the Fox?', *Critical Review* 17 (1974).

109 Ian Donaldson, *Jonson's Magic Houses: Essays in Interpretation* (Oxford: Oxford University Press, 1997), 117–18.

110 Ian Donaldson, 'Volpone: Quick and Dead', *Essays in Criticism* 21 (1971); Jonathan V. Crewe, 'Death in Venice: A Study of *Othello* and *Volpone*', *University of Cape Town Studies in English* 4 (1973); Alexander W. Lyle, 'Volpone's Two Worlds', *Yearbook of English Studies* 4 (1974); Donald Gertmenian, 'Comic Experience in *Volpone* and *The Alchemist*', *Studies in English Literature* 17, no. 2 (1977); Alexander Leggatt, *Ben Jonson: His Vision and his Art* (London: Methuen, 1981), 23–29, 275–76; Peter Womack, *Ben Jonson* (Oxford: Basil Blackwell, 1986), 138–44.

111 Alexander Leggatt, 'The Suicide of Volpone', *University of Toronto Quarterly* 39 (1969).

112 Stephen J. Greenblatt, 'The False Ending in *Volpone*', *Journal of English and Germanic Philology* 75 (1976): 94–95.

113 Ibid.: 103–04.

114 James Hirsh, 'Cynicism and the Futility of Art in *Volpone*', in *New Perspectives on Ben Jonson*, ed. James Hirsh (Madison, NJ: Fairleigh Dickinson University Press, 1997), 106.

115 Donaldson, *Magic Houses*, 113. See also Katharine Eisaman Maus, *Ben Jonson and the Roman Frame of Mind* (Princeton: Princeton University Press, 1984), 49–52.

116 Mark A. Anderson, 'Structure and Response in *Volpone*', *Renaissance & Modern Studies* 19 (1975); Duncan, *Lucianic Tradition*, 144–64; Richard Dutton, *Ben Jonson: To The First Folio* (Cambridge: Cambridge University Press, 1983), 64–74, 147–53; Cave, *Ben Jonson*, 44–68.

117 William Empson, 'Volpone', *Hudson Review* 21 (1968): 651–53 with "that" in the first sentence silently corrected to "than."

CHAPTER TWO

Volpone on the Stage

Rebecca Yearling

The title page of the 1607 quarto edition states that *Volpone* was first performed at the Globe 'in the yeere 1605', which probably means around February/March 1606. The play was put on by Shakespeare's acting company, the King's Men, and in the cast were Richard Burbage – the King's Men's star performer – and also Henry Condell, John Heminges, William Sly, Alexander Cooke, John Lowin, and perhaps Nicholas Tooley.[1] There has been much speculation regarding which part each actor played. Brian Parker suggests that Burbage may have played Volpone, Condell Mosca, Sly Voltore, Heminges Sir Politic, Lowin Peregrine and Cooke Bonario.[2] However, there are other possibilities. A surviving copy of the 1616 folio has a handwritten annotation claiming that Heminges played the part of Corbaccio, alongside Nathan Field as Voltore – but Field did not join the King's Men until 1616, so it is not known whether Heminges had played the role of Corbaccio originally, in 1606, or whether he performed different roles in the play at different times. Equally, Cooke's name appears last on the list of actors for *Volpone*, which is sometimes taken as an indication that the role in question was that of a woman: it is possible that he played either Lady Would-be or Celia. The play's music and songs may have been provided by the composer Alfonso Ferrabosco the Younger, who supplied music for several of Jonson's court masques.[3]

The play – and the production – seems to have been a success: *Volpone* was one of the plays that the King's Men took on tour to several locations in the summer of either 1606 or 1607, including Oxford and Cambridge. In the 1607 'Epistle', which he dedicates 'to the two famous universities', Jonson refers to 'their love and acceptance shewn to his poem in the presentation'.

It is not known how often *Volpone* was played over the next twenty or so years, but it was certainly performed at court on 27 December 1624, and again before the king at the newly-converted Whitehall Cockpit theatre on 19 November 1630.[4] The diary of one theatregoer, Sir Humphrey Mildmay, records another performance on 27 October 1638: 'dined att Whitehall & after dynner to the fox play = att bl: fryars . . .'[5], and this was followed up by another royal performance at the Cockpit on 8 November of the same year.

The first recorded revival of *Volpone* after the Restoration was in 1662. At some point during that year it was performed by Sir Thomas Killigrew's company, the King's Men, at the 'new new Theatre in Lincolnes Inne fields'[6]; and it was also performed at court on 16 October, in a performance attended by John Evelyn.[7] The next year, on 7 May 1663, Killigrew opened his new Theatre Royal – also known as Drury Lane, Covent Garden or The King's Theatre – in Bridges Street, and *Volpone* was performed again there, in a production starring Michael Mohun as Volpone and Charles Hart as Mosca. Mohun, a leading English actor and a full sharer in the King's Men company, was at the time mainly noted for playing villains: he had previously played Iago to Hart's Othello and Cassius to his Brutus. We do not know who played the female roles in the earlier Restoration productions, but in this production, certainly, they were performed by women: the part of Celia was taken by Ann Marshall and that of Lady Would-be by the renowned comic actress Katherine Corey, who habitually played old women's parts, mothers, governesses and bawds. When Samuel Pepys saw this production on 14 January 1665, he described it as 'a most excellent play – the best I think I ever saw, and well acted.'[8]

It was illegal at this time for two companies to own the same play, so *Volpone* was played exclusively by Killigrew's King's Men at Drury Lane for the next twenty years. However, there was nothing to stop amateur groups playing it, and there are several accounts of such productions, including one in Oxford on the 1st and 6th of January, 1663, when Anthony Wood records: 'given to see Volponey acted at the town hall by prentices and tradesmen, 6d.'[9]

One of the characteristics of the Restoration stage was a new interest in elaborate staging, scenery, costumes and particularly music, and when old plays were revived, they frequently had new songs, dances and musical interludes added to them, to the extent that some complained that the music was treated as a bigger attraction than the play itself. *Volpone* was not exempt from this treatment: at some point during the 1670s (possibly a revival at Drury Lane on 17 January 1676) a new prologue was added to the play which attacks the fashion, complaining:

Did Ben now live, how would he fret and rage
To see the music room envy the stage? [...]
In vain we chuse the best Poetick strain,
The teeming head's choice labours cull in vain,
Whilst plyant fingers quite putt down the brain.
The Fox above our boasting Play-bills shew,
Variety of musick stands below.'[10]

The play's production history during the 1680s is somewhat uncertain, as the King's Men got into financial difficulties during this time, and were in 1682 forced to close down their theatre and form a union with the other patent company, Thomas Betterton's Duke's Company, at Dorset Garden. They took their previous repertory with them: in 1691, Gerard Langbaine reports that *Volpone* 'is still in vogue at the Theatre in *Dorset-Garden*.'[11]

The union of the companies lasted until 1695, and after that, the best actors of the two companies formed yet another new company, under Betterton, which performed at a new theatre in Lincoln's Inn Fields. This collaboration was to last until 1705. Meanwhile, the Drury Lane theatre reopened under the control of Christopher Rich and Thomas Skipwith. It seems likely that Jonson's plays continued to be performed during this period, but there are no records of *Volpone* between 1691 and 1700. The next known performance is on 2 May 1700, and then again on 27 December 1700, when the *English Post* reports that, 'The Ambassador from Tripoli with his Retinue came last Friday to the King's Play-House to see a Play, called *Volpone, or the Fox*.'[12]

The play met with a hitch in 1702 when it, along with two other plays, *The Humour of the Age*, and *Sir Courtly Nice*, was accused of immorality. In *Volpone's* case, this charge was based on a single line in which Peregrine tells Lady Would-be, 'Be damn'd': a line not, in fact, in Jonson's text, but one which the actors must have added. The actors of the Drury Lane company – John Powell, John Mills, Robert Wilks, Elizabeth Verbruggen, Mariah Oldfield, Benjamin Jonson, William Pinkman, William Bullock, Philip Griffin, Colley Cibber, and Jane Rogers – were called before the Middlesex Grand Jury on 16 February 1702 to account for themselves, but all except Pinkman (also known as Pinkethman) were found not guilty.[13] There were no performances of the play that year, which Noyes suggests may be because the charge had unnerved the players.[14] However, if that was the case, their caution did not last long: in 1703, there were five productions, and *Volpone* continued to be a popular work throughout the next ten years, with some fifty-eight performances between 1700 and 1710.

Continuing the fashion from the 1670s, these performances were often played as part of a longer show, with the rest of the bill being made up of musical attractions, singing, dancing and short comic sketches. In June 1705, one performance was advertised as containing 'Purcell's *Genius of England* sung by Leveridge', and another, from November 1705, contained 'A Sonata, compos'd by the Great Archangelo Corelli for Flute and Violin, and perform'd by Signior Gasparini and Mr Paisable'.[15] As one of Her Majesty's players at Drury Lane wrote to another actor in around 1705,

> 'Volpone' or 'Tamerlane' will hardly fetch us a tolerable audience, unless we stuff the bills with long entertainments of dances, songs, scaramouched entries and what not.[16]

Nevertheless, Jonson's play continued to be produced on a regular basis throughout the period, moving several times between Drury Lane and the new Queen's Theatre at the Haymarket, as a result of the two main theatre companies' ongoing financial difficulties, and consequent repeated forming and disbanding of new companies, unions and cooperatives. Richard Steele praised a 1709 Drury Lane production in *The Tatler*, remarking that the play was so impressive that it put more recent dramas to shame:

> This night was acted the comedy, called, the *Fox*; but I wonder the modern writers do not use their interest in the house to suppress such representations. A man that has been at this, will hardly like any other play during the season [...][17]

The production Steele saw had the 'famous and heroic actor' George Powell[18] playing Volpone and Robert Wilks as Mosca – a part the latter apparently played with 'the officiousness of an artful servant'.[19] Wilks seems to have first played Mosca in around 1701, and continued to perform the part regularly until 1731, the year before his death. However, throughout at least some of this period, Powell shared the role of Volpone with the actor John Mills.

From 1713–1727, *Volpone* was played once a year, on average, and was performed before royalty twice: at Hampton Court in 1718 and at Drury Lane in 1722. It was then dropped from the Drury Lane repertory in 1727, whereupon it was taken up by John Rich's company at the relatively new Lincoln's Inn theatre.[20] The Lincoln's Inn production of *Volpone* starred the eminent comic actor James Quin as Volpone and Lacy Ryan as Mosca. Both Quin and Ryan had previously performed in productions of the play at Drury Lane, with Quin having played Voltore and Ryan having played Bonario, before they joined Rich's company. Rich's performers continued to play *Volpone* on and off until 1754, first at Lincoln's Inn and later at a new theatre in Covent Garden, which Rich opened in December 1732.

After 1727, there were no productions of *Volpone* at Drury Lane for four years, until the play was revived for a single performance in 1731, starring John Mills and Robert Wilks. There were no Drury Lane performances in 1732 or 1733, but then in 1734, the play was revived again – possibly because James Quin had rejoined the company for the 1734–1735 season, leaving the Covent Garden players. In this new production, Quin was cast as Volpone, and John Mills was relegated to playing Corvino: a move that was explained as a 'way of giving still greater novelty to this piece'.[21] Thomas Davies, who saw this production, remarks that Quin was a more impressive Volpone than Mills had been, but also that Mills made a better Corvino than Colley Cibber, who had taken the part in 1731. Cibber had 'seemed [. . .] to jest with the character,' but Mills 'was in earnest, and had a stronger voice to express passionate and jealous rage'.[22] Of the other performances, Davies notes that Mrs Clive's Lady Would-be 'gave infinite entertainment', while Mrs Butler made the relatively minor part of Celia 'extremely interesting'.

Quin stayed with the Drury Lane company for seven seasons, during which time he was replaced as Volpone at Covent Garden by the Irish actor Dennis Delane.[23] However, Delane seems to have been generally less admired in the part than Quin was, according to Quin's biographer,[24] and when Quin returned to Covent Garden, he resumed the role, which he went on to play until 1750. During this period, the play seems to have been very popular: in 1733 and 1734 there were twelve performances altogether, shared between Drury Lane, Covent Garden and the Haymarket.[25] There were productions throughout the rest of the 1730s and into the 1740s, and *Volpone* was still going strong in 1747: one writer reported that *Volpone* 'still continues to be acted, with the greatest Applause, which, without doubt, it deserves [. . .]'[26] However, the play was dropped from both the Drury Lane and Covent Garden repertories in 1754, and not played again until 1771.

During this period of neglect, the famous actor-manager David Garrick developed plans to revive *Volpone* at Drury Lane, with himself as the lead, and there were announcements in the press to this effect in both 1757 and 1769. However, although this production got as far as parts being distributed to the actors, and rehearsals may have begun, 'the play was superseded by some means not known.'[27]

In fact, there had been growing doubts about *Volpone* for some time. Critics had continued to disapprove of those aspects that Dryden, John Dennis and others had singled out back in the 1680s, such as Sir Politic's tortoise-shell, the mountebank scene and the construction of the last act.[28] However, more serious and all-encompassing criticisms were beginning to grow as the eighteenth century proceeded. David Erskine Baker, for example, commented in 1764 that although the play – along with Jonson's other works – might give pleasure to the critic in the study, 'there still runs through them all an unempassioned coldness in the language, a laboured stiffness in the conduct, and a deficiency of incident and interest in the catastrophe.'[29] Jonson's plays, in other words, were gradually falling out of key with popular taste, and coming to be seen as cold, academic and unappealing.

An attempt to redress these problems was made by George Colman in his 1771 adaptation. In Colman's hands, the play was shortened considerably; several scenes were cut from the Politic Would-be plot; contemporary Jacobean references were removed, and the language was tidied up, with most of the bawdy references removed. The revival, which opened at Covent Garden on 26 November, was generally well received, with one critic praising Colman's alterations, remarking that the 'many blamable intrusions upon delicacy of idea, and expression in the original' had now been removed, and that the play was now more appropriate 'to the professed chastity of the present age'.[30] Colman's version was performed on and off until January 1773, but then was dropped again. Fashions in theatre had changed, and Jacobean drama was beginning to fall out of favour. The vogue was for plays that were impeccable in their moral values, high on noble sentiments and low in intellectual content, and most early seventeenth century plays failed to fit that mould.

Colman tried again in the 1780s, making still more drastic revisions and cutting the Would-be plot altogether. This version, performed at the Haymarket theatre and featuring John Palmer as Volpone and Robert Bensley as Mosca, ran for eight performances in 1783 and received good reviews, both for the performances and the revised play itself. The biographer of John Bannister, who played Voltore, describes the acting as superlative: Palmer's 'declamation, his malignant mirth, his audacious love, and, in the end, his manly, uncontrollable anger, were all [. . .] irresistible,' while Bensley

was brisk and agile; his eye [. . .] was illumined with archness and satirical pleasantry; and his voice [. . .] gave out, with sonorous vivacity, the sarcastic observations which the other characters provoked.[31]

The adaptation was revived once more at Drury Lane in February 1785, again starring Palmer and Bensley. However, this production only lasted three nights before the theatre was closed, and there were no further productions of the play at all, either in adapted or original form, for another 136 years. In 1786, Thomas Davies suggested that the play was simply too difficult for modern audiences, commenting that 'the language [...] is so pedantic and stuck so full of Latinity that few, except the learned, can perfectly understand it'.[32] Jonson did not fit the spirit of the times: his play was neither unequivocally moral nor pleasingly easy.

The next production of *Volpone* was therefore not until January 1921, when the Phoenix Society revived the play at the Lyric Theatre in Hammersmith. This production was heavily influenced by William Poel's revivals of Jacobean plays using original staging and costuming: the set was largely bare, and left unchanged throughout the performance, and the text seems to have been uncut. W. B. Yeats attended one of these performances and in a letter to the Phoenix Society secretary remarks,

> *Volpone* was even finer than I expected. I could think of nothing else for hours after I left the theatre. The great surprise to me was the pathos of the two young people [Celia and Bonario], united not in love but in innocence, and going in the end their separate way.[33]

Meanwhile, T. S. Eliot, writing his 'London Letter' for *The Dial* magazine in May 1921, called the production,

> the most important theatrical event of the year in London. The play was superbly carried out; the performance gave evidence of Jonson's consummate skill in stage technique, proceeding without a moment of tedium from end to end; it was well acted and both acted and received with great appreciation.[34]

Eliot went on to say that the performance 'brought the great English drama to life as no contemporary performance of Shakespeare has done'.

Two years later, in June 1923, the Phoenix production was revived for a benefit performance for the Stage Society at the Regent Theatre in King's Cross. A review for the *Spectator* called it 'a most enjoyable comedy', because of 'the tightness of construction and neatness of the language', although the same review also complained that the play itself was a somewhat superficial work: 'The characters represent definite and docketed "humours"; there is no need to get 'inside' the words [...]'[35]

1923 also saw an amateur production by the Marlowe Society at Cambridge University, which was performed seven times in March of that year. Critical response was generally enthusiastic, although some critics expressed doubts about the farcical style in which some of the more minor parts were performed. The beast-fable aspect of the play was drawn to the audience's attention via a curtain across the back of the stage, which portrayed Aesop's fable of the fox and the crow, and the play's music and songs were mainly adapted from the surviving works of Ferrabosco.[36]

The next production was at the Cambridge Festival Theatre in 1930. Directed by Evan John, this production 'aimed at speed and gaiety, and achieved it consistently'.[37] The reviewer from *The Times* commented favourably on the delivery of the dialogue, the pacing and the lightness of touch in the actors' characterizations, but felt that the play itself had distinct 'narrowness and limitations', particularly when compared to the works of Shakespeare.[38]

Volpone was then produced again at the Birmingham Repertory Theatre in March-April 1935, with a shortened and simplified text. As the programme note put it,

> The original was couched in extravagant language and much reference to classical incident which made the play somewhat difficult for modern requirements, this has now been deleted [...][39]

Critical reviews were mixed, although most objections were to the play itself rather than to the production, with some complaining of the text's 'crudities' and feeling that, 'There is something extraordinarily wearisome in undiluted depravity, even though presented with fine jugglery of words'.[40]

This production was taken to the Malvern Festival in the summer of 1935, with a few cast changes: the actors playing Corvino, Lady Would-be, Sir Politic and Volpone himself were replaced. This time it received much better reviews, with critics seeing it as representing 'the whole comic spirit of the period at its ugly, coarse, relentless and yet brilliant best'.[41] Some of this new favour seems to have been due to the new Volpone: whereas the previous Volpone, John Clifford, had primarily emphasized the humour of the part, the replacement performer, Wilfred Lawson, brought a greater sense of menace to the role. As one reviewer commented,

> Wilfred Lawson saw to it that the farce was dominated by the sulphurous horror of an intelligence immensely alert in the pursuit of evil, and there was terror as well as laughter in the play'.[42]

Perhaps the most influential *Volpone* of the twentieth century was to come in 1938, with a Michael Macowan-directed production starring Donald Wolfit, the famed Shakespearean actor, which opened at the Westminster Theatre in January of that year. Macowan's production emphasized the beast fable aspect of the play: the characters wore outfits designed to recall the animals and birds that their names suggested, with Volpone swathed in furs, the gulls adorned in feathers and the Avocatori designed to recall owls, blinking through thick glasses, wearing 'appropriate head-dresses as they sit buzzing and squeaking on their perch', in a continuation of the play's bird metaphor.[43] Macowan also cut the Would-be subplot.

This production was a great success, with the critic for the *New Statesman* describing it as 'better than my recollection of the Phoenix Society's performance in 1921', and the *Evening News* claiming that audiences 'are never likely to see this crabbed, cruel play better done'.[44] However, it was Wolfit's performance that most reviewers singled out for special praise. Wolfit was already notorious for his dynamic, somewhat histrionic acting style, and in both this and subsequent productions of *Volpone*, he dominated the stage, with an energetic and sensuous performance, which the teenage Kenneth Tynan recalled in a letter to a friend:

> almost lovingly wolfit savoured every syllable; and in the colossal 'milk of unicorns and panther's breath' speech the house was burdened with verbal perfume. how he impressed too with the hissing delivery of his triumphant 'I am volpone and thisssss my sssslave'.[45]

Wolfit went on to play the part of Volpone repeatedly over the next twenty years. In 1940, for the Cambridge Arts Festival, he developed his own production of the play which was based on Macowan's staging but made some further alterations. He restored the Would-bes (casting a man in drag – Donald Beves, a Cambridge don – as Lady Would-be), and also directed the actors playing the Avocatori to perform as more obviously figures of fun than they had been in Macowan's staging. However, several critics felt that this latter change undermined the effectiveness of the courtroom scenes, by turning them into farce. Wolfit directed the play again in 1942, 1944, 1947, 1949 and 1953. Each of these productions differed from the others in a variety of ways (for example, the 1947 version cut Lady Would-be again, although it retained Sir Politic), but there were certain devices and bits of business that Wolfit developed and seems to have maintained throughout them all, such as his performance of the play's last moments:

the blood-curdling howl after receiving the sentence of the court, followed by the line, 'This is called the mortifying of the FOX!' and the holding on to the final hissing sibilant.[46]

The effect of Wolfit's performance was, in some ways, to turn the play into a one-man show. Alan Wheatley played Mosca in Macowan's original production, with a performance notable for its 'airy agility and whispering mephisto-gaiety',[47] but Wolfit was reportedly unhappy with this portrayal, seeing Wheatley's Mosca as too independent, too liable to distract the attention away from Volpone himself. In his own later versions, he directed his Moscas to be more subservient. As one critic complained of one of Wolfit's versions, although several other actors put in good performances, 'the requisite combination of parts hardly begins to take shape', and as a result, 'The evening's pleasure is largely confined to Mr Wolfit's playing of Volpone'.[48]

Between 1942 and 1953, Wolfit took his productions on successful tours to Canada, the USA and Egypt, where they were also met with enthusiasm. The Broadway response to the play in 1947 is typical: although Wolfit's company presented other plays on Broadway in the same season – productions of *Hamlet*, *King Lear*, *The Merchant of Venice* and *As You Like It* – *Volpone* was the only one to achieve real success, with *Time* magazine describing how 'the crowd – or, at any rate, the critics – made an excited grab' for the production,[49] praising both the play and the performances. Wolfit last played the role in 1959, in a television production directed by Stephen Harrison for the BBC 'World Theatre' series.

Wolfit's production had a huge influence upon later stage versions of *Volpone*. It became common for directors to stress the beast-fable aspect of the story and to cut the Would-bes, and common for critics to view the show as a star-vehicle, rather than an ensemble piece. It was also hard for other actors playing the part in the years immediately following Wolfit to live up to his performance: they were frequently compared to Wolfit and found wanting.

Since Wolfit, however, there have been several other notable productions in their own right. In 1944, *Volpone* was played five times at the Shakespeare Memorial Theatre in Stratford-on-Avon, with a cast starring Robert Atkins (who also directed) as Volpone and John Byron as Mosca. The Would-bes were present, although Sir Politic's tortoise-shell was cut. However, critics complained that the Atkins version 'emphasize[d] the farcical passages of the play and [. . .] abate[d] the satire'. Atkins played Volpone as a 'genial rogue [. . .] who retains our sympathy as he tumbles in and out of scrapes which are essentially harmless', and as result, the play was funny but not in any way disturbing or provocative, raising only 'comfortable laughter'.[50]

In 1952, George Devine directed Ralph Richardson as Volpone and Anthony Quayle as Mosca in a production at Stratford. The reviews were mixed: many thought it a good production, but were unsure about the slowness and gentleness with which Richardson played the part. Richardson brought out the comedy of his role, but not the savagery or depravity; he played Volpone, one reviewer remarked, as simply 'a crazy eccentric devising practical jokes, which are played with a good-humoured self-satisfaction'.[51] Another critic was harsher: Richardson, he wrote, 'substituted ponderous flatness for the spirit of glorious, gloating rascality'.[52] Either way, critics felt that some of the play's satiric edge and energy had been lost. Richardson's restraint, however, gave Anthony Quayle – who played Mosca – more of a chance to shine. Playing the part as 'oily, sly and smooth, a Zeal-of-the-Land Puritan with a touch of Uriah Heep', Quayle was 'at once plausible, comic and sinister'.[53] Meanwhile the Would-be scenes were restored, albeit to mixed effect, with one critic remarking that Wolfit's 'excision seems the more justified in that Mr. Michael Hordern and Miss Rosalind Atkinson could not, with all their talent, fully reconcile us to their presence here. The scenes [...] look like a playwright's afterthought'.[54]

The Bristol Old Vic production, in 1955, seems to have been mainly notable for its skilful deployment of the play's animal imagery. The three suitors moved, talked and stood like birds; Alan Dobie's black-clad Mosca buzzed and darted around the stage like a fly; and only Eric Porter's Volpone seemed slightly out of place. As one reviewer remarked, he 'has a lion's mane and a lion's roar that can hardly be reconciled with the sly cunning of a fox'.[55] In 1964, Tyrone Guthrie directed a vigorous *Volpone* in Minneapolis, which was described as 'bursting with color, movement, and the splendor of words'.[56] Guthrie's production again emphasized the beast-fable motif, with elaborate animal costumes and performances to match: the suitors, for example, were dressed 'in black, with beaks for noses, great feather collars to preen and puff, clawed gloves'.[57] It was also marked by spectacular physical effects. At the climax of the mountebank scene, Volpone climbed a ladder to Celia's balcony, only to meet Corvino who sent him toppling backwards into the arms of the crowd below. For all this, some complained that the production was too good-humoured, with both Douglas Campbell as Volpone and George Gizzard as Mosca 'less vividly sinister than they might be'.[58]

Four years later, Guthie was invited to direct another production at the National Theatre in London, which starred Colin Blakely as Volpone and Frank Wylie as Mosca. Again, Guthrie's production was full of entertaining stage-business: Volpone leapt out of bed at the beginning to wash his face in gold ducats, while his seduction of Celia was full of 'comic skirmishings round the room and lascivious wrestling-holds among the pillows'.[59] Again, Volpone was dressed in furs, emitting 'odd foxy yelps'[60], while the suitors were strikingly bird-like. One reviewer recalls,

> Edward Petherbridge transforming his fingers into Voltore's vulturely claws [. . .] the parrot-like verbal ticks of Graham Crowden as Sir Politick [. . .] the ravenly curve of Paul Curran's back, his whole black-cloaked body semi-circling towards Corbaccio's beak [. . .] All these were small masterpieces of inter-pretation, manifesting a controlled and consistent response towards the play as a moral fable.[61]

However, many critics were less sure about the overall style of the production, which, like the Minneapolis version, tended to emphasize the grotesque and farcical elements of the play at the expense of the language and plot. The critic for the *Sunday Telegraph* remarked, 'An enormous load of fussy business, obsessive mannerisms and grotesque posturing was plastered across the façade of the play, so that a walled-in plot could be only just heard struggling, with increasing feebleness, to escape'; while the *Daily Express* complained, 'The extravagantly costumed freaks who people the stage eventually outstay their first, startled welcome. A circus which had little to offer except its clowns would soon pall'.[62]

In 1966, Frank Hauser directed Leo McKern as Volpone at the Oxford Playhouse, in another hugely successful production. McKern had a strong physical presence, and brought 'enormous agility and great vocal skill' to the role, while critics also singled out Leonard Rossiter's performance as Corvino for praise: 'superb in his mixture of jealousy and tortured affability'.[63] It was generally agreed that the production got the balance between savagery and comedy just right. However, when the production came to London the following year, reviews were less positive: critics felt that the balance of the performances had tipped too much towards comedy, and as a result it 'muffle[d] cruelty and present[ed] the deadly sins as [. . .] eccentricities'.[64]

A production directed by David William at the Stratford Festival in 1971 sought to emphasize the grotesquerie and decadence of the play. In this version, Volpone's opening invocation to his gold was 'back[d] up with responses from the mass and with a procession of monks who then strip off for an orgy in black leather and masks', among whom the Volpone – played by William Hutt – wandered, clad in black pyjamas and smoking a cigarette.[65]

However, probably the most notable production of the 1970s was the Peter Hall-directed revival at the National Theatre in London in 1977, with Paul Scofield as Volpone, Ben Kingsley as Mosca and John Gielgud as Sir Politic. This version aimed for greater realism than some previous productions had done. As one reviewer remarked,

> Peter Hall's production of *Volpone* is no symbolic menagerie, no routine animation of the beastly meanings behind the names of the characters, but a fleshing-out of the artifice, a humanising of the fable. The passions, in keeping with the taming of the allegory, are brought down to life-size from the grand caricatures they sometimes appear.[66]

Scofield's Volpone was in keeping with this interpretation, more restrained and less theatrical than many. However, although some critics found his performance impressive, others complained that, like Ralph Richardson in 1952, he was *too* restrained. As John Barber commented in *the Daily Telegraph*,

> What I missed was the manic Jonsonian tension [...] Perhaps the laughter was too good-humoured, the sensuality too polite. Scofield himself too noble a figure.[67]

As with the Devine production, Hall kept the Would-be scenes, although again, one reviewer complained that they were tedious at times, and added, 'Gielgud somewhat ruefully told me later that he found it "difficult to see much that was funny in the role".[68]

In 1983, Bill Alexander directed a production at The Other Place in Stratford-on-Avon, which was later transferred to The Pit in London. This version ran for three and three-quarter hours, and included both the subplot and other frequently cut or shortened aspects, such as the performances of Volpone's three fantastics. The Volpone, played by Richard Griffiths, met with mixed responses: several critics felt he was better at the more flamboyant scenes than the more intimate and sensuous ones, which made sequences such as the attempted seduction of Celia less powerful than they might have been.[69] However, other members of the cast were praised highly, particularly Miles Anderson's Mosca, Nigel Cooke's 'bookish booby' of a Bonario, and Bruce Alexander's Sir Politic, played as 'an Elizabethan Inspector Clouseau; his pockets crammed with every paper except the one he wants, his eyes ranging the Rialto for spies'.[70]

In 1990, Nicholas Hytner directed a new production of *Volpone* at the Almeida theatre, starring Ian McDiarmid as a 'sensuous, athletic' Volpone, and Denis Lawson as Mosca. Of particular note in this production was Cate Haner's Celia, which she played not as the usual virtuously bland innocent but as 'an indignant spitfire of a girl who is not unaffected by the sight of Volpone's treasure'.[71] Again, Hytner cut the Would-be subplot.

The most recent notable production of *Volpone* was in 1995, at the Royal National Theatre. This version starred Michael Gambon as Volpone and Simon Russell Beale as Mosca, and the strong cast and lively nature of the production were commented on by virtually all critics. Gambon's 'raddled, Pagliacci-faced Volpone' was highly praised, as was Russell Beale's 'blackly hilarious' Mosca, who gave 'a brilliant masterclass in beady disingenuousness'.[72] The gulls were also skilfully differentiated:

> the icily amoral Voltore (Stephen Boxer) [. . .]; the doddery Corbaccio (Trevor Peacock); and the control-freak Corvino (Robin Soans), whose strangulated voice is both birdlike and lifelike.[73]

Nevertheless, some ended up feeling that it was all a bit much:

> Warchus's desire to fill the vastness of the theatre with all these marvellous things displays the law of diminishing returns [. . .] Every costume tries to top the last, and the acting starts at such a pitch that its impact becomes exhausting [. . .] Overwhelmed by spectacle, we come out reciting the set.[74]

Warchus, like Wolfit and Guthrie before him, seemed to some critics to lack trust in the play's own ability to amuse. Instead, he played up the spectacle, and added extra stage business, such as an opening dumb-show in which Volpone is chased through the house by a pack of legacy-hunters. Nevertheless, the production won him an Olivier award nomination, and its popularity with audiences showed that *Volpone* still had the power to attract packed houses, nearly four hundred years after its first performance.

In general, of all these twentieth-century productions of *Volpone*, the most admired and appreciated ones seem to be those in which the balance of the play is felt to be right. The energy and pace must not be allowed to drop, as then the performance drags, but equally should not be too fast, as then the poetry cannot be heard or understood. Moreover, as the anonymous *Times* critic for the 1935 Malvern festival production put it, 'There is a tendency in revivals which are not first rate to empha-size the farcical portions of the play'.[75] Some directors seem to be aiming to turn *Volpone* into a lighthearted romp, but critics often feel that this is to distort the play's essence, reduce its point and risk becoming simply repetitive and exhausting. For example, one reviewer complained of a

January 1948 revival by the New York City Theatre company that the director

> worked on the theory that maximum movement, however aimless, and maximum noise, however unmotivated, would guarantee hilarity and convince the audience that *Volpone*, a Real Classic, was just as funny as a Marx Brothers movie.[76]

In terms of costuming, animal-influenced outfits have been in fashion ever since the first Wolfit production, although some critics feel that to emphasize this aspect of the play too much may be more of a hindrance than a help, as they risk making people forget about the humanity of the characters and see them only as caricatures. As Robert Macdonald commented of the Guthie productions, 'It is difficult to condemn real vultures for behaving like vultures.'[77] Meanwhile, modern dress may work well: the 1955 Joan Littlewood production at the Theatre Royal, Stratford East, employed modern dress in order to emphasize the continuing relevance of Jonson's themes, with Mosca, for example, appearing as 'the most plausible, cigarette-sucking spiv that ever grew from dead-end kidhood'.[78]

The sets for *Volpone* allow much scope for creativity and the use of symbolism. Emphasizing Volpone's wealth by providing him with an extravagant setting is common: the 1952 Devine production, for instance, had a spectacular collection of sets, designed by Malcolm Pride: a Grand Canal, complete with gondolas, an imposing Senate and a gold-panelled bedroom for Volpone; while in order to change these sets, 'the stage ascended, dived, capered sideways, did everything in fact, but sit up and beg'.[79] Such use of technology can bring out the theatricality of Jonson's play. However, there also seems to a tendency for productions, particularly those with a large budget, to overdo the spectacle, leaving reviewers complaining of sensory overload and the losing of the plot beneath the special effects. The 1990 Hytner production, by contrast, chose to conceal Volpone's wealth, with a set 'surrounded by a canal of shallow water', filled with 'a heap of chests, cases and barrels, all locked.' According to John Peter, a *Sunday Times* theatre critic, 'No other production I've seen brought out so eloquently the deadly, impotent power of Volpone's treasure.'[80] Meanwhile, the set for the 1999 RSC production, directed by Lindsay Posner, emphasized the bird-catching metaphor of Volpone's activities, featuring 'a huge cabinet full of glistening treasures in the foreground, plucked birds hanging up in the dim area behind.'[81]

Of all the changes made in production, the most common is to cut the Would-bes. There seems to be no way to win with these characters: when they are cut, as they were in the Hauser and Hytner productions, and several of Wolfit's, critics complain that refusing to deal with the Would-bes 'is a form of abdication and evasion'.[82] However, when they are present – as they were in the Devine and Hall productions – critics (and even the actors and directors themselves) frequently call them tedious and unfunny. It is only rarely – as in Bill Alexander's production – that their presence seems really to be relished.

It is also relatively common to cut, or radically reduce, the role of Volpone's trio of fantastics, although some productions exploit the potential of these characters as sources of additional humour and/or grotesquerie: as in a production at the Royal Exchange Theatre in Manchester in 2004, when they were transformed into a 'dude', a nun and a sexy nurse, and were required to 'clown[] around with the knocka-bout physicality of *commedia dell'arte*, [while] adding, in the musical interludes, some good imitations of bad Italian television',[83] or the 1969 Birmingham Rep production, directed by Michael Simpson, in which they were presented during the attempted rape of Celia, adding to the sense of menace by looking on with 'leering approval'.[84]

The last scene and the epilogue are another aspect of the play that clearly makes directors uneasy. Several directors have cut the epilogue[85] or even replaced it with scenes in which – for example – Volpone escapes from his guard and runs away (Bristol, 1972, dir. Richard David). Tyrone Guthrie in particular seems to have been uncertain about how the play 'should' end, and experimented several times with alternative endings throughout his productions' run. In his early Minneapolis staging, he inserted a madrigal to be sung by the entire cast before Volpone's epilogue. When he directed his 1968 London version, he dropped both madrigal and epilogue, leaving only the final sentencing, which was accompanied by laughter from the Avocatori. There have also been attempts at providing alternative, symbolic endings, such as that in an adaptation by Pirie Macdonald at the Seattle Repertory theatre in 1969, which substituted for Volpone's epilogue a blind man walking across the stage: perhaps intended to symbolize Blind Justice.

Volpone has been filmed several times: in 1948 by Stephen Harrison; as a three-part production for schools, adapted by Michael Simpson, in 1965; as part of the TV series 'Play of the Week', in 1960; as a TV film in 2003; and as adapted by Donald Wolfit in 1959. It has been performed and broadcast six times on BBC radio.[86] There have been various foreign-language film and TV versions, including the 1988 Italian film, *Il Volpone*, directed by Maurizio Ponzi and set in modern Liguria, and TV films broadcast in Norway, Germany, Hungary and France.

The play has been also been the subject of numerous adaptations, of which the most influential was the 1926 rewrite by Stefan Zweig.[87] Zweig cut many scenes from Jonson's original text and added several others, but his main change was to alter the relationship between Volpone and Mosca in such a way as to turn Mosca into the play's hero. This Mosca – who has been working with Volpone for only eight weeks when the play begins – is a playful, good-humoured man, who believes that wealth should be distributed rather than hoarded. When he is made Volpone's heir towards the play's end, he promptly spends all the money on a feast for the neighbourhood, while Volpone flees the city.[88] Meanwhile, Zweig makes Volpone himself rather less attractive: more miserly, misanthropic and cowardly than in Jonson's version. Zweig cuts Volpone's dwarf, eunuch and androgyne, cuts the Would-be subplot and gives Bonario and Celia animal names to make them fit better with the rest of the characters. Bonario is thus rechristened 'Leone' (lion) and Celia, 'Colomba' (dove). Zweig also gives Volpone a mistress, in the form of the prostitute Canina, whom he may have based on Doll Common in *The Alchemist.*

Zweig's adaptation was hugely popular, especially in Germany and France, throughout the 1930s,[89] and it formed the basis for Maurice Tourneur's 1939 film *Volpone*, starring Louis Jouvet, and also George Antheil's 1953 opera of the same name.[90] In Zweig's hands, the play became a lighter, less disturbing work[91] and some found this to their tastes. One reviewer, for example, remarked, 'As rewritten by an up-to-date European, author Jonson's somewhat mechanical morality becomes a gleeful and raucous farce, lacking the solemnity of a classic and imbued instead with precisely the caustic and colloquial violence which it had for its original audiences in 1605', while another applauded Zweig's bravery in being willing to challenge Jonson's authority and give an old play a new interest and relevance for a modern audience.[92]

However, many other critics have attacked Zweig's version, complaining that it oversimplifies the play and so weakens both its moral lesson and its dramatic interest. Volpone becomes a miser rather than a game player – interested in hoarding wealth rather than in the fun of acquiring it – and thus loses much of his imaginative sympathy for the audience, while turning Mosca into an (eventual) hero lessens the play's sense of moral unease. As one remarked, 'Of this fine, strong comedy, with its dark exhuberance and its riches of language, Herr Stefan Zweig has stolen the theme, lost the spirit and mangled the plot.'[93] Zweig's version may be 'a more compact and tidy play', but it is also 'a pretty watery brew' when considered along side the '*champagne brut*' of the original.[94] Critics condemn the Tourneur film on similar grounds, with Jonas Barish commenting,

It is a stroke of irony that would doubtless have stung Jonson to fury that his massive onslaught on fraud should itself survive in a counterfeit version, and that a play which exposes greed as the ugliest of passions should reach the public in a diluted form because of the venality of the box-office.[95]

Nevertheless, Zweig's version has continued to be frequently produced throughout the twentieth century and on into the twenty-first, seeming particularly popular in America.

Zweig's approach has, moreover, set a pattern for other modern adaptations of *Volpone*, which typically attempt to transform the play into something more conventional, more manageable, both in dramatic and moral terms, than is the original play.[96] One common approach has been to turn the play from satire into a comic romp, in which questions of morality hardly arise at all. This was the case with the 1962 musical version, *Foxy*, whose book was written by Ian McLellan Hunter and Ring Lardner Jr., with a score by Robert Emmett Dolan and Johnny Mercer. *Foxy* turned *Volpone* into a farce, set in the Canadian Yukon during the 1898 gold rush. Written as a vehicle for the comedian Bert Lahr, it involved much broad physical humour and slapstick, with Foxy himself portrayed, despite his greed, as essentially a 'loveable old codger'.[97] Despite a star-turn from Lahr that won him a Tony Award, *Foxy* was not a great success.[98]

Another mid-twentieth-century adaptation which similarly changed the play's tone from satire to bawdy farce was *Sly Fox*, written by Larry Gelbart in 1976. This adaptation is set in nineteenth-century San Francisco (like Hunter and Lardner, Gelbart evidently thought that a gold-rush setting was appropriate), and although the basic plot is very similar to that of *Volpone*, Gelbart adopts many of the changes that Zweig originally made to the play, such as the removal of the Would-bes, the changed relationship between the Volpone and Mosca characters and the Volpone-character's mistress, who here becomes the witty Miss Fancy. Indeed, as he confessed to the *New York Times*, 'To this day, I've never seen or even really read *Volpone* [. . .] I worked from an English translation of Zweig's German adaptation of Ben Jonson's play in English. He streamlined it; he made some good changes'.[99] However, Gelbart does make one alteration to Zweig: whereas in Zweig's play, Mosca is left in possession of the wealth, in *Sly Fox*, he is outwitted one last time by Sly, who leaves him with only an empty money-chest.

Gelbart's adaptation was a successful one: the original production, starring George C. Scott as Foxwell, ran for 495 performances, with the *New York Times* critic, Clive Barnes, commenting, 'Be warned, a man might die laughing at *Sly Fox*'.[100] The play also did moderately well when it was revived in 2004, running for over six months and one hundred and seventy performances, despite somewhat mixed reviews. Although some critics found the play funny, others complained that the show was somewhat dated and the humour too broad.[101]

In 1955, Thomas Sterling used *Volpone* as the basis for a novel, entitled *The Evil of the Day*. This book follows the initial set-up of Jonson's play – a wealthy man summons three individuals to his 'death-bed', claiming that he is about to name his heir – but radically changes the storyline from this point onwards, as one of the heirs is found murdered, and the novel turns into a murder mystery. Sterling's book was adapted in 1959 by the playwright Frederick Knott as the comedy-thriller *Mr Fox of Venice*, and Knott's play was subsequently adapted yet again in 1967 as the film *The Honey Pot*, directed by Joseph Mankiewicz. However, all three of these versions bear little resemblance to Jonson's play, outside of the basic situation and the Venetian setting.

A more recent operatic version of *Volpone*, by composer John Musto and librettist Mark Campbell, premiered in March 2004 at The Barns performance space in the Wolf Trap National Park for the Performing Arts in Virginia. Musto and Campbell's version, 'an unfaithful adapta-tion', cut Jonson's five acts down into two, provided a romance between Celia and Bonario, turned Corvino into a woman – Corvina – and added a subplot involving a Parisian brothel-owner, Erminella, seeking her long-lost son in Venice: a son who turned out to be Mosca. This version provided a happy ending for Volpone, Mosca and Erminella, who escape together on a boat to Genoa. Campbell also replaced virtually all of Jonson's text with his own rhyming, pseudo-Elizabethan lyrics. However, despite all these changes, Musto and Campbell's version retains the idea – lost in many other adaptations – that Volpone himself is more motivated by the pleasure of the game of deception than by his inherent lust for gold. The production received positive notices, with the *Washington Post* praising it as 'a detailed and ingenious study of greed', presented with 'exactly the right blend of clarity, lightness and vivid action'.[102]

The tendency, then, among both producers of the original play and those writing and producing adaptations, has been to soften and sim-plify the play, to make it more purely comic. The problems that critics and audiences have traditionally had with Jonson's original *Volpone* were well summed up by Coleridge in 1836, when he complained that it was 'impossible to keep up any pleasurable interest in a tale, in which there is no goodness of heart in any of the prominent characters [. . .] If it were possible to lessen the paramountcy of Volpone himself, a most delightful comedy might be produced, by making Celia the ward or niece of Corvino, instead of his wife, and Bonario her lover'.[103] Although adaptors have varied in their responses to these 'problems', it is notable that the areas they have tended to change most drastically are the same ones: they update and simplify the difficult language; they alter the conclusion to make it less harshly moralistic, usually letting Volpone and Mosca escape their punishments; they turn Celia and Bonario into lovers, as Coleridge wanted; they create a 'hero' in the form of Mosca; they cut the Would-bes, but add other female characters, such as a love interest for Volpone.[104]

This approach is, however, condemned by most modern critics, who insist that cruelty and moral ambiguity is a key aspect of the play, and so should be acknowledged in production. Much of Jonson's interest as a dramatist lies in his provocativeness, his refusal to make judgement easy for his spectators, or allow them to relax into automatic or mindless responses to the drama. Audiences may occasionally be troubled by *Volpone*'s lack of sympathetic characters, or the savagery of its satire, but all the evidence suggests that that is exactly what Jonson intended. To make the play safer, gentler, or more straightforwardly 'commercial', turning it into Coleridge's 'most delightful comedy', does seem rather to miss the point.

Despite all this, though, *Volpone* has proved its continuing theatrical viability over the years. Whether performed on a largely bare stage, as in the first performances at the Globe, or with the elaborate, mechanical sets and complicated special effects of some more recent productions, whether played as a grotesque beast-fable or a more low-key and naturalistic study of human selfishness and greed, *Volpone* has continued to attract audiences; and in the years since the 1921 Phoenix revival, the play has become the most frequently produced play of the Jacobean and Caroline period, outside of the works of Shakespeare.[105]

Notes

1 Tooley's name does not appear on the printed cast list, but a Jacobean handwritten annotation in a copy of the 1616 folio suggests that he played Corvino at some point. Tooley had joined the King's Men in 1605.

2 Brian Parker, 'Introduction', *Volpone; or The Fox*, The Revels Plays, 2nd edn. (Manchester: Manchester University Press, 2000): 42.

3 Of Ferrabosco's songs for *Volpone*, only his version of Act III's 'Come My Celia' has survived, although several critics have cast doubt on whether this setting was actually used in the original production of the play, given the complexity of the music. See David Fuller, 'Ben Jonson's Plays and Their Contemporary Music,' *Music & Letters* 58.1 (1977): 66.

4 Herford and Simpson, *Ben Jonson* Vol. IX (Oxford: Oxford University Press 1950): 196.

5 Quoted in Gerald Eades Bentley, 'The Diary of a Caroline Theatergoer,' *Modern Philology* 35.1 (1937): 68. Bentley notes how, in this period, *Volpone* was commonly referred to by its subtitle, 'The Fox'.

6   R. G. Noyes, *Ben Jonson on the English Stage 1660–1776*, Harvard Studies in English
     XVII (New York: Benjamin Bloom, 1966): 40–41. Noyes' account of the play's stage
     history between 1660 and 1785 is a comprehensive one, and I am indebted to his
     work for much of my information in this section. Unless otherwise stated, my sources
     for accounts of late seventeenth and eighteenth century productions of *Volpone* are
     Noyes, and also Herford and Simpson, *Ben Jonson* Vol. IX, 196–208.

7   John Evelyn, entry for 16 October 1662, *The Diary of John Evelyn*, Vol. 3: 1650–1672,
     ed. E. S. De Beer (Oxford: Clarendon Press, 1955): 341.

8   Samuel Pepys, entry for 14 January 1665, *The Diary of Samuel Pepys*, Vol. 6:
     1665, ed. Robert Latham and William Matthews (London: G. Bell and Sons,
     1972): 10.

9   Anthony Wood, quoted in Noyes, *English Stage* 44.

10   Noyes dates this prologue to between 1673 and 1676, when the vogue for operatic
     versions of early modern plays was at its height. Robert Gale Noyes, 'A Restoration
     Prologue for *Volpone*', *Modern Language Notes* 52.3 (1937): 199–200.

11   Gerard Langbaine, *An Account of the English Dramatick Poets* (1691), quoted in
     Noyes, *English Stage* 50.

12   *English Post*, 27–30 December 1700.

13   The actors' names and details of this case are taken from the reports of the Kings'
     Bench Proceedings for Monday 16 February 1702, as reported in the updated
     version of *The London Stage 1660–1800*, part 2: 1700–1729, ed. Judith Milhous
     and Robert D. Hume. This revised edition has not yet been published, but can be
     found online at <http://www.personal.psu.edu/users/h/b/hb1/London%20Stage%20
     2001/> [accessed 10 March 2009]

14   Noyes, *English Stage* 55.

15   Quoted in *The London Stage 1660–1800*, Part 2: 1700–1729, ed. Emmett L Avery,
     Vol. 1 (Carbondale IL: Southern Illinois University, 1960): 95, 106.

16   Quoted in Noyes, *English Stage* 57.

17   Richard Steele, *The Tatler*, 26–28 May 1709.

18   Richard Steele, *The Tatler*, 14–16 April 1709.

19   Richard Steele, *The Spectator*, 5 May 1712.

20   This theatre had opened in 1714.

21   William Cooke, *Memoirs of Charles Macklin Comedian* (1804; New York: Benjamin
     Blom, 1972) 380.

22   Davies, *Dramatic Miscellanies*, quoted in Noyes, *English Stage* 68. William Cooke
     borrows this judgement of Cibber's and Mills' performances from Davies almost
     verbatim in *Charles Macklin* 380.

23   Delane took over the part of Volpone in 1736.

24   Anonymous, *The Life of Mr James Quin, Comedian* (1766), quoted in Noyes, *English
     Stage* 84.

25   The Haymarket performances were due to the fact that, in September 1733, certain
     of the leading Drury Lane players rebelled against what they saw as oppression by
     the theatre's patentees and decided to form their own breakaway group, who played
     at the Haymarket. This new company performed a season of twelve of Jonson's plays,
     but then returned to Drury Lane in March 1734.

26   'A Compleat List of all the English Dramatic Poets' (1747), quoted in Noyes, *English
     Stage* 86.

27   Cooke, *Charles Macklin* 381.

28   See, for example, Richard Hurd, 'A Dissertation Concerning the Provinces of the
     several Species of the Drama' (1753), *Critical Heritage* 442.

29 David Erskine Baker, *The Companion to the Play-house* (1764), *Critical Heritage* 494–95.

30 Anonymous, *The Theatrical Review* (November 1771), *Critical Heritage* 516.

31 John Adolphus, *Memoirs of John Bannister, Comedian*, quoted in Noyes, *English Stage* 99.

32 Davies, *Dramatic Miscellanies* (1783–1784), *Critical Heritage* 558.

33 W. B. Yeats, Letter to the Phoenix Society, 8 February 1921, *The Letters of W. B. Yeats*, ed. Allan Wade (London: Rupert Hart-Davis, 1954) 665.

34 T. S. Eliot, *The Dial* 70, June 1921.

35 A. P., *The Spectator*, 7 July 1923.

36 Herford and Simpson, *Ben Jonson* Vol. IX, 204.

37 Anonymous, *The Times*, 28 April 1930.

38 Ibid.

39 Ejner J. Jensen, *Ben Jonson's Comedies on the Modern Stage* (Ann Arbor, Michigan: UMI Research P, 1985) 55.

40 A. C. M., *Birmingham News*, 30 March 1935.

41 Anonymous, *Manchester Guardian*, 2 August 1935.

42 Anonymous, *The Times*, 31 July 1935.

43 D. W., *Punch*, 2 February 1938.

44 Desmond MacCarthy, *New Statesman*, 29 January 1938; J. G. B., *Evening News*, 26 January 1938.

45 Kenneth Tynan, Letter to Julian Holland, 9 December 1944, *Kenneth Tynan: Letters*, ed. Kathleen Tynan (London: Weidenfeld and Nicolson, 1994) 55. Lack of capitalisation Tynan's own.

46 Ronald Harwood, *Sir Donald Wolfit CBE, His Life and Work in the Unfashionable Theatre* (New York: St. Martin's Press, 1971) 126.

47 Desmond McCarthy, *New Statesman*, 29 January 1938.

48 Anonymous review of *Volpone* at the King's Theatre, Hammersmith. *The Times*, 13 October 1953.

49 Anonymous, 'Shakespeare Outfoxed,' *Time*, 10 March 1947.

50 Anonymous, *The Times*, 7 June 1944.

51 T. C. Worsley, 'The Fox', *New Statesman*, 26 July 1952.

52 Harold Conway, *Evening Standard*, 16 July 1952.

53 Worsley, *New Statesman*; Anonymous review of *Volpone*, *The Times*, 16 July 1952.

54 Clifford Leech, 'Stratford 1952', *Shakespeare Quarterly* 3.4 (1952): 357.

55 Peter Rodford, *Plays and Players*, January 1956.

56 Richard Christiansen, *Chicago Daily News*, 18 July 1964.

57 Thomas Willis, *Chicago Tribune*, 8 September 1964.

58 Harold Clurman, *The Nation*, 10 August 1964.

59 Ronald Bryden, 'View-halloo *Volpone*,' *The Observer*, 21 January 1968.

60 Henry Popkin, 'Black Comedy Still Has Too Much,' *The Times*, 17 January 1968.

61 Anonymous, 'Comedies with happy endings,' *Tribune*, 26 January 1968.

62 Herbert Kretzmer, Herbert, 'Prancing, dancing, giggling – endless,' *Daily Express*, 17 January 1968; Alan Brien, 'Volpone gets the business,' *Sunday Telegraph*, 21 January 1968.

63 Anonymous, *The Times*, 21 September 1966; Ian Donaldson, *The Guardian*, 21 September 1966.

64 Benedict Nightingale, *Plays and Players*, March 1967.

65 Irving Wardle, *The Times*, 10 August 1971.

66 Ned Chaillet, '*Volpone*', *Plays and Players*, June 1977.

67 John Barber, *Daily Telegraph*, 27 April 1977.

68 Don D. Moore, untitled review of *Volpone* on April 26 1977, *Educational Theatre Review* (1978): 115.

69 See, for example, Irving Wardle, 'Biting wit of the biter bit,' *The Times*, 6 October 1983, which complains, 'Like many bulky actors, Mr Griffiths lacks sensuality.'

70 Wardle, *The Times*, 6 October 1983.

71 John Peter, 'Jonson's Finest, Lost in Action,' *The Sunday Times*, 8 April 1990.

72 Paul Taylor, *The Telegraph*, 29 July 1995.

73 Katherine Duncan-Jones, 'No Exit From Venice,' *TLS*, 18 August 1995.

74 Robert Hewison, *The Sunday Times*, 6 August 1995.

75 Anonymous, *The Times*, 31 July 1935.

76 Francis Mason, 'A Note on the Theatre,' *The Hudson Review* 1.2 (1948): 256.

77 Robert Macdonald, *The Scotsman*, 22 January 1968.

78 Stephen Williams, *Evening News*, 4 March 1955.

79 Conway, *Evening Standard*, 16 July 1952.

80 Peter, 'Jonson's Finest.'

81 John Gross, 'There are times when Oscar is a bit of a trial,' *Sunday Telegraph*, 28 March 1999.

82 Peter, 'Jonson's Finest.'

83 Lynne Walker, 'The fox has all the lines', *The Independent*, 2 November 2004.

84 W. H. W., *Birmingham Evening Mail*, 26 February 1969.

85 For example, this happened in the 1995 Warchus production, which ended with Volpone and Mosca beginning to undergo their assigned punishments, cutting Volpone's epilogue and also cutting his line, 'This is called mortifying of a fox.'

86 1944, adapted by Eric Linklater, broadcast on 19 March 1944; 1953, adapted by Arthur Goring and Derek Blomfield, broadcast on 18 February 1953; 1955, arranged by H. A. L. Craig and retitled *The Fox and the Gold*, broadcast on 21 February 1955; 1957, broadcast on 17 June 1957; 1971, broadcast on 9 May 1971; 2004, broadcast on 28 March 2004 and 17 April 2005.

87 Zweig's version was translated into English by Ruth Langner in 1928.

88 Zweig's interpretation is clearly motivated by twentieth-century political concerns. The adaptation's scheme is broadly Marxist in intent, as Mosca becomes a kind of representative of the exploited masses, who ultimately manages to restore wealth to the ordinary people to whom it belongs.

89 Zweig's text was translated into French by Jules Romain, and first opened at the Paris Théâtre d'Atelier in December 1928. For productions of this adaptation in Germany, and also France and America, during the 1920s and 30s, see Purificación Ribes, 'Stefan Zweig's *Volpone, eine lieblose Komödie* on Stage in Austria and Germany (1926–1927),' *Ben Jonson Journal* 14 (2007): 61–77.

90 Tourneur's film did not, in fact, make many changes to Zweig's text: it is more a filmed play than a full cinematic adaptation, although it does (as might be expected) attempt to bring the action more into the outdoors. The casting is of some interest, however – Volpone was played by Harry Bauer, who typically specialised in Semitic roles, such as Shylock, and played Volpone as a Jewish stereotype, complete with false nose.

91 An author's note instructs the actors to perform the play 'as a *commedia dell' arte*, lightly, quickly, caricatured rather than realistic; *allegro con brio*'.

92 Anonymous, 'New Plays in Manhattan', *Time*, 23 April 1928; B. M. Steigman, 'Goodly Offering', *The English Journal* 18.3 (1929): 248–49.

93 Peter Fleming, *The Spectator*, 30 January 1932.

94 Thomas Barbour, review of a 1957 New York Rooftop Theatre production of Ruth Langner's translation of Zweig's *Volpone*. 'Revivals and Revisions: Theatre Chronicle,' *The Hudson Review* 10.2 (1957): 261–62.

95   Jonas Barish, 'Introduction,' *Volpone* (New York: Appleton-Century-Crofts, 1958): x.

96   See David McPherson's 'Rough Beast into Tame Fox,' which shows how the persistent trend of adaptations of *Volpone* has been to make the play more conventional. David McPherson, 'Rough Beast Into Tame Fox: The Adaptations of *Volpone*,' *Studies in the Literary Imagination* 6.1 (1973): 77–84.

97   Victor Gluck, 'Foxy in Concert', Review of the 2000 Musicals Tonight revival, *Back Stage*, December 2000.

98   Although it ran for seven weeks in the summer of 1962, in a theatre in Dawson City in the Yukon, the box-office receipts were poor. It was subsequently revived on Broadway, with several new songs and new choreography, in 1964, where it ran for seventy-two performances.

99   Larry Gelbart, interviewed by Emily Nussbaum, 'The Sly Fox of *The Sly Fox*,' *The New York Times*, 28 March 2004.

100 Clive Barnes, *The New York Times*, 15 December 1976.

101 See, for example, Ben Brantley, 'Theater Review: Stealthy, Wealthy, Joke-Wise', *The New York Times*, 2 April 2004.

102 Joseph McLellan, 'A Wolf Trap, A Comic *Volpone* That Truly Sings,' *Washington Post*, 12 March 2004.

103 Samuel Taylor Coleridge, *Notes and Lectures Upon Shakespeare and Some of the Old Dramatists*, Vol. I. (London: William Pickering, 1849): 278.

104 Interestingly, to my knowledge, no adaptation has turned Bonario into the play's unequivocal hero – perhaps because even when rewritten, he remains a somewhat pallid and charmless character.

105 R. B. Parker and David M. Bevington, Introduction, *Volpone*, The Revels Student Edition (Manchester: Manchester UP, 1999): 18.

CHAPTER THREE

The State of the Art

Robert C. Evans

Introduction

Surely the most important development in recent scholarship on Ben Jonson's *Volpone* (as, indeed, on all scholarship in general) has been the rise of the internet. And, almost just as surely, increasing improvements in internet resources will continue to transform work on Jonson's play, as on so much else. Of course, so rapid, unpredictable, and unrelenting is the progress of online technologies that any individual attempt to describe the impact of the internet on literary research becomes anachronistic almost as soon as it is written. Nevertheless, a constant effort will be made throughout this chapter to indicate how the internet has already opened up new possibilities for students of Jonson's great drama and how it may open up even newer and richer possibilities in the future. I also hope to use this chapter to outline the kinds of developments that have taken place in the study, performance and influence of *Volpone* in the first years of the twenty-first century, and I hope, as well, to suggest some opportunities for further work, many of them centred on the world wide web.

Of all the recent developments in internet resources, one of the most exciting has been the growth of 'search-inside-the-text' features of various online sites. The electronic version of the Modern Language Association Bibliography, for instance, now makes it possible to search the entire texts of an increasing number of scholarly articles, and the same is true of numerous other resources, such as Literature Online (LION), the Literary Resource Centre, JSTOR, Project Muse and countless others. Equally helpful are such 'electronic library' sites as Netlibrary, ebrary, Questia and the Literary Reference Centre, many of which offer searchable versions not only of the full texts of academic articles but also of the full texts of academic books. Perhaps the most exciting development of all, however, has been the growth of such free 'search-inside-the-text' resources as those offered by Google books and by the various versions of amazon.com (including amazon.co.uk, amazon.fr, amazon.ca and so on). Access to these resources (unlike access to many of the other sites already mentioned) is presently free and seems likely to remain so, and the fact that both amazon and Google books focus on providing searchable versions of monographs makes them especially valuable.

Google books, in fact, is adding millions of new titles to its database each year, including full-text, downloadable versions of many books and journals that have long been out of copyright. Increasingly easy access to growing numbers of books and articles from the seventeenth, eighteenth, nineteenth and early twentieth centuries now makes it possible for almost anyone to do research of a sort that could have been conducted, in the past, only at the very best academic libraries – research which even then would have been enormously time-consuming if not impossible. At present, a key term – such as 'Volpone' – can be searched in seconds, resulting (at least in the case of Google books) in 'hits' from thousands of sources, in numerous languages, printed over hundreds of years. (This is not even to mention what happens when one searches that same term on the 'web' in general, using basic search engines.) Google books not only provides access to the complete versions of millions of texts that are out of copyright, but it also often provides surprisingly full access to numerous recent texts that are very much in copyright. And, even when individual pages are excluded from the 'limited preview' feature of Google books, those same excluded pages can often be accessed by using the handy Google books link to amazon. com. Moreover, even when Google books provides only a 'snippet' preview of books contained in its database, it will still frequently indicate the page numbers on which the searched term appears, or it will at least indicate that the searched term appears *somewhere* inside a particular book. The book can then be ordered via interlibrary loan. Thanks to such resources as Google books and amazon.com, it is now possible for students and scholars to do in seconds the kinds of searches that would only have been possible, in the past, by leafing through all the pages of millions of books in the world's largest libraries. In short, in the first decade of twenty-first century, the possibilities for scholars have been almost totally transformed and wonderfully enriched. And things are only likely to get better.

In the recent past, when one wanted to do serious academic research on *Volpone*, one would have begun by searching such resources as the online MLA Bibliography or Literature Online. At present, however, it would be irresponsible to stop with those resources or even with any of the other resources available at most academic libraries (such as online catalogues, which now increasingly list not only relevant books but also the contents of essay collections). These days, it makes great sense to search Google books and amazon.com as well, since searches of those sites will turn up much additional information – information that cannot be accessed in any other way. In the following pages, having relied in part on such internet searches, I hope to indicate the kind of work that has been done on *Volpone* from 2001 to early 2010 in the following areas of concentration: (1) overviews; (2) sources and parallels; (3) historical contexts; (4) themes; (5) economics; (6) reception; (7) performances and performance issues; (8) influence and adaptations; (9) artistry and craft; and (10) editions. My goal is to be as comprehensive as possible, calling attention to as many different useful sources as I can. After offering this survey, I will conclude by suggesting some possibilities for future work on Jonson's dramatic masterpiece.

Overviews

Overviews of comments on *Volpone* contained in nearly a hundred books published between 1886 and 1999 are included in my own *Ben Jonson's Major Plays: Summaries of Modern Monographs* (2000), and much of the same material is covered in a differently organized survey of scholarship on the play published in 2010 as part of the recurring 'Jonson and His Era: Overviews of Modern Research' feature of the *Ben Jonson Journal*.[1] In addition, Douglas A. Brooks, before his untimely death, completed a masterful survey titled 'Recent Studies in Ben Jonson (1991–mid-2001)', which contains one-and-a-half pages summarizing comment on the play, not to mention scattered references elsewhere in his valuable article.[2] In his very useful *Complete Critical Guide to Ben Jonson* (2002), James Loxley devotes six concentrated pages to *Volpone* (69–74), suggesting (among other interesting comments) that the play 'exceeds the framework its didactic purpose imposes, opening the text up to the possibility of a burlesque of its own moralizing',[3] and Loxley also addresses such issues in the play as 'transgression and transformation', the identification of wealth with the cultivation of desire, the enactment of 'the link between desire and money in the experience of consumption', and the general 'triangulation of money, theatricality and desire'. Elsewhere in his book, Loxley touches on such other aspects of the work as its use of the carnivalesque, the importance of its Dedicatory Epistle, its depiction of erotic disorder, its exploration of gender, its focus on shape-shifting, and its presentation of the role of the state.[4] Even more comprehensive, however, is the discussion contained in Sean McEvoy's recent book *Ben Jonson, Renaissance Dramatist* (2008), which includes a chapter on the play more than twenty pages in length.[5] That chapter opens with a section on 'Contexts' that deftly sketches both historical and literary influences, including the importance of the play's setting, its status as a city comedy, its political implications, and the ambiguity of its presentation of the 'amorality and theatricality of the free market'.[6] McEvoy next discusses 'The Play' itself, emphasizing its focus on such matters as 'the dissolution of identity', its use of dramatic irony, Mosca's use of asides, the ambiguous presentation of Celia (who can even seem a bit 'masochistic'), the ways Lady Would-be can be seen as a parody of the title character, and the fact that Volpone himself seems to enjoy dressing up.[7] Throughout his discussion, McEvoy is careful to cite the work of numerous previous critics, and indeed a separate section on 'Critical Approaches' offers a fine survey of the variety of ways in which the play has been interpreted.[8] Finally, McEvoy offers a substantial discussion of 'The Play in Performance', touching not only on individual productions but also commenting more generally on varied kinds of approaches. McEvoy notes, for instance, the dangers of excessive reliance on stage business, the importance of high energy and pacing, and the traits of successful portrayals of Mosca.[9] All in all, McEvoy offers a lucid but solid overview – one that is likely to satisfy seasoned Jonsonians while also being extremely helpful to beginning students as well.

Sources and Parallels

Raphael Lyne's 2006 article '*Volpone* and the Classics' offers a crisp survey of its topic, discussing the playwright's general debts to the Greeks and Romans and suggesting how Jonson's characters take the classics far less seriously than did Jonson himself and therefore how the behaviour of those characters often falls short of classical ideals. Lyne explores classical precedents for Jonson's emphasis on metamorphosis, and he concludes his survey by suggesting that classical influences on the play often contribute to its complexity in ways that militate against any simple interpretations.[10] Bruce Boehrer, in two pieces from 2001 and 2002, relates Corvino's behaviour to Ovidian precedents (particularly in *Amores* 2.19),[11] while John Creaser comments in passing in 2002 that in Roman plays no threat to punish a '*servus* is ever carried out, whereas in *Volpone* Mosca is condemned to lifelong servitude in the galleys'.[12] Meanwhile, Erich Segal in 2001 notes a number of parallels between *Volpone* and both classical and biblical sources, particularly in the presentation of Celia,[13] while Jacob Blevins in 2004 contrasts Catullus's song to Lesbia with Volpone's use of it when he tries to seduce Celia:

'Lesbia is quite a willing participant; Celia is not. Rape is an option for Volpone; Catullus' lover claims that he wants a real relationship based on something more than physical desire'. Blevins suggests that Jonson wrote at the beginning of a trend in which neo-classical poets imitated the words of their classical predecessors but not necessarily their sentiments.[14] In any case, Stephen Orgel noted in 2002 that 'a great deal of Renaissance art offered its patrons precisely the pleasures of recognition', and he argued that this is one of the reasons that the song to Celia clearly alludes to Catullus's famous lyric.[15]

An important medieval source is the subject of a lengthy article from 2005 by Christopher Baker and Richard Harp titled 'Jonson's *Volpone* and Dante'. Baker and Harp emphasize the importance of fraud as a sin in both works, note how both texts combine comedy and punishment, compare the structures of the epic and the play (which place Satan and Volpone at their respective centres), and suggest how Jonson's scene about Scoto the mountebank shares similarities with Dante's treatment of a sinner named Manto. In addition, they compare Jonson's Celia to Dante's Beatrice and Jonson's Mosca to a sinner named Mosca dei Lamberti. Volpone himself (they note) shares striking similarities to a Dantean sinner named Gianni Schicchi, and they also compare the careers of Jonson and his Italian forbear.[16] More briefly, Denis Kezar in 2001 suggested another parallel between Jonson's play and early Christian literature, arguing that *Volpone* 'can be read as a generic farce of the *ars moriendi* tradition, exposing in its vulpine title character and his central prop (a faux deathbed) the easily abused nexus between dying and acting',[17] while Brandie R. Siegfried in 2006 asserted that 'Celia's seduction is arranged in terms of the banquet of sense' tradition and that 'Celia responds by demonstrating her preference for both Heroic Virtue and Christian Holiness'.[18] Meanwhile, Glynne Wickham in 2002 noted the ways Mosca functions as the kind of conventional vice figure often found in medieval and Renaissance literature.[19]

Other recent commentators have pointed to other possible influences on Jonson's play by a variety of Renaissance sources. Thus, Rocco Coronato argued in 2005 that the 'usage of the domestic scene in *Volpone* recalls the Spanish tradition of the *scena aperta*',[20] while in the same year Bella Mirabella outlined ways in which the mountebank scene in Jonson's play probably reflects performances by real contemporary mountebanks.[21] Similarly, in 2007 Jan Frans van Dijkhuizen suggested that the mountebank scene echoed the vocabulary of contemporary anti-possession tracts, and he also noted that the symptoms of Voltore's demonic possession resemble those described in contemporary pamphlets.[22] Focusing on a different scene from the play, Jason Lawrence in 2005 noted that it 'has become a critical commonplace to suggest that Lady Would-be's opinions of Guarini in *Volpone* contain a barely concealed allusion' to Samuel Daniel's play *The Queenes Arcadia*, but Lawrence suggested that 'no one has fully appreciated the depth of Jonson's attack. Jonson deliberately uses Lady Would-be's parade of Italian authors to expose systematically the wide range' of Daniel's sources. Lawrence argued that this 'concerted effort to expose the sources of a successful university play by means of another play performed at, and dedicated to, both universities clearly demonstrates Jonson's strong disapproval of both the method and extent of his rival's eclectic borrowing in the process of dramatic composition.'[23]

Relations with another contemporary dramatist – Thomas Middleton – are the topic of various recent comments. Thus, Celia Daileader argued in 2007 that Volpone's sick-room reflects the influence of Middleton's *A Mad World, My Masters* (rather than vice versa),[24] just as Valerie Wayne argued that *Volpone* was influenced by Middleton's *A Trick to Catch the Old One*,[25] while MacDonald P. Jackson noted similarities between *Volpone* and *The Revenger's Tragedy* (but without asserting which came first).[26] Finally, recent comments on the relationship between *Volpone* and works by Shakespeare include Richard Andrews' claim that whereas Shakespeare tends to be sympathetic even to his most ridiculous characters, *Volpone* contains 'a level of pitiless contempt for practically everybody which goes even beyond Mediterranean models',[27] while Andrew Gurr speculated that Jonson's 1607 epistle to *Volpone* may have been influenced by a recent court performance of *King Lear*.[28] Stanley Wells compared Mosca to Robin Goodfellow and noted the similarity between the theatrical self-consciousness of Jonson's play and a particular moment in *Twelfth Night*.[29] Robert Logan suggested that Jonson may have been inspired to imitate Marlowe by observing Shakespeare's earlier example.[30] Andrew Hadfield speculated that Jonson's depiction of Venetian justice may have been a response to the success of *Othello*;[31] Lois Potter noted that among other resemblances (including the Venetian setting), *Volpone* and *Othello* each features two major protagonists (Volpone and Mosca; Othello and Iago);[32] and Ian Donaldson commented on the significance of handkerchiefs in both dramas.[33]

Historical Contexts

Recent commentary on the historical contexts of *Volpone* ranges from brief and scattered observations to highly detailed discussions, including Richard Dutton's important new book exploring the play in connection with the Gunpowder Plot. Among the briefer comments are Linda Woodbridge's claim in 2001 that the harsh treatment of Volpone at the end of the play 'embodies the period's desperate need to pin down any kind of slipperiness with punishments producing immobility'.[34] Slightly fuller comments on legal matters by Laurie Shannon in 2002 dealt with the play's reflection of contemporary sumptuary laws and their relevance to changes of costume,[35] while Edward Gieskes, as part of a broader discussion of laws and lawyers in the work, argued that the text reflects anti-lawyer literature of its era, that its legal concerns are more English than Italian, that the scrutineo is presented as the chief legal authority within the text, and that the play shows how the law could be used to perpetrate injustice.[36] Finally, in a highly suggestive article from 2007, Frances Teague argued that Jonson chose an Italian setting for his courtroom in order to avoid the appearance of obvious allusions to the legal fallout of the Gunpowder Plot. Teague noted that public hearings are often used to help resolve the plots of Jonson's plays, although *Volpone* makes the fullest use, of any of his works, of a court-room setting. Most interestingly, Teague suggested that the Avocatori are generally conscientious in their conduct and that they legitimately decide in favor of the plaintiffs who make the most convincing case. The Avocatori are not flawless, Teague contended, but they come off better than court personnel in various other works by Jonson. Meanwhile, Teague's comments on Jonson's own attitudes toward the Gunpowder Plot presented him as basically sympathetic to the conduct of the government – a position at variance with the recent claims of Richard Dutton.[37]

Dutton's arguments have been developed over a number of years in a variety of articles, many of which are included, revised, and expanded in his new book titled *Ben Jonson, Volpone, and the Gunpowder Plot*.[38] Essentially, Dutton argues that Jonson's text (especially the 1607 quarto and its prefatory epistle) reflects the playwright's disdain for Robert Cecil, Earl of Salisbury, the widely unpopular chief advisor to King James who was suspected by many of using the discovery of the Gunpowder Plot to his personal advantage and to the special disadvantage of English Catholics, including Jonson himself. Dutton's book is the product of much research and extended reflection, and obviously I cannot do justice to it in my brief summary here. Suffice it to say that it is one of the most thought-provoking discussions of the play to appear in a long time, and that even those who are not entirely convinced by its central claims will find it highly stimulating and well worth reading. The book includes chapters on the play in relation to Jonson's life and to the prefatory epistle; on the commendatory verses that precede the quarto text and on the theme of 'metempsychosis'; on the specific satire of Sir Politic Would-be; on the relations between the play and beast fables; on the relevance of the Venetian setting; and on patronage, plots, and demonic possession. Frances Teague's article (mentioned above) reaches different conclusions about the relations between *Volpone* and the Gunpowder Plot than Dutton does, and another dissenting opinion is implied at the end of a 2010 article by James Bednarz.[39] In the process of defending the standard assumption that Volpone was probably indeed performed at Cambridge soon after it was written (an assumption which has recently been disputed), Bednarz wonders whether such a performance would have been likely if Cecil – influential at the University and in the town – had indeed been a recognizable target of the play. Dutton's contentions, then, have already begun to stimulate the kind of reaction and response that always greet a major piece of provocative scholarship. However, Dutton's basic claims – especially his emphasis on the importance of Jonson's Catholicism – do find some support in a recent article by Dennis Flynn, who stresses the friendship between Jonson and John Donne. Donne, according to Flynn, shared Jonson's religious sympathies and may have been a more important source of information about Venice than has hitherto been recognized. Flynn explores the relationship between Donne, Jonson and Sir Henry Wotton (the English ambassador at Venice, who may have been a partial model for Sir Politic Would-be). However, the most important implication of Flynn's argument for Dutton's claims about Cecil and the Gunpowder Plot is his contention that 'both Jonson and Donne in these years favored toleration for Catholicism, in opposition to the dominant policy of Salisbury'.[40]

Legal matters and the relevance of the Gunpowder Plot have been just two of a variety of concerns of recent historical critics. Lukas Erne, for instance, compared and contrasted the title pages of Jonson's play and Marlowe's *Tamburlaine*, while Henry Woudhuysen also focused on the history of printed texts in commenting on the unusual inclusion of blank leaves at both the beginning and end of the 1607 quarto.[41] Andreas Mahler suggested that Sir Politic Would-be may in fact be the very first tourist ever depicted on stage,[42] while Paul Yachnin related Celia's handkerchief to contemporary conventions of 'gentrified wooing'.[43] Mario DiGangi, in a passing comment, suggested that 'Mosca is intelligible not as a sexual transgressor who happens to be a servant, but as a transgressive servant who happens to be erotically involved with his master'. According to DiGangi, the 'homoerotic affection between Mosca and Volpone signifies as disorderly because it becomes a vehicle through which Mosca can transcend his low place in the social hiearchy'.[44] Meanwhile, Farah Karim-Cooper discussed how Volpone's praise of Celia's appearance draws on, mocks and modifies his culture's traditional standards of beauty, and she also discussed how the mountebank scene is relevant to contemporary concerns with beauty and national identity.[45]

The mountebank show, in fact, has been the focus of several recent historically oriented discussions. Sarah Knight, for example, argued that 'Jonson used Bacon's critique of the mountebank as imposter as the backcloth for his portrait' of Scoto of Mantua, contending as well that he drew on other contemporary anti-mountebank polemics. Volpone (said Knight) 'pretends to be a medical mountebank, but the learning he professes and his attitudes towards textual authority establish the prototype of a more specifically academic pretender to learning.'[46] M. A. Katritzky used Jonson's play as evidence of the traits of early modern mountebank shows, although she noted that Volpone's costume as Scoto was not necessarily historically accurate.[47] Discussion of Volpone as mountebank almost inevitably involves discussion of *Volpone* and medicine, and this topic has indeed been the focus of a number of historical scholars. Especially important in this regard has been the work of Tanya Pollard, who in 2004 stressed the similarities in this play between the roles of actors and doctors, arguing that the play parodies contemporary medical charlatans while also parodying theatre itself. She emphasized the importance of purgation as a theme in the play and argued that Volpone's performances function like the drugs he tries to sell.[48] Many of these arguments are also included in a book by Pollard published in 2005.[49]

Also concerned with issues of disease and medicine in *Volpone*, Jonathan Gil Harris argued in 2004 that the play presents disease as migratory and invasive, thus resembling the soul described in the 'metempsychosis' episode. Like Pollard, Harris emphasized the importance of drugs in the work, noting that drugs were often considered exotic in Jonson's day and were frequently associated with the rich. Harris discussed drugs and disease in the work in association with Venice's status as a port city connected with foreign trade and potential foreign contamination, and he linked the latter condition to Jonson's satire of the Would-bes.[50] Finally, another commentator concerned with the play's presentation of disease is Byron Lee Grigsby, who discussed how the play reflects changes in attitudes toward diseases and their treatment in the period. More specifically, Grigsby contended that *Volpone* 'demonstrates both the role of syphilis as a representation of sinful sexuality and the belief that leprosy reflects sins of the community.'[51]

Several recent historically oriented critics have discussed *Volpone* in relation to issues of theatrical collaboration. Thus, Grace Ioppolo suggests that comments by Jonson in the Prologue imply that in the playhouses of the time, 'the main author reigned above co-adjutors (helpers or assistant writers), novices (inexperienced or probationary writers), and journeymen (writers who were newly qualified, having finished their apprenticeships) [...]. Also included in Jonson's hierarchy of collaborators is the 'Tutor', which may have been his rebuke of established dramatists such as Heywood, who later mended or doctored other authors' manuscripts'.[52] A similar point was made by Neil Carson,[53] but a particularly full and especially suggestive treatment of the issue of collaboration in the play was undertaken by Gregory Chaplin.[54] Chaplin emphasized how *Volpone* broke with the collaborative practices common in the theatre of Jonson's day. Chaplin stressed the tensions inherent in collaboration (at least for a writer such as Jonson), and he also explored the ways in which collaboration and its tensions become important themes within *Volpone* and in various later Jonsonian plays. According to this view, Mosca and Volpone are themselves collaborators whose relationship fractures by the end of the work. Chaplin's article – which is very clearly written and full of shrewd insights – is a splendid example of the ways in which historically grounded scholarship can be brought to bear on the artistic details of a literary text.

Themes

Thematic critics – who tend to be interested in literary works mainly for the ideas they explore or express – have found much to intrigue them recently in *Volpone*. Mathew Martin, for instance, in 2001 connected Jonson's play to such matters as utopia, dystopia, Platonic politics, and skepticism concerning the 'unalienated or just self'.[55] Martin argued that the play emphasizes the 'unreliability of sense perception' as well as the fallibility of reason, maintaining that in this work 'the mind possesses no inner light of truth and has access to no transcendent realm of ideas from which the standards of truth might be obtained'.[56] *Volpone* explores (according to Martin) such issues as the relation between money and death, the distance between word and flesh, the relations between the body and consumption, and the sudden imposition – at the end of the work – of a kind of Platonic justice that is at variance with the tone of the rest of the text.[57] Similar issues were also examined by Andrew Hiscock, who argued (among much else in a very lengthy chapter) that Jonson 'attempts to generate moral impulses in his audience by dramatizing a world which has lost all ability to do so'.[58] Jonson's audience, according to Hiscock, 'is asked to attend to the complex operations of urban colonization as the morally deviant and criminal strategies of masterless men [...] gradually reorganize the power relations of Venice and reinterpret them to their own advantage'.[59] Indeed, a 'city in flux serves as an excellent backdrop for the success of a man [Volpone] who celebrates the fact that he fails to make any investment in his own society'.[60]

Similar issues were explored in a lengthy article by Katharine Eisaman Maus, although from a more explicitly religious perspective. Maus connected Volpone's behavior with traditional notions of idolatry, arguing that the 'religious framework' of Jonson's thinking 'has received little attention' – a claim that seems true not only of *Volpone* but of this author's work in general.[61] Linking the play also to various writings about gift-giving, Maus claimed that 'Volpone uses his treasure to remind himself that he is, uniquely and by terms of a game he has designed himself, a pure recipient. He breaks the social and spiritual rules that require reciprocation; and initially he does so without apparent incurring any penalty'.[62] In the course of developing this more general argument, Maus offered a number of intriguing asides, as when she noted that 'Volpone avoids confronting the necessity of death by continually rehearsing that death' or when she contended that although Celia is 'generally considered a pallid placeholder', she is in fact 'a strong-minded character who plays not only a pivotal role in the plot but an important thematic role as well'.[63] In her final pages, Maus stressed the importance of patronage as an implied theme of this drama.

Other themes that have been the subject of recent attention include issues of desire, sex and gender. Thus, in the course of a few pages, Ronald Huebert managed to make a number of quite suggestive comments about masculinity in Jonson's play. He argued, for instance (in contrast to other recent commentators) that the bond between Volpone and Mosca is not erotic but instead resembles that between a team captain and his star player. Competitive masculine energies are displayed by most of the major characters, including the leading pair, but Volpone and Mosca know how to exploit those energies in others. Most of the males in Jonson's play associate manliness with domination, but by the end of the play Volpone begins to feel his own manliness threatened.[64] Also commenting on issues of gender and sexuality was Ian Frederick Moulton, who noted similarities between Jonson's play and the erotic writings of Aretino and who asserted that the 'image of the aroused spectator applauding expert erotic performers is one to which the play returns repeatedly; a fascination with the erotic nature of theatrical display lies at the heart of *Volpone*'.[65] Moulton (in contrast to Huebert) claimed that 'there are hints throughout the play that Volpone has erotic relations with men as well as women', and in fact Moulton asserted that 'Volpone's ambivalent gender position and his erotic attractiveness are explicitly linked to his theatricality' – a theatricality that attracts both men and women.[66] Even gold (Moulton maintains) 'is gendered both masculine and feminine' in Jonson's play.[67] Also commenting on issues of gender, Mary Beth Rose argued that 'Volpone's phallic heroism seeks to monopolize all gendered subject positions – to exist simultaneously as both subject and object of the gaze'. She noted that Volpone often places himself in female subject positions, making himself the focus of male desire, almost like a Petrarchan mistress.[68] Meanwhile, in a book concerned explicitly with *The Gendering of Men*, Thomas King also mentioned *Volpone*, stressing the ways in which Celia is subjected to patriarchal control and arguing that 'Jonson's play opposes two economies of reproduction, the sexual and the pederastic, construing the latter as unnatural'.[69] In a discussion of male friendship in the play, Tom MacFaul supported the widespread assumption that the relationship between Volpone and Mosca may be sexual and suggested that Mosca's growing power may symbolize the ways a ruling class (represented by Volpone) may weaken itself by failing to be more active on its own behalf.[70] Finally, in comments on the weakness and decay of the patrilineal ideal in this text, Lynne Dickson Bruckner suggested that the 'difficulty of maintaining a secure paternal line' is exposed repeatedly in this play, particularly 'through the roaming eroticism that characterizes Volpone's house'.[71]

However, although issues of sexuality and gender have received much attention from thematic commentators on *Volpone* in the past ten years, other topics – including animal imagery, old age, exorcism, laughter and allegory – have also been the subjects of varied comments. Thus, Bruce Boehrer discussed the Would-bes in connection with Renaissance ideas about parrots, arguing that they are 'a pair of dramatic characters who seem to be drowning in irrelevant detail, who are so impressionable that everything is of equal importance to them, and who are thus forever doomed to miss the point of action and conversation'.[72] Boehrer developed this parallel even more fully in 2004, suggesting that Jonson was innovative in his use of the word 'pol', that Lady Would-be 'seems to hear and repeat everything while understanding nothing', and that the playwright uses parrot imagery for 'satire of women and over-privileged ninnies . . . that also combines with Jonson's anti-Italian prejudice'.[73] More recently, in another comment on animal imagery, Charlotte Scott suggested that the 'bestial qualities of the characters in *Volpone* [. . .] are somewhat complicated by their non-bestial counterparts, suggesting that the idea of the human is always in contention'.[74]

Issues of old age in the play were mentioned briefly by Brian Gibbons in 2004. Gibbons suggested that the 'savage energy' of *Volpone* 'is more comprehensible against the background of [contemporary] preachers' constant admonitions to treat old age as a time to renounce the things of the world and purify one's heart'.[75] Hilaire Kallendorf, commenting on exorcism in the play, emphasized the importance of the 'coach' figure in the drama's exorcism and also discussed exorcism as 'a synechdoche for curing the body politic'.[76] Finally, in a fairly dense discussion of the theme of allegory in Jonson's play, Madhavi Menon argued that *Volpone* 'contributes to a study of allegory in three ways: it emphasizes the importance of a veil, it suggests the relationship between disease and the condition of being veiled, and it points to the inevitable fact that this disease, far from being contained, will erupt at several moments and in different registers throughout the play'.[77]

Economics

Issues of money and economics are obviously central to *Volpone* – so much so that Lanse Minkler has published a book for economists and businessmen in which Volpone (as the personification of selfishness) is repeatedly contrasted with Don Quixote (the representative of morality).[78] Treatments of economic themes in *Volpone* have recently been offered by Lea Knudsen Allen, by Oliver Hennessey and by Alison V. Scott. Thus, Allen compares Volpone's bedroom to Venice itself as a centre of trade and commerce, and she also discusses at length the ways in which Scoto's powder of Venus acquires exotic value – a value that Scoto produces 'by ascribing to his powder a famous lineage and a series of geographical displacements. As a rhetorical effect of representing objects as things from afar embedded in discourses of desire and foreignness, exoticism derives not merely from being in places that are remote, but also from movement through space'.[79]

In a quite lengthy discussion of the play, Oliver Hennessey comments on Venice as a site of varied transgressions, discusses Lady Would-be's relevance to economic issues, and wonders why Volpone risks his wealth by behaving as disruptively as he does. In the course of developing his own explicitly 'postmodern' argument, Hennessey challenges the worth of much previous commentary, although he does make an interesting suggestion in passing about the value of Ernest Becker's famous book from 1973, *The Denial of Death*, for the insights it might provide into Jonson's drama. Hennessey's own approach, however, is mainly rooted in the ideas of the economist Tibor Scitovsky, who tried to explain why wealthy people are often bored. From this perspective, Mosca (for instance) can be seen as a kind of professional tutor whose job is to stimulate Volpone's desires (and alleviate his boredom) by providing him with novel entertainments. Volpone thus becomes dependent on Mosca: 'When is Volpone happy? Whenever he is successfully imitating Mosca's skilled labour. In other words, part of the pleasure of this activity for Volpone is the novelty of dressing down'. For Hennessey, the play offers a 'robust critique of feudal elitism'.[80]

Alison V. Scott, meanwhile, sees the play as a satire not only on greed but on self-indulgence, so that 'Jonson in his characterization of Volpone examines how, in the socio-economic climate of early modern England, the sin of avarice was giving way to the practice of luxury'. [. . .] Volpone is thus brought to his undoing, not by the hardening and hoarding processes of *avaritia*, but by the softening and transformative processes of *luxuria*; in wanton disregard for protecting his 'substance', Volpone wastes it in Ovidian-styled dissipation'.[81] Scott traces the history of commentary on both sins, shows how Celia is linked both to her husband's avarice and to Volpone's love of luxury, and demonstrates how Celia's resistance to Volpone reflects Christian teachings about both kinds of temptation. Scott shows how Volpone's luxury is self-destructive, ambivalent, and relevant to early modern concerns about the possibilities of fraud in a capitalist economy. All in all, her discussion of economics in the play manages to be both rigorously grounded in theology and history as well as lucid in its phrasing.

Performances and Performance Issues

Volpone, as a stage production, apparently pleased its first audiences, and it has done so repeatedly throughout the centuries when it has been well presented. Recent discussions of the play as a work for the stage have been extensive. Bruce R. Smith discusses implied and explicit stage cues in the text (especially involving the use of curtains),[82] and Alan Dessen discusses such matters as the complexity of gender roles in one scene of the play, the importance of the age of the actor who originally played Lady Would-be, and the relevance of that actor's most recent roles before *Volpone* was originally staged.[83] Finally, Jeremy Lopez, in a detailed discussion of the Would-be subplot, emphasizes its impact on the stage and argues that the pleasure this portion of the play provides 'lies in its allowing the audience to imagine its own active, physical participation in the cruelest and most delightful kind of mere theatricality'.[84]

A helpful listing of more recent performances of *Volpone* (including both amateur and professional productions and those done on stage, film, and radio) can be found at a website hosted by the University of Warwick,[85] while Jeremy Lopez lists five productions (from 1948–1972) reviewed in two major academic journals.[86] *Volpone* is regularly discussed in the annual 'Census of Renaissance Drama Productions' published in the journal *Research Opportunities in Medieval and Renaissance Drama*,[87] and information about a wide variety of productions is now increasingly available on the internet,[88] including numerous articles and reviews.[89] These internet sources often include photographs and sometimes even video clips, and of course *Volpone* is already turning up more and more, in various ways, on online video sites, such as YouTube.com.[90] As the internet continues to develop, the problem will not be finding references to performances of *Volpone* but finding, organizing and preserving those references in systematic ways.

References in recent books to performances of *Volpone* are numerous, varied and often intriguing. They include, for instance, Annette Fern's passing allusion, in a book on American puppetry, to a noted marionette theatre's production of the play,[91] Charles Marowitz's reference to a late 1940s Actors' Lab production 'which *Life* magazine described as containing "some of the finest acting to be seen in America today",[92] references to three different U.S. productions (from the 1940s, 50s, and 60s) in the newest *Oxford Companion to the American Theater*,[93] and Michael Green's tantalizing reference to a very fine South African production of *Volpone* staged by Leonard Schach in the 1950s or 60s.[94] Various recent commentators discuss the famous 1955 British production directed by Joan Littlewood, which was favorably reviewed by Kenneth Tynan (among others),[95] while Thomas S. Hischak has lately noted that a 1957 Off-Broadway production directed by Gene Frankel was 'widely applauded'.[96]

One of the most interesting aspects of recent references to modern productions of *Volpone* is the frequency with which members of minorities or other marginalized groups are mentioned. Thus, in addition to Joan Littlewood, Nina Vance was another early female director of the play (she staged productions in 1961 and 1962),[97] while one recent reference book lists a number of African-American actors who have performed in the work.[98] Another such book mentions that the play is part of the repertory of the U.S. National Theater of the Deaf,[99] while several sources comment on the involvement of dwarfs either in the play itself or in works inspired by it.[100] Yet productions of the play have also left their traces in recent writings by or about socially prominent persons as well, including many famous actors. A biography of Paul Scofield, for instance, quotes him as calling it 'a real performer's play, [...] with a whole range of marvellous parts', and the same biography reports how the audience would 'gasp' each night when Scofield, as Volpone, seemed about to rape Celia.[101] Several recent books discuss Leo McKern's involvement in various productions of the play in the 1960s, especially his reluctance to be upstaged by Laurence Olivier, who had hoped to play Mosca to McKern's Volpone.[102] Even more recently, Michael Gambon has commented on his performance of the title role and on his perception of the way the play evolves.[103]

Influence and Adaptations

Recent scholarship has suggested that *Volpone* began influencing other
writings almost from the start, including works by Jonson himself.
Charles Cathcart argues for the impact of Jonson's play on such other
dramas as Edward Sharpham's *Cupid's Whirligig*, Lording Barry's
Ram-Alley, and also *The Family of Love* (authorship uncertain).[104] Carol
A. Morley suggests that *Volpone* is one of a number of famous plays
alluded to in *Herod and Antipater*, a drama by Gervase Markham and
William Sampson,[105] while a recent editor of Margaret Cavendish notes
the influence of Jonson's play on Cavendish's *Nature's Pictures*.[106] The
influence of *Volpone* on writings by Aphra Behn has been discussed
by Carolyn D. Williams,[107] and the play's impact on Behn, Thomas
Killigrew, and the Earl of Rochester has been noted by M. A. Katritzky.[108]
The editors of works associated with George Villiers, Second Duke of
Buckingham, offer extensive discussion of Jonson's influence on the
play titled *Sir Politick Would-be*, which is also touched on more briefly
by John J. Richetti.[109] Marc Galanter mentions a 1692 English work
titled *Dum Thrivo Vivo* (apparently still in manuscript) that 'depicts
a lawyer as a fox in robes' and that refers to 'Sly Volpone';[110] Diane Dugaw
detects the influence of Volpone on John Gay's *Three Hours after
Marriage*;[111] and Tom Lockwood hears echoes of Jonson's play in
Sheridan's *School for Scandal*.[112] Meanwhile, Ivan Cañadas has argued
for the influence of *Volpone* on a work by Mary Wollstonecraft.[113]

One of the most surprising aspects of recent writings about *Volpone*
is the realization that versions of the work have so often been set to
music. The eminent British composer William Walton apparently
considered writing an opera based on *Volpone*, and the avante-garde
American composer George Antheil did in fact create such an opera – a
work which can now be listened to in its entirety on the internet.[114]
More recently, another opera loosely based on the play – composed by
John Musto, with a libretto by Mark Campbell – has not only been
successfully staged on multiple occasions but has now also been
recorded and issued on CD.[115] Other classical composers who wrote
music associated with one or another version of the play include
Louis Gruenberg, Marc Blitzstein, Domenick Argento and Louis
Applebaum.[116] Another recent reference work mentions an opera by
Francis Burt and theatre music by Nicolae Beloiu.[117] One of the most
intriguing facts about musical adaptations of *Volpone*, however, is the
knowledge that a version of the play was staged in the early 1960s as a
musical comedy (*Foxy*) for Broadway – a musical starring the great
comedian Burt Lahr. Although Lahr won a Tony award for his performance in the title role, the production was one of the most famous flops

in Broadway history, and no professional recording of the production was ever made.[118] In late 2000, however, *Foxy* was revived in a small-scale production by a company known as Musicals Tonight, and reviews of their production, as well as a 2002 CD recording of songs from their version of the work, are now available.[119] Most intriguing, however, is the fact that numerous copies of a bootleg recording of the original Broadway production are owned by members of an internet website called Castalbumcollector.com, and so it is indeed now possible to hear the venerable Lahr in live performance of his award-winning role.[120]

Volpone, then – more than any other work by Jonson – seems to have inspired the talents of numerous other artists, including not only other dramatists but also other writers, composers, filmmakers and even puppeteers. Surely this will continue to be the case, and indeed the rise of the internet will make it easier and easier for adaptors to share their work with a world-wide audience.

Artistry and Craft

Ironically, the category of commentary that seems to have received least attention from recent students of *Volpone* is the category that is arguably most important: the category dealing with the play's craftsmanship, or with its features or successes as a work of art. *Volpone*, after all, is presumably worthy of all the attention lavished on it (including all the study of sources, themes, historical contexts, reception, influence and so on) because it is a highly skilful piece of writing. If it were merely another text from the Renaissance (however interesting as an historical document or statement of ideas) it would surely not command the kind of attention, respect and even affection it has always attracted. Yet recent discussion of *Volpone* as a compelling demonstration of Jonson's talent as a writer and of his skill as a playwright has been relatively rare. Perhaps critics feel that all that can be said on this subject has been said already; perhaps they feel that the artistic merits of the play are so obvious that they need little sustained attention. Surely part of the explanation involves the general move away from critical 'formalism' during the last several decades. Whatever the reasons, it is striking that attention to the artistry and craft of *Volpone* has been the subject of so little extended discussion in recent writing about the play. Passing comments on the skill and structure of the work can be found in many essays and books, but detailed exploration of these topics is relatively rare.

Frederic Bogel does discuss how the 'dramatic reversals of Jonson's play move from one dimension of the satirist's identity to another, opposing, dimension', and in this sense he thinks that the 'structure of Act I is paradigmatic. The act breaks sharply into two distinct units: I.1

and I.3–5', so that Act I 'ends not simply with Volpone beginning to occupy the position of the suitors, like a satirist become the victim of his satiric targets, but with a radical skepticism about the stability and determinateness of position itself'.[121] Similarly concerned with matters of construction is Henry S. Turner, who discusses how the play's use of space affects its structure. Turner argues that *Volpone* 'reflects Jonson's attempt to adapt the methods of scenographic composition to a five-act structure, such that the act assumes the same modelling function that an individual scene might also have'. He discusses the skilful introduction of the various characters, and he also suggests that Jonson is more indebted to English structural models than his invocation of Roman authorities might imply.[122] Thomas Rand comments on the ways Sir Pol's plan for detecting plague not only echoes Scoto's speech about his oil but also foreshadows Mosca's final speech about gold.[123]

Perhaps the most interesting – and certainly the most detailed – recent discussion of the formal aspects of Jonson's play is Murray Roston's essay '*Volpone*, Comedy or Mordant Satire?' Roston argues that 'until the actual moment when Volpone attempts to force himself upon Celia – a moment when, I propose to argue, the entire ambience of the play undergoes a profound change – the mood is one of sheer fun and good humor'.[124] In developing this contention, Roston explores various classical and Renaissance parallels for the tone and methods of Jonson's work, arguing, for instance, that the 'time-honored comic theme of the cuckolded husband not only supplies the main theme but also is entertainingly reflected in the subplot, although this has never been noted'.[125] Roston believes that the method Jonson 'adopted to ensure the morality of the play's message was to temper the secular comedy by providing a heavily didactic ending', and he suggests that the 'terminology employed in the rape scene highlights the transition from a secular to a religious setting'.[126] As these brief quotations will suggest, Roston's style is eminently clear and free of jargon, and his essay manages to combine informed study of Jonson's sources and historical contexts with pertinent comments about the actual tone(s) and artistry of the play. It would be helpful to have more such work, since it is work of this sort that is likely to help non-Jonsonians appreciate why *Volpone* has always commanded such affection and respect.

Editions

The period covered by the present article (2001–2009) is framed, on the outside, by the publication of two major editions of *Volpone* – R. B. Parker's revised version for The Revels Plays series (1999) and Richard Dutton's edition for the Cambridge University Press *Ben Jonson* (expected publication date: 2010).[127] Other editions published between 2001 and 2009 tended to be reissues of earlier printings, but two English-language versions did offer innovations. Thus, Richard Harp's revised version of *Ben Jonson's Plays and Masques* in the Norton Critical Editions series, besides offering much valuable contextual material, also reprinted Jonas Barish's famous article on the double plot of the play as well as portions of a lengthy article showing that Volpone was often linked, by people in the seventeenth century, with the enormously wealthy money-lender Thomas Sutton.[128] This latter topic merits further investigation, especially since a good deal of documentary evidence from the period supports the claim. Meanwhile, Robert N. Watson, in a very useful version of the play for the New Mermaids series, offered a superb introduction covering such matters as biography, genre, the major characters, the subplot, the conclusion, the stage history, and the choice of copy texts. Among many intriguing comments in Watson's edition is his suggestion that one 'unrecognized basis for Jonson's plot is the tradition of moot cases at the Inns of Court', as well as his observation that at the end of the play, 'Volpone and Mosca betray each other, but in a deeper sense they are both betrayed by Jonson'. Watson's discussion of the effects of different kinds of punctuation in the quarto and folio versions (and indeed his discussion of those two versions in general) is very suggestive, and his decision to offer a clear paraphrase of Jonson's dedicatory epistle should prove helpful to many readers.[129]

One of the most useful editions of *Volpone* ever prepared remains, as yet, 'unpublished', although it can easily be ordered both in book form and as a searchable PDF file. This is Michael W. Stamps' 2004 dissertation (prepared under the supervision of Richard Harp) titled *Ben Jonson's* Volpone: *A Critical Variorum.*[130] This exceptionally helpful and impressively comprehensive work (which runs to over 500 pages) offers an appendix offering a wide range of topics, including such matters as the texts; the first publishers and printers; sources, analogues and influences; and (in exhaustive detail) numerous kinds of criticism. The play itself is very fully annotated, and although the edition is not yet entirely complete (and is now several years out of date), it is a superb undertaking (especially in its searchable electronic version), and I shall have more to say about it below.

Prospects and Suggestions

Volpone has always been not only one of Jonson's most popular plays (if not in fact *the* most popular) but has also always been one of the most popular non-Shakespearean works of the period. So much critical work has already been done on *Volpone*, and so much is still being done, that it seems imperative that a critical variorum edition of the work should not only be published in book form but should be issued online, where it can be continuously supplemented. Fortunately, Michael Stamps has provided the groundwork for such a project; all that remains now is to make sure that his edition (perhaps revised and updated) gets into print and (even more important) that it is put online in some formal way so that our sense of the scholarship on *Volpone* can be constantly brought up to date in an organized and coherent fashion. A digital '*Volpone* Variorum Project' thus seems the most useful undertaking one could imagine for the twenty-first century and beyond. Such a project would allow scholars and students to see very easily what has already been said (sometimes over and over) about the play and would also thus stimulate new directions and new developments in scholarship.

Also worth pursuing would be a number of other kinds of editions, modelled after the kinds that exist for Shakespeare's most popular plays. Both Oxford and Cambridge University Presses, for instance, offer versions of Shakespeare's work intended for students, and surely if any non-Shakespearean play could prove profitable in such a format, it would be *Volpone*.[131] An edition of *Volpone* modelled on the Folger Library's Shakespeare volumes (with their detailed glosses and plentiful period illustrations) would also be helpful, as would (for that matter) something along the lines of the 'No Fear Shakespeare' volumes, which 'translate' Shakespeare into modern English and thus make his works more comprehensible to beginning students. An edition of Volpone similar to the newer editions of Shakespeare for CliffsNotes (part of the CliffsComplete series) would be helpful to students, while teachers would benefit from an edition similar to the ones appearing as part of the Folger Library's 'Shakespeare Set Free' series. One can even imagine illustrated versions of *Volpone* (along the lines of any number of illustrated – and indeed even 'classic comic' style – editions of Shakespeare). Whatever would make the play more accessible to students and 'regular' readers would be worthwhile and would help to keep Jonson more a living author rather than a merely venerated 'classic'.

Audio versions of *Volpone* (along the lines of the Caedmon or Arkangel Shakespeare series) would be highly helpful to students. The only recording apparently available at present is on cassette; in this version the play is 'acted' by one person in a fashion unlikely to stimulate much interest in the work.[132] Similarly dry and somewhat underwhelming is the brief film *Ben Jonson*, which touches very briefly on *Volpone* while offering a general overview of Jonson's career.[133] Ideally, the best way to bring the play alive for contemporary students and other audiences would be to film a good production of the work. Fortunately, the possibility of such a film now seems in the offing, thanks to a British group called Stage on Screen, which plans to issue, in 2010, a DVD of a performance of *Volpone*, not to mention DVDs of other productions of classic plays (including *The Alchemist*).[134] It remains to be seen how successful this effort will prove, but anything would arguably be better than the virtual nothing that now exists. It seems sad that most of the video *Volpone*s presently available on DVD are in French rather than English. Fortunately, the growth of the internet – and especially the rise of such video sites as YouTube – makes it increasingly likely that productions of *Volpone* staged by amateur groups, college companies, and/or small professional theatres will be filmed and widely shared. Likewise, the rise of file-sharing sites makes it increasingly likely that good amateur audio versions of the play will be recorded and made widely accessible. No longer will Jonsonians (or those interested in any other 'classic' artist) need to depend on large corporate entities (whether in publishing, theatre, or other media) to produce high-quality works by or about their subjects of interest. Good work can and undoubtedly will increasingly be 'published' online. In an ideal world, practically everything of interest to Jonsonians – including books, articles, films, recordings and pedagogical aids – will be available on the internet at little or no price. Jonson himself, who eagerly embraced relatively new media in his own day (including printed books and the professional theatre) would surely endorse such an ideal if he could be with us here and now to do so.

Notes

1   Robert C. Evans, *Ben Jonson's Major Plays: Summaries of Modern Monographs* (West Cornwall, CT: Locust Hill Press, 2000); for the section on *Volpone*, see pp. 136–49. See also Evans, 'Jonson and His Era: Overview of Modern Research: *Volpone*', *Ben Jonson Journal* 17 (2010), 97–114.

2   Douglas A. Brooks, 'Recent Studies in Ben Jonson (1991–mid-2001)', *English Literary Renaissance* 33.1 (2003), 110–52.

3   James Loxley, *The Complete Critical Guide to Ben Jonson* (London: Routledge, 2002), p. 70.

4   Loxley, pp. 71, 72–73, 223.

5   Sean McEvoy, *Ben Jonson: Renaissance Dramatist* (Edinburgh: Edinburgh University Press, 2008).

6   McEvoy, pp. 52–57; see esp. p. 55.

7   McEvoy, pp. 57–59.

8   McEvoy, pp. 63–68.

9   McEvoy, pp. 68–75.

10 Raphael Lyne, 'Volpone and the Classics', in *Early Modern English Drama: A Critical Companion*, ed. by Garrett A. Sullivan, Jr., et al. (New York: Oxford University Press, 2006), pp. 177–88.

11 Bruce Boehrer, 'Ovid and the Dilemma of the Cuckold in English Renaissance Drama', in *Ovid and the Renaissance Body*, ed. Goran Stanivukovic (Toronto:

University of Toronto Press, 2001), pp. 171–88; see esp. p. 181. See also Bruce Thomas Boehrer, *Shakespeare among the Animals* (New York: Palgrave, 2002); see esp. pp. 95–96.

12 John Creaser, 'Forms of Confusion', in *The Cambridge Companion to Shakespearean Comedy*, ed. Alexander Leggatt (Cambridge: Cambridge University Press, 2002), pp. 81–101; see esp. p. 83.

13 Erich Segal, *The Death of Comedy* (Cambridge, MA: Harvard University Press, 2001), pp. 377–81, esp. pp. 375–77.

14 Jacob Blevins, *Catullan Consciousness and the Early Modern Lyric in England: From Wyatt to Donne* (Aldershot: Ashgate, 2004), p. 117.

15 Stephen Orgel, *The Authenthic Shakespeare, and Other Problems of the Early Modern Stage* (New York: Routledge, 2002), p. 93.

16 Christopher Baker and Richard Harp, 'Jonson's *Volpone* and Dante', *Comparative Drama* 39.1 (2005), 55–74.

17 Dennis Kezar, *Guilty Creatures: Renaissance Poetry and the Ethics of Authorship* (New York: Oxford University Press, 2001), p. 153.

18 Brandie R. Siegfried, 'Dining at the Table of Sense: Cavendish, Shakespeare, and *The Convent of Pleasure*', in *Cavendish and Shakespeare, Interconnections* (Aldershot: Ashgate, 2006), pp. 63–83; see esp. p. 67.

19 Glynne Wickham, *Early English Stages 1300–1660, Volume 4: Requiem and an Epilogue*, 2nd edn (New York: Routledge, 2002) pp. 88–89.

20 Rocco Coronato, 'Ferrara in *Volpone*', in *Babylon or New Jerusalem? Perceptions of the City in Literature*, ed. Valeria Tinkler-Villani (Amsterdam: Rodopi, 2005) pp. 27–42; see esp. p. 37, n. 25.

21 Bella Mirabella, '"Quacking Delilahs: Female Mountebanks in Early Modern England and Italy', in *Women Players in England, 1500–1650: Beyond the All-Male Stage* (Burlington, VT: Ashgate, 2005), pp. 89–105; see esp. 94–97.

22 Jan Frans van Dijkhuizen, *Devil Theatre: Demonic Possession and Exorcism in English Renaissance Drama, 1558–1642* (Cambridge: D. S. Brewer, 2007), pp. 113–14.

23 Jason Lawrence, *'Who the devil taught thee so much Italian?' Italian Language Learning and Literary Imitation in Early Modern England* (Manchester: Manchester University Press, 2005), pp. 99–100.

24 Celia R. Daileader, 'The Courtesan Revisited: Thomas Middleton, Pietro Aretino, and Sex-Phobic Criticism', in *Italian Culture in the Drama of Shakespeare and His Contemporaries: Rewriting, Remaking, Refashioning* (Aldershot: Ashgate, 2007), pp. 223–38; see esp. p. 236.

25 Valerie Wayne, '*A Trick to Catch the Old One*', in *Thomas Middleton and Early Modern Textual Culture: A Companion to the Collected Works*, ed. Gary Taylor and John Lavagnino (New York: Oxford University Press, pp. 354–55.

26 MacDonald P. Jackson, '*The Revenger's Tragedy*', in *Thomas Middleton and Early Modern Textual Culture: A Companion to the Collected Works*, ed. Gary Taylor and John Lavagnino (New York: Oxford University Press, pp. 360–63; see esp. pp. 362–63.

27 Richard Andrews, 'Shakespeare and Italian Comedy', in *Shakespeare and Renaissance Europe*, ed. Andrew Hadfield and Paul Hammond (London: Thomson Learning, 2005), pp. 123–49; see esp. p. 139.

28 Andrew Gurr, 'Headgear as a Paralinguistic Signifier in *King Lear*', *Shakespeare Survey* 55 (2002): 43–52; see esp. p. 45, n. 7.

29 Stanley Wells, *Shakespeare & Co.* (New York: Pantheon, 2007), p. 148.

30 Robert A. Logan, *Shakespeare's Marlowe: The Influence of Christopher Marlowe on Shakespeare's Artistry* (Aldershot: Ashgate, 2007), pp. 156–57.

31 Andrew Hadfield, *Shakespeare and Republicanism* (Cambridge: Cambridge University Press, 2005), p. 309, n. 45.

32 Lois Potter, *Othello: Shakespeare in Performance* (Manchester: Manchester University Press, 2002), p. 7.

33 Ian Donaldson, 'Looking Sideways: Jonson, Shakespeare, and the Myths of Envy', in *Shakespeare, Marlowe, Jonson: New Directions in Biography*, ed. Takashi Kozuka and J. R. Mulryne (Aldershot: Ashgate, 2006), pp. 241–57; see esp. p. 252.

34 Linda Woodbridge, *Vagrancy, Homelessness, and English Renaissance Literature* (Urbana: University of Illinois Press, 2001), p. 56.

35 Laurie Shannon, *Sovereign Amity: Figures of Friendship in Shakespearean Contexts* (Chicago: University of Chicago Press, 2002), pp. 132–36.

36 Edward Gieskes, *Representing the Professions: Administration, Law and Theater in Early Modern England* (Newark: University of Delaware Press, 2006), pp. 143–47.

37 Frances Teague, 'Ben Jonson and London Courtrooms', in *Solon and Thespis: Law and Theater in the English Renaissance*, ed. Dennis Kezar (Notre Dame, IN: University of Notre Dame Press, 2007), pp. 64–77.

38 Richard Dutton, *Ben Jonson, Volpone and the Gunpowder Plot* (Cambridge: Cambridge University Press, 2008).

39 James P. Bednarz, 'Was *Volpone* Acted at Cambridge in 1606', forthcoming in the *Ben Jonson Journal* (2010).

40 Dennis Flynn, 'Donne's "Amicissimo, et Meritissimo Ben: Jonson" and the Daring of *Volpone*', *Literary Imagination*, 6.3 (2004), 368–89; see esp. p. 387. For a more specialized discussion of Donne's praise of Jonson's play, see David Kovacs, 'Donne's Latin Poem on Jonson's *Volpone*: Some Observations and a Textual Conjecture', *International Journal of the Classical Tradition*, 12.4 (2006), 563–68.

41 Lukas Erne, *Shakespeare as Literary Dramatist* (Cambridge: Cambridge University Press, 2003), pp. 37–41; H. R. Woudhuysen, 'Early Play Texts: Forms and Formes', in *In Arden: Editing Shakespeare*, ed. Ann Thomson and Gorden McMullen (London: Thomson Learning, 2003), pp. 48–61; see esp. p. 53.

42 Andreas Mahler, 'Point of Reference or Semantic Space: Functions of Venice in Early Modern English Drama', in *German Shakespeare Studies at the Turn of the Twenty-First Century*, ed. Christa Jansohn (Newark: University of Delaware Press, 2006), pp. 161–79; see esp. p. 171.

43 Paul Yachnin, 'Wonder-effects: Othello's Handkerchief', in *Staged Properties in Early Modern English Drama*, ed. Jonathan Gil Harris and Natasha Korda (Cambridge: Cambridge University Press, 2006), pp. 316–34; see esp. p. 318.

44 Mario DiGangi, 'How Queer Was the Renaissance?', in *Love, Sex, Intimacy, and Friendship Between Men, 1550–1800*, ed. Katherine O'Donnell and Michael O'Rourke (London: Palgrave Macmillan, 2007), pp. 128–47; see esp. p. 136.

45 Farah Karim-Cooper, *Cosmetics in Shakespearean and Renaissance Drama* (Edinburgh: Edinburgh University Press, 2006), pp. 24–25 and 155–56.

46 Sarah Knight, '"He is indeed a kind of Scholler-Mountebank"', in *Shell Games: Studies in Scams, Frauds, and Deceits (1300–1650)*, ed. Mark Crane et al. (Toronto: CRRS Publications, 2004), pp. 59–80; see esp. pp. 65–66.

47 M. A. Katritzky, *Women, Medicine and Theatre, 1500–1750: Literary Mountebanks and Performing Quacks* (Aldershot: Ashgate, 2007), pp. 104 and 80.

48 Tanya Pollard, '"No Faith in Physic": Masquerades of Medicine Onstage and Off', in *Disease, Diagnosis, and Cure on the Early Modern Stage*, ed. Stephanie Moss and Kaara L. Peterson (Aldershot: Ashgate, 2004), pp. 29–41; see esp. pp. 45–49.

49 Tanya Pollard, *Drugs and Theater in Early Modern England* (Oxford: Oxford University Press, 2005), pp. 43–53.

50   Jonathan Gil Harris, *Sick Economies: Drama, Mercantilism, and Disease in Shakespeare's England* (Philadelphia: University of Pennsylvania Press, 2004), pp. 108–35.

51   Byron Lee Grigsby, *Pestilence in Medieval and Early Modern English Literature* (New York: Routledge, 2004), pp. 166–69; see esp. p. 166.

52   Grace Ioppolo, *Dramatists and Their Manuscripts in the Age of Shakespeare, Jonson, Middleton, and Heywood: Authorship, Authority, and the Playhouse* (New York: Routledge, 2006), p. 32.

53   Neil Carson, *A Companion to Henslowe's 'Diary'* (Cambridge: Cambridge University Press, 2004), pp. 59–60.

54   Gregory Chaplin, '"Divided amongst Themselves": Collaboration and Anxiety in Jonson's *Volpone*', *ELH* 69.1 (2002), pp. 57–81.

55   Mathew R. Martin, *Between Theater and Philosophy: Skepticism in the Major City Comedies of Ben Jonson and Thomas* Middleton (Newark: University of Delaware Press, 2001), p. 23. For a similar point, see Frederic V. Bogel, *The Difference Satire Makes: Rhetoric and Reading from Jonson to Byron* (Ithaca: Cornell University Press, 2001), who argues that the play 'suggests that the idea of character as indelible and determinate, and as something given rather than constructed, may [. . .] be an illusion' (p. 94).

56   Martin, pp. 24 and 26.

57   Bogel also comments on the ambiguities and ambivalences of the conclusion (p. 105).

58   Andrew Hiscock, *The Uses of This World: Thinking Space in Shakespeare, Marlowe, Cary and Jonson* (Cardiff: University of Wales Press, 2004) pp. 142–70; see esp. p. 151.

59   Hiscock, p. 156.

60   Hiscock, p. 159.

61   Katharine Eisaman Maus, 'Idol and Gift in *Volpone*', *English Literary Renaissance* 35.3 (2005), 429–53; see esp. p. 432.

62   Maus, p. 441.

63   Maus, pp. 443 and 445. On issues of characterization, see also Ruth Lunney, *Marlowe and the Popular Tradition: Innovation in the English Drama before 1595* (Manchester: Manchester University Press, 2002), who argued that although the play features characters who are often 'richly elaborated or overdetermined', our 'interest in them remains primarily ethical, not psychological' (p. 129).

64   Ronald Huebert, *The Performance of Pleasure in English Renaissance Drama* (New York: Palgrave Macmillan, 2003), pp. 55–58.

65   Ian Frederick Moulton, *Before Pornography: Erotic Writing in Early Modern England* (Oxford: Oxford University Press, 2001), p. 207.

66   Moulton, pp. 208–09.

67   Moulton, p. 208.

68   Mary Beth Rose, *Gender and Heroism in Early Modern English Literature* (Chicago: University of Chicago Press, 2002) pp. 16–17; see esp. p. 16.

69   Thomas Alan King, *The Gendering of Men, 1600-1750: The English Phallus*, Vol. 1 (Madison: University of Wisconsin Press 2004), pp. 137–39; see esp. p. 139. See also Vol. 2: *The Gendering of Men, 1600-1750: Queer Articulations* (Madison: University of Wisconsin Press, 2008), p. 75.

70   Tom MacFaul, *Male Friendship in Shakespeare and His Contemporaries* (Cambridge: Cambridge University Press, 2007), pp. 103–05.

71   Lynne Dickson Bruckner, 'Ben Jonson's Branded Thumb and the Imprint of Textual Paternity', in *Printing and Parenting in Early Modern England*, ed. Douglas A. Brooks (Aldershot: Ashgate, 2005), pp. 109–30; see pp. 115–17, esp. p. 117.

72   Bruce Boehrer, *Shakespeare among the Animals*, p. 129. See also pp. 95–96.

73   Bruce Thomas Boehrer, *Parrot Culture: Our 2500-Year-Long Fascination with the World's Most Talkative Bird* (Philadelphia: University of Pennsylvania Press, 2004), pp. 66–68.

74   Charlotte Scott, 'Still Life? Anthropocentrism and the Fly in *Titus Andronicus* and *Volpone*', *Shakespeare Survey*, 61 (2008), 256–68; see esp. p. 267.

75   Brian Gibbons, 'The Representation of Ageing in Shakespeare and Jonson', in *Old Age and Ageing in British and American Culture and Literature*, ed. Christa Jansohn (Münster: LIT, 2004), pp. 39–49, esp. 44.

76   Hilaire Kallendorf, *Exorcism and Its Texts: Subjectivity in Early Modern Literature of England and Spain* (Toronto: University of Toronto Press, 2003), pp. 29–32; see esp. p. 32.

77   Madhavi Menon, *Rhetoric and Sexuality in English Renaissance Drama* (Toronto: University of Toronto Press, 2004), pp. 140–45; see esp. p. 142.

78   Lanse Minkler, *Integrity and Agreement: Economics When Principles Also Matter* (Ann Arbor: University of Michigan Press, 2008), pp. 2–3; see also pp. 11, 22, and 74.

79   Lea Knudsen Allen, '"Not Every Man Has the Luck to Go to Corinth": Accruing Exotic Capital in *The Jew of Malta* and *Volpone*', in *Global Traffic: Discourses and Practices of Trade In English Literature and Culture from 1550–1700*, ed. Barbara Sebek and Stephen Deng (New York: Palgrave MacMillan, 2008), pp. 95–114; see pp. 101–05, esp. p. 104.

80   Oliver Hennessey, 'Jonson's Joyless Economy: Theorizing Pleasure and Motivation in Volpone', *English Literary* Renaissance, 38.1 (2008), 83–105; see esp. pp. 100 and 103.

81   Alison V. Scott, 'Censuring Indulgence: Volpone's "Use of Riches" and the Problem of Luxury', *AUMLA*, 110 (2008), 1–14; see esp. pp. 1–2.

82   Bruce R. Smith, *The Key of Green: Passion and Perception in Renaissance Culture* (Chicago: University of Chicago Press, 2009) esp. pp. 223 and 233–34.

83   Alan C. Dessen, *Rescripting Shakespeare: The Text, the Director, and Modern Productions* (Cambridge: Cambridge University Press, 2002), esp. pp. 23–24.

84   Jeremy Lopez, *Theatrical Convention and Audience Response in Early Modern Drama* (Cambridge: Cambridge University Press, 2003), pp. 203–05; see esp. p. 204.

85   *Elizabethan and Jacobean Drama:* Volpone – *Stage History* <http://www2.warwick.ac.uk/fac/arts/ren/elizabethan_jacobean_drama/ben_jonson/volpone/stage_history>.

86   Jeremy Lopez, 'Census of Renaissance Drama Performance Reviews in *Shakespeare Quarterly* and *Shakespeare Survey*, 1948–2005', *Research Opportunities in Medieval and Renaissance Drama* 45 (2006), 41–104.

87   See, for example, James Shaw, 'Census of Renaissance Drama Productions', *Research Opportunities in Medieval and Renaissance Drama*, 44 (2005), 116–41, esp. 125–27, and James Shaw, 'Census of Renaissance Drama Productions', *Research Opportunities in Medieval and Renaissance Drama*, 45 (2006), 105–56, esp. pp. 128–34.

88   See, for example, information concerning such performances as the following: a 2001 production in Austin, Texas by The Bedlam Faction (*http://www.bedlamfaction.com/volpone_reviews*); a November 2004 production at Queen's University in Canada (*http://www.queensu.ca/drama/library/volpone/volpone.htm*); a 2007 production by the Utah Shakespearean Festival (*http://www.bard.org/Education/studyguides/volpone/index.html*); a production by Theatre Babel that was touring in 2008 and 2009 (*http://www.theatrebabel.co.uk/info.html*). This last web site is especially interesting since it contains a video clip.

89 See, for example, articles or reviews dealing with the following performances: a 2002 production in Sydney (*http://www.smh.com.au/articles/2002/06/19/10238644 54123.html*); a 2004 production at Minnesota State University (*http://media.www. msureporter.com/media/storage/paper937/news/2004/11/11/VarietytheatreDance/ volpone.A.Timeless.Tale.Of.Greed-2020012.shtml*); a 2004 production in Manchester (*http://www.independent.co.uk/arts-entertainment/theatre-dance/reviews/volpone-royal-exchange-theatre-manchester-531682.html*); and a 2008 production in Vancouver (*http://www.straight.com/article-141087/volpone*).

90 A search of YouTube in August 2009, for instance, turned up a clip from a 2000 production at Lipscomb University (*http://www.youtube.com/watch?v=T_QMk_ bHyOo*); a clip from a production in Spanish, dated 1999–2002 (*http://www.youtube. com/watch?v=xTbUirys9Lc*); a clip concerning a 2008 production in Spanish (*http:// www.youtube.com/watch?v=kW8on80WaX8*); a clip from a 2008 production in French (*http://www.youtube.com/watch?v=JTBjccYiwfQ*); and an extract from an undated production in French of the adaptation of the play by Jules Romains (*http:// www.youtube.com/watch?v=UBCwJArIzL4*). A particularly entertaining production (at least if the clips are any indication) seems to have been staged outdoors in Stockholm in 2007 (*http://www.youtube.com/watch?v=0_Ut_lTGz-Y*; *http://www. youtube.com/watch?v=gmxeXyzLqQk*). Also available on YouTube (*http://www. youtube.com/watch?v=XJNf3aKXVrk*) is a clip from the 2003 French version starring Gerard Depardieu – a version which is now available on DVD, but apparently (as yet) without English subtitles.

91 Annette Fern, 'The Marionette Theatre of Peter Arnott at Harvard University', in *American Puppetry, Collections, History and Performance*, ed. Phyllis T. Dircks (Jefferson, NC: McFarland, 2004), pp. 177–88, esp. p. 179.

92 Charles Marowitz, *The Other Chekov: A Biography of Michael Chekov, The Legendary Actor, Director, and Theorist* (New York: Applause, 2004), p. 221.

93 Gerald Bordman and Thomas S. Hischak, *The Oxford Companion to American Theatre*, 3rd ed. (New York: Oxford University Press, 2004), pp. 160, 223, and 281.

94 Michael Green, *Around and About: Memoirs of a South African Newspaperman* (Claremont, SA: David Philip, 2004), p. 43.

95 Lesley Wade Soule offers a nicely detailed paragraph on the Littlewood production; see her article 'Joan Littlewood' in *The Routledge Companion to Directors' Shakespeare*, ed. John Russell Brown (London: Routledge, 2008), pp. 251–68, esp. 260. Dominic Shellard quotes extensively from Tynan's review of the Littlewood staging in his book *Kenneth Tynan: A Life* (New Haven: Yale University Press, 2003), p. 112. Tynan himself, commenting on the Littlewood version, remarked that 'I decline to think there is much poetry worth saving in *Volpone*' and praised Littlewood for 'rightly refus[ing] to impose "the Shakespeare voice" on Jonson's versified prose'; see his *Theatre Writings*, ed. Dominic Shellard (London: Nick Hern, 2007), p. 53. See also Yael Zarhy-Levo, *The Making of Theatrical Reputations* (Iowa City: University of Iowa Press, 2008), pp. 70–71.

96 Thomas S. Hischak, *Enter the Playmakers: Directors and Choreographers on the New York Stage* (Lanham, MD: Scarecrow, 2006), p. 45. For Hischak's comments on productions in 1928 and 1930, see p. 92.

97 Anne Fliotsos and Wendy Vierow, *American Women Stage Directors of the Twentieth Century* (Urbana: University of Illinois Press, 2008) p. 423.

98 Anthony D. Hill and Douglas Q. Barnett, *Historical Dictionary of African-American Theater* (Lanham, MD: Scarecrow, 2009), pp. 60, 66, and 141.

99 C. Lee Jenner, 'National Theatre of the Deaf', in *The Cambridge Guide to American Theatre*, ed. Don B. Wilmeth, 2nd edn (Cambridge: Cambridge University Press, 2007), p. 471. See also *http://www.lifeprint.com/asl101/topics/nationaltheaterofthedeaf.htm*.

100   Betty M. Adelson describes two dwarf actors who appeared in the play and also a
      series of artworks by the artist Jack Levine modeled on characters in the drama; see
      The Lives of Dwarfs: Their Journey from Public Curiosity to Social Liberation (New
      Brunswick, NJ: Rutgers University Press, 2005), pp. 163–64. The director Roger J.
      Porter describes the disappointment of one dwarf whom Porter at first rejected as
      too tall to have a role in the play; see *Self-same Songs: Autobiographical Perform-
      ances and Reflections* (Lincoln: University of Nebraska Press, 2002), p. 66.

101   Garry O'Connor, *Paul Scofield: An Actor for all Seasons* (New York: Applause, 2002),
      pp. 260–61.

102   Don Chapman, *Oxford Playhouse: High and Low Drama in a University City*
      (Hatfield: University of Hertfordshire Press, 2008), p. 194. See also George Whaley,
      Leo 'Rumpole' McKern: The Accidental Actor (Sydney: University of New South
      Wales Press, 2009), pp. 139–40. For two references to televised productions,
      including one in 1967 starring McKern, see Horace Newcomb, ed., *Encyclopedia of
      Television*, 2nd edn, 4. Vols (New York: Fitzroy Dearborn, 2004), pp. 1454 and 2181.

103   Mel Gussow, *Michael Gambon: A Life in Acting* (New York: Applause, 2004),
      pp. 143–44; for Simon Russell Beale's comment that Mosca does all the work in the
      play, see p. 223.

104   Charles Cathcart, *Marston, Rivalry, Rapprochement, and Jonson* (Aldershot: Ashgate,
      2008), pp. 50, 56–57, 76, 85, 93, 139, and 141.

105   Carol A. Morley, ed., *The Plays and Poems of William Heminge* (Rutherford, NJ:
      Fairleigh Dickinson University Press, 2006), p. 100, n. 125.

106   Margaret Cavendish, *Political Writings*, ed. Susan James (Cambridge: Cambridge
      University Press, 2003), p. 17, n. 28.

107   Carolyn D. Williams, '"This Play Will Be Mine A[rse]": Aphra Behn's Jonsonian
      Negotiations', in *Jonsonians: Living Traditions*, ed. Brian Woolland (Aldershot:
      Ashgate, 2003), 93–106; see esp. 103–05.

108   Katritzky, *Women, Medicine and Theatre, 1550–1750*, pp. 152–54 and 170.

109   Robert D. Hume and Harold Love, ed., *Plays, Poems, and Miscellaneous Writings
      Associated with George Villiers, Second Duke of Buckingham*, 2 vols (Oxford: Oxford
      University Press, 2007), vol. 2, pp. 125–35. See also John J. Richetti, *The Cambridge
      History of English Literature, 1660–1780* (Cambridge: Cambridge University Press,
      2005), p. 429.

110   Marc Galanter, *Lowering the Bar: Lawyer Jokes and Legal Culture* (Madison:
      University of Wisconsin Press, 2005), p. 262.

111   Diane Dugaw, *'Deep Play': John Gay and the Invention of Modernity* (Newark:
      University of Delaware Press, 2001), p. 134.

112   Tom Lockwood, *Ben Jonson in the Romantic Age*, p. 40.

113   Ivan Cañadas, 'The Influence of Ben Jonson's *Volpone* on Mary Wollstonecraft's
      Maria, or The Wrongs of Women', ANQ, 19.3 (2006), 7–10.

114   On Walton, see Irene Morra, *Twentieth-Century British Authors and the Rise of
      Opera in Britain* (Aldershot: Ashgate, 2007), p. 58.

115   For an excellent overview of information about the 2004 staging of the Musto/
      Campbell opera, see Quimby Melton, 'Recent Reviews', pp. 275–78. For briefer com-
      mentary on the 2007 revival, see Amy M. Green, 'Recent Ben Jonson Theatrical
      Events and Productions', *Ben Jonson Journal*, 15.1 (2008), 106–09, esp. pp. 107–08.
      Additional information about the opera can be found quite easily on the Internet;
      much of it is surveyed by Melton. The double-CD recording of a 2007 live perform-
      ance of the opera was released in the summer of 2009; it includes the full libretto.
      See John Musto, *Volpone: An Opera in Two Acts Unfaithfully Based on Ben Jonson's
      Comedy* (Wolf Trap Recordings; www. wolftrap.org).

116 Charles J. Hall, *Chronology of Western Classical Music*, 2 Vols. (New York: Routledge, 2002), pp. 15, 119, 154, 882, 964, and 1025; on Antheil, see pp. 15 and 933. For numerous passing references to Blitzstein's music for *Volpone*, see Leonard J. Lehrman, *Marc Blitzstein: A Bio-Bibliography* (Westport, CT: Praeger, 2005). On Applebaum, see Walter G. Pitman, *Louis Applebaum: A Passion for Culture* (Toronto: Dundurn, 2002), pp. 239, 365, and 460.

117 See the *International Who's Who in Classical Music: 2003* (London: Europa, 2003), pp. 59, 113, 271, and 421.

118 For recent commentary on *Foxy*, see (for instance), Ethan Mordden, *Open a New Window: The Broadway Musical in the 1960's* (New York: Palgrave, 2002), pp. 78–80; Philip Furia, *Skylark: The Life and Times of Johnny Mercer* (New York: St. Martin's, 2003), pp. 225–30; and Gene Lees, *Portrait of Johnny: The Life of John Herndon Mercer* (New York: Pantheon, 2004), pp. 249–53.

119 For a sampling of the reviews, see *http://www.musicalstonight.org/REVfoxy.html*; the single CD was issued by Original Cast Records (*www.originalcastrecords.com*).

120 See *http://castalbumcollector.com/recordings/3693/lists*; I am grateful to several members of this list for sharing information with me.

121 Bogel, *The Difference Satire Makes*, pp. 87–89.

122 Henry S. Turner, *The English Renaissance Stage: Geometry, Poetics, and the Practical Spatial Arts 1580–1630* (New York: Oxford University Press, 2006), pp. 262–64, esp. 264.

123 Thomas Rand, 'Jonson's *Volpone*', *The Explicator*, 62.2 (2004), 77–80.

124 Murray Roston, *Tradition and Subversion in Renaissance Literature: Studies in Shakespeare, Spenser, Jonson, and Donne* (Pittsburgh: Duquesne University Press, 2007), pp. 135–70, esp. 138.

125 Roston, p. 148.

126 Roston, pp. 161–62.

127 Ben Jonson, *Volpone*, ed. R. B. Parker, rev. ed. (Manchester: Manchester University Press, 1999); the Dutton edition will be published as part of the forthcoming Cambridge edition of Jonson's works.

128 Richard Harp, ed., *Ben Jonson's Plays and Masques*, 2nd edn (New York: Norton, 2001); see Jonas Barish, 'The Double Plot of *Volpone*' (pp. 399–411) and Robert C. Evans, 'Thomas Sutton: Ben Jonson's Volpone?' (pp. 411–21).

129 Robert N. Watson, ed., *Volpone* (New York: Norton, 2003), esp. pp. xi, xxiii, xxxi–xxxiii, 163–71.

130 Michael Wayne Stamps, *Ben Jonson's 'Volpone': A Critical Variorum Edition* (Ann Arbor: UMI Dissertation Services, 2004).

131 See, for instance, the 'Oxford School' edition of *Hamlet*, ed. Roma Gill, rev. ed. (Oxford: Oxford University Press, 2002) or the 'Cambridge School' edition of Hamlet, ed. Richard Andrew and Rex Gibson, 2nd edn (Cambridge: Cambridge University Press, 2005).

132 *Volpone, by Ben Jonson*, narrated by Flo Gibson (ISBN 1-155685-549-4; www.audiobookcontractors.com).

133 *Ben Jonson* (Princeton, NJ: Films for the Humanities and Sciences, 2004).

134 See *www.stageonscreen.com/volpone.htm*.

CHAPTER FOUR

New Directions: Jonson's Literary Theatre: *Volpone* in Performance and Print (1606–1607)

James P. Bednarz

The first edition of BEN: IONSON / his / VOLPONE / or / THE FOXE
– as the title page of the first quarto of 1607 describes it – occupies a
prominent position in recent criticism as an example of Jonson's
entrenched anti-theatrical prejudice.[1] Here, contemporary scholars,
inspired by Jonas A. Barish's seminal essay 'Jonson and the Loathèd
Stage', find evidence of a playwright who rejects the debased commercial theatre as he strives to establish his stage-plays as literature through
print. 'Jonson's stress on the enduring literary merits of his works, as
opposed to their brief stage life', writes W. David Kay, 'is nowhere
seen more clearly than in the printed text of his comedy *Volpone*'.[2] What
supposedly had caused Jonson to reject the authority of performance
and the value of theatre? Building on both Barish's essay and Elizabeth
L. Eisenstein's optimistic appraisal of the print revolution as a source
of intellectual stability, Richard C. Newton suggests that Jonson was a
writer who sought 'permanence and liberation from performance'
because he realized that the status of theatre in his own culture was too
low to sustain a literary career, especially insofar as it was a medium that
delegated too much power to actors and audiences. A play in performance, Newton argues, is 'always in process, always being interpreted for
the needs of the social group that as an audience "possesses" it', so that it
was only through publication that Jonson could claim ownership and
proclaim completeness and permanence for his work.[3] It is for this
reason that Timothy Murray even contends that Jonson's effort to 'assert
control' over the 'corruption and foulness' of theatre caused his 'major

contribution to literary history' to be in his role 'as an editor instead of a writer'.[4]

The main problem with this widely accepted hypothesis, however, is that it misrepresents Jonson's complex and variable attitude toward performance, especially by fostering the false assumption that the first quarto of *Volpone*, published at the inception of the major phase of his dramatic career, was counter-theatrical. On the contrary, a more thorough examination of its prefatory material or 'paratexts' (its dedication and 'Epistle' to Oxford and Cambridge Universities and the set of commendatory poems by a distinguished group of writers including Francis Beaumont and John Donne) reveals how Jonson and his admirers took advantage of its recent theatrical successes, associated with these prestigious institutions, to confirm his literary merit.

Nowhere in his opening epistle does Jonson construe the printed version of *Volpone* as a stable and authoritative text that compensates for the liability of performance. In fact, the opposite is true. For those privileged academic auditors who had been present at either of these early performances at Oxford and Cambridge the play's quarto provided a souvenir of those outstanding theatrical occasions, and for the rest of its readers it carried the implicit endorsement – or so Jonson tells us – of its original learned audiences. Rather than erasing signs of its theatrical origin, *Volpone*'s publication memorializes these gratifying theatrical occasions when its performance by the King's Men ratified, to Jonson's satisfaction, his status as a poet. Print, in this instance, did not negate but re-mediate performance. So that while it would be wrong to deny that Jonson recurrently denounced the stage's imputed vices throughout his long career in commercial drama, it would be equally erroneous to assume that he did not also occasionally take pride in the performance of his plays and view their production as a measure of his literary stature. At the opening of his epistle, Jonson writes that no person has ever had 'a wit so presently excellent as that it could raise itself' without the help of 'commenders, and favourers to it' (lines 1–3), as he acknowledges how significant he found the adulation of these select auditors who fused academic and theatrical domains.

Barish had originally insisted that Jonson's 'well-articulated antitheatricalism' was matched by 'a less acknowledged but nonetheless potent theatricalism' which contributed to the 'high tension and precarious equilibrium' of his comic masterpieces.[5] Yet outside of David Riggs' evocation of Scoto of Mantua as Jonson's anti-type within the drama, this balance is seldom repeated in recent studies of his career that recurrently assume his almost absolute estrangement from theatre.[6] The purpose of this essay is consequently to restore Barish's sense of balance to our perception of Jonson's reliance on both performance and print in his bid to define himself as an ideal poet in the paratexts of *Volpone*. Reading the first quarto more accurately requires situating it in what Robert Weimann defines as a 'circulation of authority' that progresses 'from writing to playing and, simultaneously, from playing to writing, with both circuits connected to a crucial court of special appeal and cultural patronage – the responding, judging, applauding audience'.[7] Because here Jonson not only enlists *Volpone*'s theatrical reception to help justify his reputation as an ideal 'poet', but also construes the formal 'laws' of 'Time' and 'Place' upon which he professes his literary art to be based in terms that apply solely to the performance of his plays.

It is understandable why critics who focus exclusively on the title-page of the first edition of *Volpone* might erroneously conclude that Jonson was attempting to disguise the play's theatrical origin. At a time when it was customary to find the name of the acting company rather than that of its author on the title-pages of contemporary plays, Jonson, who exercised an extraordinary degree of editorial control over the publication of his drama, emblazoned his own name in ostentatiously large type and omitted any reference to the King's Men, who had performed it. But this typographic substitution of author for actors does not appear to be based on his determination to erase the theatrical nature of his play because any reader who opens the first quarto to glance at its dedication immediately discovers Jonson's testimony to the favourable reception that *Volpone* received at Oxford and Cambridge when the King's Men seem to have performed it in 1606, perhaps as part of their summer touring:

TO THE MOST NOBLE
AND MOST AEQUALL
SISTERS
THE TWO FAMOUS UNIVERSITIES,
FOR THEIR LOVE
AND
ACCEPTANCE
SHEWN TO HIS POEME
IN THE PRESENTATION:
BEN: JONSON
THE GRATEFULL ACKNOWLEDGER
DEDICATES
BOTH IT, AND HIMSELFE.

Fusing both productions, Jonson describes his play as a poem-in-presentation, a work of art enacted before spectators whose appreciation is crucial to its reception. And in the 'Epistle', composed at his house at Blackfriars on 11 February 1607, dedicating both his masterpiece and himself to Oxford and Cambridge, he thanks them for their enthusiastic response, re-defining the King's Men's theatrical success as the poet's personal triumph.[8] He had realized the dream of a poet's theatre. He only praises what he has achieved, he argues, in order to 'justify' the taste of these judicious scholars that might otherwise have been called into question in 'an age wherein poetry and the professors of it hear so ill on all sides' (line 10). It is important to remember that when Jonson refers to Oxford and Cambridge as most 'noble' and 'aequall', he is not only commenting on their comparable academic status but also using the latter adjective as an English equivalent for the Latin 'aequus' in order to stress that they were 'just' or 'equitable' in appreciating his work.[9] In commending them as equal, he subtly commends himself. In such a negative cultural context, he further explains, even their academic 'authority' needed explication, and it was to this end that he proffers the epistle's eloquent defence of his art and life. In the first quarto of *Volpone*, Jonson took full credit for both performed and printed versions of his comedy, and its title-page, read in light of his sequent dedication and epistle, might be taken to signify his responsibility for the play's appearance in both media. All one has to do to discover this is just open the quarto.

It is unfortunate, however, that we know so little about these two performances that Jonson recalls with such affection in both the first quarto of 1607 and the First Folio of 1616 (which eliminates the commendatory poems). He seems to imply that these productions were sponsored by the universities, but this does not seem to have been the case. There were, however, two reasons why Jonson might have felt justified in acknowledging their largesse, even though *Volpone* was probably neither sponsored by the universities nor presented on their property. First, in 1606 the universities' vice-chancellors would have had to allow performances by the King's Men in both towns, at a time when prohibition, especially at Cambridge, was common. He was thankful for what he construed as the universities' tacit approval that his work conformed to their standards. And second, the performances at Oxford and Cambridge were probably so well attended by gownsmen that Jonson construed their presence as a synecdoche for both institutions.[10] A precedent for this exaggeration is provided by the title-page of the 'bad' first quarto of *Hamlet*, published in 1603, which brags that Shakespeare's play had been acted not only in 'the City of London' but also at 'the two Universities of Cambridge and Oxford'. Here, the suburb of Southwark is upgraded to the city of London, and the towns of Cambridge and Oxford (or their suburbs) become proxies for the universities they adjoin. Three years later, in 1606, *Volpone* might have been presented as part of the King's Men's summer tour, an event that coincided that year with plague in London.

We know that the town paid the King's Men for having visited Oxford in July of 1606, and it was at this time that the production of *Volpone* which Jonson celebrates might have been acted in either the town hall (which doubled as the guildhall) or a local inn.[11] In 1610, Henry Jackson, who held an M.A. from Corpus Christi College and was appointed a fellow in 1612, observed the King's Men's performances of *The Alchemist* and *Othello* in what was possibly the same place. But REED has found no corroborating evidence of the King's Men at Cambridge in 1606.[12] At the time, Cambridge was more vigilant than Oxford in protecting its precincts from invasions by professional players.[13] From 1570 onward, the university which had secured by statute the right to ban public entertainment from within five miles of the town centre prohibited commercial entertainment of all kinds, from bear-baiting to stage plays. A letter that James I signed on 23 July 1604, prepared by Robert Cecil, the earl of Salisbury, who was lord secretary, specifically granted Cambridge's chancellor and vice-chancellor unchallengeable authority – over all but the king's pleasure – in restraining any entertainment either at the university or in the town and its environs, and the letters patent that James subsequently issued to the university on 4 March 1605 affirmed this right. The activities to be forbidden included such unprofitable and idle pastimes as 'common plays' and 'comedies and tragedies in the English tongue'.[14] University administrators were even given the right to jail offenders. It is no coincidence that Cecil, at whose request James signed the letter of authorization, was the chancellor of Cambridge from 1601 to 1612.

Yet enforcement remained selective. In the summer of 1606, Richard Clayton, who was then vice-chancellor, forced Thomas Greene and John Duke, members of Queen Anne's Men, to abandon their plan for a performance at the town hall, even though the actors objected that they had secured the permission of John Edmonds, the mayor, who had already given them its key and had approved the building of a stage and the removal of glass windows that might accidentally be broken. Subjected by the vice-chancellor to litigation in the university's Commissary's Court, Greene and Duke were compelled on 25 July to sign a notarized document legally binding them 'and their whole company' from performing 'any manner of plays or interludes' within a five-mile radius of both the university and town on penalty of paying the Chancellor the sum of twenty pounds.[15] If, as it seems likely, *Volpone* had been acted in the Cambridge area at about the same time or soon after, Jonson would have been right to have been proud of his achievement, and his victory would have been a triumph for both the poet and professional theatre.

Doubting that *Volpone* was performed at Cambridge during this period, due to ingrained administrative disapproval for commercial entertainment and especially the contemporaneous pressure brought to bear upon Greene and Duke, Alan H. Nelson, editor of its REED volume, suggests that: 'Perhaps the dedication expresses a hope that the printed book now offered for the judgment of the universities will have a good reception'.[16] But Jonson states that he is dedicating his work in print to the universities because of the 'love and acceptance' they have already 'shown'. He is not addressing future prospects but is recalling, as he writes in the epistle, 'your affections past' (line 115) for a play that had been 'seen' (line 95). What is more, Esmé Stuart's commendatory poem (quoted in its entirety later in this essay) corroborates Jonson's claim in describing how *Volpone* had been 'endued with spright | Of action' in 'both Minerva's cities'. If, on the strength of this internal evidence, we reject Nelson's conjecture, it is because it is impossible to believe that Jonson and Stuart were blatantly lying about these performances, however exaggerated their statements might be.[17] Why would they foolishly risk their reputations in fabricating something that at the time could be so easily verified? It seems far more plausible to assume that Jonson was sincerely grateful to both universities for what he calls 'the bounty of your act' (line 8).

Volpone would consequently only have been staged at Cambridge by securing the chancellor or vice-chancellor's approval, and this would have been a particularly high profile decision in light of the mayor's problem with the university about Queen Anne's Men.[18] In 1606, Cecil, the university chancellor, was also Jonson's patron, and, as a result, the poet might have interpreted the administrative decision to allow the King's Men's performance at 'Cambridge' as a tacit endorsement of his drama.[19] It would have been an unusually magnanimous gesture for either Cecil or his vice-chancellor to permit the King's Men to act *Volpone*, and what probably facilitated the decision was Jonson's patronage by the chancellor. On 24 July 1606, the day before Greene and Duke were effectively banished from Cambridge, Cecil paid Jonson thirteen pounds, six pence, for helping to welcome King James and his brother-in-law Christian IV of Denmark to his estate at Theobalds, as part of what David Riggs calls an effort to maintain the poet 'within his clientage network'.[20] One therefore wonders to what extent this act of favouritism – allowing the King's Men to perform at Cambridge while banning Queen Anne's Men – can be reconciled with Richard Dutton's recent suggestion that throughout the play Jonson savagely satirizes Cecil.[21] Jonson's comedy would have premiered by March of 1606 at the Globe, and whatever political satire it offered would still have been a hot topic by the time it reached Cambridge. Wouldn't Cecil have heard about any personal attack on him in Jonson's play by then? And even if he were completely oblivious to Jonson's supposedly caustic topicality or had no prior knowledge of what the company would perform, why would the King's Men have wanted to antagonize him by mocking him in *Volpone* at Cambridge?

The King's Men, in any case, apparently found Jonson's erudite comedy to be a hit at both academic venues. During their visit to Cambridge in 1591–1592, the Queen's Men had set up 'bills' or posters on the gates of the colleges announcing their presence in nearby Chesterton, and one wonders if the King's Men used a similar, but perhaps less aggressive, advertising campaign to publicize Jonson's comedy in 1606.[22] The success of *Volpone* before Oxford and Cambridge audiences must have been especially gratifying for Jonson, since *Sejanus*, his prior play for the King's Men (written with an unknown collaborator) in 1603 had failed at the Globe. Sejanus, Tiberius's henchman, had been torn apart by an angry mob, and Jonson, in his Folio dedication of the play to his patron Esmé Stuart, Seigneur d'Aubigny (a cousin of James I, with whom the poet was living in 1604), admitted that when his *'poem' Sejanus* was first performed, it *'suffer'd no less violence from our people here, than the subject of it did from the rage of the people of Rome'* (H&S, 4:349). So that when Jonson published a revised version of *Sejanus* in 1605 as a single-authored play with scholarly annotations, print certainly provided him with a welcome alternative to performance. 'Although *Volpone* was a stage success', Joseph Loewenstein, suggests, 'the quarto imitates and elaborates that of *Sejanus* in proposing itself as counter-theatrical'.[23] But as a result of their radically different receptions, the strategy of bibliographic self-vindication revealed in the first quarto of *Sejanus* is, instead, directly opposed to the program of theatrical self-authorization encountered two years later in the first quarto of *Volpone*. Because just as the theatrical failure of *Sejanus* prompted Jonson to savour the solace of print, the success of *Volpone* encouraged him to conceive of its publication as a printed memento of ideal productions that had verified its value as literature and his status as a laureate poet. The 'most learned Arbitresses', Jonson exults in his epistle to *Volpone*, 'have seen, judged, and to my crown, approved' (line 95). In *Self-Crowned Laureates*, Richard Helgerson writes that Jonson could only attempt 'to make himself a laureate dramatist by combating drama'.[24] The genre was still too near the base of Parnassus, Helgerson concludes, for Jonson to consider it to be a proper vehicle for artistic self-advancement, through which he could be symbolically crowned with laurel. But in the epistle to *Volpone*, Jonson, on the contrary, construes theatrical success as a sign of literary investiture.

'The idea of a playhouse full of educated theatergoers struck a responsive chord in Jonson', notes Riggs. 'Here, at last, were flesh-and-blood spectators whom he could address without scorn or condescension'.[25] Indeed, Esmé Stuart, who witnessed the fiasco of *Sejanus*' debut, was so pleased with *Volpone*'s success that he even refers to the play's quarto as the exhibition of its corpse in his commendatory poem 'To my worthily-esteemed Mr. Ben Jonson', which idealizes the play's joint performances – in 'Minerva's cities', places sacred to the goddess of wisdom – as its finest realization:

> Volpone now is dead indeed, and lies
> Exposed to the censure of all eyes
> And mouths; now he hath run his train and shown
> His subtle body where he best was known –
> In both Minerva's cities, he doth yield
> His well formed limbs upon this open field;
> Who, if they now appear so fair in sight,
> How did they when they were endued with spright
> Of action? Yet in thy praise let this be read:
> The Fox will live, when all his hounds be dead.
>
> (lines 1–10)

No matter how 'fair' readers might find the well-formed limbs – the relatively clean lines of Jonson's plot – Stuart argues, those who have encountered *Volpone* dead – in the field of print – can only imagine how beautiful this 'Fox' had been when it ran its 'train' through Oxford and Cambridge. Jonson's 'most noble and most equal sisters' are combined by Stuart in the equally benign feminized ideal of Minerva, and although he sees the comedy's performances in her 'cities' as its finest moment, he finds consolation in the paradox that even in its present deadened form *Volpone* will outlive the memory of those 'hounds', Jonson's detractors, who pursued him. In evoking its performances at Oxford and Cambridge, the poem even manages to preserve Jonson's ambiguity about its actual venue, since his phrase 'Minerva's cities' can be read as either a metaphoric reference to the universities or as a hyperbolic description of the towns. Publication revived the dead fox, but as a kind of sportsman's trophy, embalmed in print, suspended in a kind of life-in-death that lacked the 'spright | Of action'. Rather than emphasizing the play's movement from the playhouse to the printing house, D. D. (probably Sir Dudley Digges), in another commendatory poem, 'To my good friend, Mr. Jonson', similarly celebrates a comedy that had 'so pleased judicious eyes' with 'ancient comedy's | Fashions' (lines 4–5). Because of plague, London theatres had been closed from July to December 1606 and for all of 1607, except for a week in April, so that the published text of *Volpone* might have acquired an additional level of interest when it first appeared from nostalgic playgoers deprived of seeing Jonson's masterpiece performed. The poet's fond remembrance of his comedy's welcome reception might have even acquired a greater depth of affection in lieu of his present circumstance in February 1607, without a public venue to build on his success.

One of the prime difficulties that twenty-first century readers encounter in understanding the theatrical emphasis of Jonson's epistle stems from the peculiar critical terminology it utilizes in describing a good 'playwright' as a 'poet', a 'play' as a 'poem' and all 'literature' as 'poetry'. Although early modern usage varied, Jonson's literary vocabulary parallels the norm set by Sir Philip Sidney's *Apology for Poetry* and George Puttenham's *Art of English Poesy*, based on Aristotle's *Poetics* and Horace's *Art of Poetry*. Aristotle had employed the term 'poetry' (meaning 'something made') in a manner that elided dramatic and non-dramatic literary kinds, even as he concluded that tragedy was a higher form of 'poetry' than epic. Horace, whose treatise Jonson had translated twice, repeated Aristotle's usage, which would occupy a central place in English literary criticism until 'poetry', as a universal rubric describing all creative writing, was finally supplanted by the term 'literature' in the eighteenth century. In describing *Volpone* as a 'poem' when he dedicated the first quarto of his play to Oxford and Cambridge, Jonson was certainly not seeking to discount the play's theatrical origin but was availing himself of a classically influenced critical tradition in which acted drama played a central role. Lukas Erne is consequently wrong in suggesting that early modern dramatists systematically used the word 'poem' to designate the written or printed versions of their work and 'play' to denote its enactment.[26] Usage in the period was far more variable; early modern dramatists referred to 'plays' as 'poems' in either medium. In *Every Man Out of His Humour*, for example, Jonson, without any attempt to differentiate performance from publication, writes that in the comedy of Aristophanes 'this kind of Poem appeared absolute'.[27] Jonson calls *Volpone* his 'poem' in print, just as in his Prologue, written for performance, he similarly refers to the 'play' (line 2) as one of 'his poems' (line 7). It is these 'poems' that constitute 'dramatic, or, as they term it, stage poetry' (line 33). Shakespeare, using the same vocabulary, but to different ends, several years earlier in *Hamlet*, had Polonius show his tolerance for theatrical diversity by accepting both 'the scene individable', structured according to the laws of time and place and the 'poem unlimited', a different kind of drama that violated neoclassical decorum.[28]

When Jonson calls himself a 'poet' in the epistle, he is not isolating himself conceptually from theatre. Instead, he uses the word to distinguish between two kinds of dramatists: the 'poets', such as himself, who were intent on restoring the 'ancient forms and manners' of drama; and the 'poetasters' and 'playwrights' who ignorantly deformed it. In an effort to indicate how English Renaissance writers often combined attention to both dramatic and non-dramatic formats throughout their careers, Patrick Cheney has effectively deployed the hyphenated form 'poet-playwright' to elucidate and document this widespread phenomenon. And insofar as it helps to emphasize the intricate interlacement of poems and plays in their work, this nomenclature has had a salutary effect on contemporary scholarship. But, as Cheney realizes, this compound rests on a distinction between 'poet' and 'playwright' that is anachronistic, and although it helps us understand what early modern English writers did, it obscures to some extent the theoretical divisions *they* made.[29] During the Elizabethan and Jacobean periods, as we have seen, the word 'poet' was regularly applied to writers of lyric and drama. 'Poet' rather than 'playwright' was the term customarily used for dramatists, in line with Sidney's and Jonson's nomenclature. Philip Henslowe consistently paid 'ready money' to 'poets', alongside 'players', 'plasterers', 'carmen', 'laborers' and 'grooms of Her Majesty's Chamber' in his *Diary*. When John Marston began his career as a commercial dramatist in September of 1599, Henslowe designated him 'the new poet'. This was not based on a special regard for Marston; it was Henslowe's ordinary usage. On 21, 24 and 26 February, 1602, he similarly paid four unnamed 'poets' for their collaborative work on the second part of *The Black Dog*, and on 12 March compensated John Day and 'his fellow poets' for an unnamed play, before paying Anthony Munday, later in the year, whom he describes as a 'poet', for his comedy *The Widow's Charm*.[30]

Jonson's terminological innovation, however, was to divide contemporary dramatists between 'poets' who were ideal practitioners of the art of 'poetry' and debased 'poetasters' or 'playwrights'. The function of a 'good poet', he explains, is to be an 'interpreter and arbiter of nature, a teacher of things divine no less than human, a master in manners', who 'can alone (or with a few) effect the business of mankind'. If others were not willing to concede that he had achieved this ideal in *Volpone*, he complains, it was for two causes beyond his control: the bad drama of 'poetasters' who degraded the reputation of professional theatre and the malicious slander of spectators and readers who found dangerous social commentary in his plays. But just as he could not be blamed for how bad most drama had become, neither should he be held responsible for the absurd notion that his work contained covert satirical attacks on contemporary individuals, societies or nations. He was innocent on both counts, he insists, and his play deserved to be taken on its own merits.

For Jonson, a 'poet-playwright' would have been a walking contradiction, since a great dramatist was a 'poet' and a bad one was a 'playwright' or 'poetaster'. The difference between a 'poet' and a 'play-wright' was not based on their choice of genre; it was qualitative. One might despise 'playwrights' and admire dramatic 'poets'. The *Oxford English Dictionary* records the first use of the word 'playwright' as being M. Clifford's reference to the 'damned Trade of Playwright' in 1687, but this is inaccurate, since, as Ian Donaldson observes, Jonson probably coined the term, brandishing it as a sign of obloquy in the titles of *Epigrams* 49, 68 and 100. There, it serves as a nickname for John Marston, the original 'playwright'. 'The early usage is scornful', Donaldson notes, citing further appearances of the word by Cygnus 'on common play-wrights' in his verses on *Sejanus* (1605) and Henry Fitzjeffrey on Webster as 'playwright-cartwright' in *Notes from Blackfriars* (1617). In the latter year, John Davies of Hereford, perhaps influenced by Jonson's epigrams (which he could have read in manuscript or in the Folio of 1616), repeated the word in the concluding line of Epigram 225 of *Wit's Bedlam* (F7ᵛ). For Jonson, a 'playwright' practised a base trade instead of pursuing an artistic vocation. The term shared the vituperative tone of 'parcel-poet', another of his coinages, this one designating a serial collaborator in the theatre, a 'poet' who is incapable of sustaining the more prestigious literary status of single authorship.[31] Hugh Holland accordingly praises Shakespeare as 'the Famous Scenic Poet' in his com-mendatory sonnet at the opening of the Shakespeare First Folio as he requests readers whose hands have 'so clapt' (line 1) at his plays – 'Which made the Globe of heav'n and earth to ring' (line 4) – to wring them now in grief at his loss. And John Dryden's later discussion of Shakespeare and Jonson as 'dramatic poets' in *An Essay of Dramatic Poesy* shows the influence of this now extinct usage that has been replaced by our current insistence that 'poets' write lyric and narrative verses, while 'playwrights' produce drama.

Along with being characterized as counter-theatrical, the first quarto of *Volpone* has also typically been seen as the first of Jonson's published texts to demonstrate a dogmatic neoclassicism in its adherence to the 'rules of art' necessary for the creation of viable drama. Indeed, according to Timothy Murray, Jonson's advocacy of neoclassical decorum paralleled and supplemented his preference for publication, since he conceived of the typographically stabilizing instrument of print and the intellectually stabilizing force of method as coordinate means of converting anonymous unredeemable theatrical events into timeless art.[32] There are, however, three problems with this formulation. First, as we have seen, the *Volpone* quarto of 1607 does not repudiate perform-ance. Second, the quarto does not express a consistent advocacy of the 'rules' but engages in a dialectic of 'law' and 'liberty' that confounds consistent systemization. And third, the first two of Jonson's specific rules – among the three 'laws of Time, Place, Persons' (Prologue, line 31) – apply solely to the play in performance, indicating that he recognized performance itself as a valid artistic medium distinct from print. Jonson's appreciation of these 'laws' was accordingly both flexible and inherently theatrical.

Until the pioneering work of Richard Dutton, the first edition of *Volpone* was thought to mark the point in Jonson's career at which he became a strict advocate of neoclassical theory. James D. Redwine, for example, had insisted on the need to distinguish between 'pre-*Volpone*' and 'post-*Volpone* criticism', arguing that, 'The importance of *Volpone* criticism can scarcely be stressed too often – it marks a turning point in the development of Jonson's critical theory'.[33] In *Volpone*, Redwine concludes, Jonson's former attitude of 'respectful independence' had calcified into a doctrinaire affirmation of neoclassical principles. Brian Parker repeats this opinion in his introduction to the Revels edition of the play, where he similarly assumes that the 'Epistle and Prologue to *Volpone* record an important stage in Jonson's critical development, a new reliance on classical standards that is different from the independence claimed in the Introduction to *Every Man Out*' (37). What prompted Redwine's and Parker's assessment is clear. *Volpone*'s Prologue announces Jonson's commitment to remedying common theatrical errors that delight the 'rout' with a more valid theorized practise that mixes 'profit' with 'pleasure' (line 8),

> And so presents quick comedy refined,
> As best critics have designed;
> The laws of Time, Place, Persons he observeth,
> From no needful rule he swerveth.
>
> (lines 29–32)

Sixteenth-century Italian critics, analysing Aristotle's *Poetics*, had extrapolated sets of rules in systems that were both varied and fungible, and it was to this neoclassical movement, previously adapted by Sidney in *An Apology for Poetry*, that Jonson turned to master the rules of art. These so-called laws of dramatic composition became touchstones of theatrical reform that allied the poet with the most respected contemporary literary criticism. In criticism of the second half of the seventeenth century, especially due to the influence of Pierre Corneille's *On the Three Unities: Of Action, of Time, and of Place*, these three laws have come to define neoclassical doctrine. Based on Corneille's discussion of the 'three unities', Dryden in *An Essay of Dramatic Poesy* retrospectively defined *Epicoene* as Jonson's 'perfect' play. In *Volpone*, however, Jonson, who wrote before the 'three unities' were standardized, joins 'time' and 'place' to 'persons' instead of 'action', in an approach to theory that is more eclectic and tentative, offering criteria and precedents that multiply, contract and change in different contexts.

Two of the three laws that Jonson explicitly lists in his Prologue are based on prescriptive interpretations of observations in Aristotle's *Poetics*. The law of time was derived from Aristotle's assertion that 'tragedy attempts, as far as possible, to remain within one circuit of the sun, or, at least, not depart from this by much. Epic poetry, however, has no limit in regard to time'. And the law of persons was grounded in his division of tragedy and comedy along class lines. Comedy, being 'an imitation of baser men', was said to exclude the high-born characters proper to tragedy.[34] In *Every Man Out*, *Cynthia's Revels* and *Poetaster*, Jonson had included two queens, an emperor and their courts; his new comedy excluded nobles. Unlike the laws of time and persons, however, there is no mention of a law of place in *The Poetics*. This law was a sixteenth-century rule popularized by Ludovico Castelvetro, who insisted that time and place should be jointly controlled by dramatists in order to increase the credibility of acted events. And it was through Castelvetro's influence on Sidney and Jonson that the phenomenological categories of time and place became central to English neoclassicism's invention of performance criticism during the early modern period.

But before examining how the Prologue's laws of time and place are relevant *solely* to their theatrical milieu, since they are based entirely on the experiential conditions of performance, I want to stress the need to balance a sense of Jonson's advocacy of the rules of art in *Volpone* against his simultaneous admission that his work deliberately violated 'the strict rigour of comic law' (lines 100–101). Because long before readers of the first quarto of *Volpone* come upon the Prologue's neoclassical strictures, they are informed in the epistle that the play's punitive 'catastrophe' technically violates 'comic law' in refusing to end happily:

> And though my catastrophe may in the strict rigour of comic law meet with censure as turning back to my promise, I desire the learned and charitable critic to have so much faith in me to think it was done of industry; for with what ease I could have varied it nearer his scale, but that I fear to boast my own faculty, I could here insert. But my special aim being to put the snaffle in their mouths that cry out we never punish vice in our interludes &c., I took more liberty; though not without some lines of examples drawn even in the ancients themselves.

Volpone has the sternest ending of any Jonson comedy: the eponymous trickster-villain is sentenced to end his life in a hospital for incurable diseases and his accomplice Mosca is condemned to the galleys. According to Jonson, however, deliberate violation of the rules could be justified by a poet who had a more important goal: to vindicate theatre. And even this formal violation, he argues, conformed to 'some lines of example drawn even in the ancients themselves'. 'I took the more liberty,' Jonson insists, to prove that it was 'the office of a comic poet to imitate justice and instruct to life' (69). For each unique play, Jonson implies, some laws are 'needful' and others disposable, and the poet assumes the liberty to keep or break laws as he sees fit. So that if he begins his epistle with a condemnation of the 'too much license of poetasters in this time', he ends it not with an affirmation of timeless literary laws but with a declaration of the poet's informed 'liberty'. He will, he tells readers, keep or break any law that does not meet his needs, in the service of higher principles. If Jonson's commitment to neoclassical theory led him to imagine a Greco-Roman heritage of laws that governed literary composition, he always simultaneously acknowledged that tradition was innovation, since thoughtful writers had to continually adjust their use of the past to meet the new criteria of contemporary taste and circumstance. Jonson's neoclassicism allowed for a synthesis of imitation and innovation, as the poet worked within what he recognized as received authority, reserving the right to fit ancient formulae to modern needs.

Readers of the first quarto of *Volpone* who were familiar with the first quarto of Jonson's prior play *Sejanus*, published two years earlier, might have recalled that the earlier work was introduced with a similar admission of deliberate artistic transgression. In defending *Sejanus*, Jonson had previously admitted that there too he had written an irregular drama that was susceptible to attack, in this case because he had disregarded the law of time and omitted the chorus:

> First, if it be objected, that what I publish is no true *Poem*; in the strict Laws of *Time*. I confess it: as also in the want of a proper *Chorus*, whose Habit, and Moods are such, and so difficult, as not any, whom I have seen since the *Ancients*, (no, not they who have most presently affected Laws) have yet come in the way of. Nor is it needful, or almost possible, in these our Times, and to such Auditors, as commonly things are presented, to observe the old state, and splendor of *Dramatic Poems*, with preservation of any popular delight. (H&S, 4:350)

One understands why Jonson feared that long-winded choruses between acts might drain some of the 'popular delight' from his plays, but why did he feel free to violate the law of time in *Sejanus* (a play whose action extends for more than a day) and then make it one of the 'needful' laws that validate the structure of *Volpone*? If the law of time is indispensable in *Volpone* why isn't it relevant to *Sejanus*? Jonson never answered these questions, although in the earlier play he had promised to clarify his position further in a now lost treatise entitled *Obervations upon Horace his Art of Poetry*. Because of his literary crime of breaking the law of time in *Sejanus*, Jonson concedes that his work was 'no true poem', although he apparently assumed it was good and that he had broken this dramatic law for the right reason. Yet all of this consequently produces a strangely arbitrary sense of what it means to obey a literary law. One can only speculate about the extent to which Jonson recognized his double bind: that while he claimed to be dependent on the rules, their selection and application depended on his changing assessment of which laws were valid and which were not for any given play. The problem, as Jonson saw it, was to discover which of the classical rules were necessary or possible in works addressed to his contemporaries. The ancients, he concluded in a memorable phrase in *Discoveries*, were 'Guides, not Commanders' (H&S, 8:567). The poet-critic had to be discerning in these matters, knowing when to imitate, adjust, or innovate in order to achieve desired dramatic effects. In doing so, he realized that he would never satisfy the purists, and this led to a series of explanations as to why he had deliberately broken with traditions that he felt were unnecessary or counterproductive in contemporary drama. Near the end of his career, in his commendatory poem to Richard Brome's *The Northern Lass* (1632), Jonson lauded himself as the great neoclassical reformer of popular drama, whose precedent still mattered when he praised his protégé's 'observation of those comic laws | Which I, your master, first did teach the age' (*UV*, 38, 7–8). What Jonson would, on this occasion, however, leave unmentioned is his own errant record and odd sense of law: his recurrent violations of the supposedly invariable principles of art.

Jonson's reflections on himself and his work in the first quarto of *Volpone* are further amplified by the eleven commendatory poems that praise his neoclassical program of theatrical reform and reflect on his dialectical relation to the ancients. Edward Bolton, addressing both universities in Latin in, commends Jonson – quoting his motto '*Tanquam explorator*' ('as an explorer') – for being the first man to have studied Greek and Roman antiquity in order to create a learned drama for Britain. John Donne, also dignifying the quarto with a Latin verse, concurs with Bolton by proposing the paradox that Jonson is an innovator in following the ancients. In his epistle, Jonson had expressed his intention to 'reduce the ancient forms' and 'manners of the scene', and T. R. (probably Thomas Roe) echoes this language when he lauds Jonson's success in restoring 'ancient forms' (line 7) to counter a renaissance of vice. Francis Beaumont in 'To my dear friend Mr. Benjamin Jonson, upon his FOX', however, is the only respondent who specifically cites any of the neoclassical 'laws' that Jonson claims to have followed. Had he been required to justify Jonson's drama, Beaumont states, he

> would have shown
> To all the world the art which thou alone
> Hast taught our tongue: the rules of time, of place,
> And other rites, delivered with the grace
> Of comic style, which, only, is far more
> Than any English stage hath known before.
>
> (lines 11–16)

Beaumont's reduction of Jonson's three rules to two – time and place, omitting person – isolates from the welter of critical precepts two elements of drama that pertain only to its performance. Aside from time and place, all other formal strictures are covered obliquely under the vague rubric of 'other rites'. In this unique consideration of time and place as conceptual conditions of theatre, performance criticism begins in England with neoclassical criticism's emphasis on spectatorship. As I have previously mentioned, although Aristotle suggests what became known as the law of time, Castelvetro, whose influence on Sidney affected Jonson, invented the law of place. Unlike Sidney or Jonson, Castelvetro believed that drama was autotelic, rightly concerned only with delighting, not teaching, its audience. But his impact on dramatic theory was decisive for both Sidney and Jonson in so far as they both emphasized the material conditions of the 'English stage' when they speculated (no matter how inadequately) about the relation between drama and its mode of production. Elaborating on why the laws of time and place were so important, Castelvetro's *Poetica* explains that drama is staged 'in a small space and in a small space of time', insisting that the dramatist, unlike the writer of epic, has to produce fictions that respond to the phenomenology of theatre.[35] Aristotle had determined that tragedy did not depend on public performance and actors, but Castelvetro nevertheless influenced Sidney and Jonson to conceive of dramatic enactment as requiring a set of rules necessary for its transformation into 'art'.

Of all English critics, Sidney had the greatest impact on Jonson, especially in the severity of his indictment of contemporary drama in *An Apology for Poetry*, written between 1581 and 1583. Sidney finds many reasons for attacking contemporary 'play-makers and stage-keepers' who have made the theatre 'odious', but he devotes most of his critique to the charge that new English plays were 'faulty both in time and place, the two necessary companions of all corporeal actions.'[36]

How 'absurd it is in sense, even sense may imagine,' he observes, 'and art
hath taught, and all ancient examples justified.' Sidney never imagines
what it is like to read a play. Instead his focus is on the difference
between the liberty of narration – 'reporting' – for which he prescribes
no constraints and the ontology of performance – 'representing' – which
must adjust to a medium that involves bodies interacting in time
and space in a spectacle addressed to an audience whose experience is
similarly constructed. Sidney's only regret was that his favorite contemporary play, Norton and Sackville's *Gorbuduc*, was faulty in this respect,
the first of many regrets voiced over the course of the next two hundred
years that some good plays just did not fit the laws.

The laws of time and place supposedly prevented plays from being
inundated by streams of tangential action covering continents and
lasting generations. Affirming that 'the stage should always represent
but one place, and the uttermost time presupposed in it should be, by
Aristotle's precept and common reason, but one day,' Sidney famously
parodies the mimetic excesses of a typical popular drama:

> you shall have Asia of the one side, and Afric of the other, and so
> many under-kingdoms, that the player, when he cometh in, must
> ever begin with telling where he is, or else the tale will not be
> conceived [...]. [O]rdinary it is that two young princes fall in love.
> After many traverses, she is got with child, delivered of a fair boy,
> he is lost, growth a man, falls in love, and is ready to get another
> child, and all this in two hours' space: which, how absurd it is in
> sense, even sense may imagine, and art hath taught, and all the
> ancient examples justified, and at this day, the ordinary players in
> Italy will not err in.[37]

He had apparently read George Whetstone's dedication to his verse
drama *Promos and Cassandra*, published in 1578, which set a precedent
for his attention to the laws of time and place. Whetstone had condemned contemporary plays for being 'vain, indiscreet, and out of order',
since the typical English dramatist 'grounds his work on impossibilities',
as 'in three hours runs he through the world, marries, gets children,
makes children men, men to conquer kingdoms, murder monsters;
bringeth gods from heaven, and fetcheth devils from hell.'[38] A good play
was one in which play time and real time, play space and real space,
were as identical as possible. The point as Jonson saw it, at his most
doctrinaire, following Sidney, was that in order to be didactic drama
had to be plausible, and for it to be plausible, it would have to conform
ideally to the strictest ontological standards. It was this set of choices
that coincided for him with another form of 'realism': the rise of

trenchant urban satire as an antidote for the deceptive myths of romantic fiction. But in his drive for greater realism, he was apparently not disturbed by the fact that two or three hours did not extend, as it does in *Volpone*, from sunrise to sunset, or that a single stage represented four different locations close to the piazza of San Marco in Venice. His theoretical commitment to neoclassical form was largely symbolic.

Challenging the current fable that Jonson considered writing for the theatre *solely* to be a subliterary occupation and that he welcomed publication exclusively as an ennobling alternative to a debased theatrical culture, I have called attention to a cross current of critical discourse in the first quarto of *Volpone* attuned to the medium for which it was originally conceived. There is no question that Jonson understood the value of the monumentalizing function of publication and was fond of denouncing absurd theatrical practices, but the extent to which he perceived a vital connection between theatrical and what we now call 'literary' culture has rarely been noted. Jonson scholars regularly insist that he understood that being a theatre poet could never make him a laureate and that he consequently channelled his literary ambitions exclusively into publication. Through the magic of print, we are told, Jonson transformed popular plays into literature. By the end of the sixteenth century in England, however, a growing number of theatre professionals and informed enthusiasts – sometimes reluctantly and with qualifications – began to consider commercial drama to be a powerful artistic medium through which one might obtain a literary reputation that combined performed and published works. It would be foolish to deny that a virulent anti-theatrical prejudice voiced by London civic authorities, puritan zealots and disaffected intellectuals threatened the very existence of commercial theatre or to ignore the social stigma associated with actors. But while one should acknowledge that Jonson expresses considerable sympathy with some of this critique, he often expressed an intention to renovate not abolish performance.

It is wrong to conclude that Jonson, from the first quarto of *Volpone* to the First Folio, envisions himself as being only adequately represented in print. He was, as David M. Bergeron suggests, a writer both 'committed to the theater' and 'aware of an emerging reading audience'.[39] For some participants, early modern commercial theatre performances had become more than what Wendy Wall characterizes as 'illegitimate and vulgar trivial events', 'subject to multiple sites of production and protean textual practices', 'associated with a socially suspect cultural domain'.[40] When he had his name printed in large letters across the title-page of *Volpone*, he appropriated *both* its performed and published versions. And even as the Jonson First Folio instantiated his drama as literature, it featured performance histories on the title-pages of all nine plays as well as cast lists naming the actors who had originally appeared in them, commemorating theatrical premieres with a remembrance of what had been lost through re-inscription in print. It was among these lists that we find Jonson's final tribute to those members of the King's Men who had originally acted in *Volpone*, a list that must have included some if not all of the 'principal comedians' who had performed it at Oxford and Cambridge: Richard Burbage, Henry Condell, William Sly, John Heminges, John Lowin and Alexander Cooke.

In his epistle, Jonson laments that bad dramatists have made poetry 'the lowest scorn of the age' and observes that this situation 'hath not only rap't me to present indignation, but made me studious, heretofore; and by all my actions to stand off, from them' (lines 93–94). In recent criticism, Jonson's decision to 'stand off' from the poetasters has been misinterpreted as an unmitigated rejection of 'the present trade of the stage', which was fatally infected by 'ribaldry, profanation, blasphemy' (line 34).[41] Yet Jonson specifically states that his intention is to reform dramatic poetry. 'I shall raise the despised head of poetry again', he writes, 'and, stripping her out of those rotten and base rags wherein the times have adulterated her form, restore her to her primitive habit, feature and majesty, and render her worthy to be embraced and kissed of all the great and master spirits of our world' (lines 118–22). While he disliked much of what he saw in the commercial theatre, he nevertheless warned readers against indiscriminately maligning 'the reputations' of those 'honest and learned' writers (line 87) who wrote for the common players while resisting the scene's bad influences. 'That all are embarked in this bold adventure for hell' was not only 'a most uncharitable thought', he objected, but 'uttered, a malicious slander' (lines 38–39).

Notes

1 All quotations from the play, the epistle, and the commendatory poems are cited from *Volpone, or The Fox*, ed. Brian Parker (Manchester: Manchester University Press, 1999). The dedication, however, is quoted directly from the first quarto. Richard Dutton includes facsimiles of this material in *Ben Jonson, Volpone, and the Gunpowder Plot* (Cambridge: Cambridge University Press, 2008), between pages 12 and 13.

2 W. David Kay, *Ben Jonson, A Literary Life* (New York: St Martin's Press, 1995), 87. Elsewhere, however, Kay acknowledges that Jonson sought "to win a genuine literary reputation based in large part on writing for the theater" (146, n. 39).

3 Richard C. Newton, "Jonson and the (Re)Invention of the Book," in *Classic and Cavalier: Essays on Jonson and the Sons of Ben*, ed. Claude J. Summers and Ted-Larry Pebworth (Pittsburg: Pittsburg University Press, 1982), 32.

4 Timothy Murray, *Theatrical Legitimation: Allegories of Genius in Seventeenth-Century England and France* (New York: Oxford University Press, 1987), 44.

5 Jonas A. Barish, "Jonson and the Loathèd Stage," in *A Celebration of Ben Jonson*, ed. William Blissett, Julian Patrick, and R. W. Van Fossen (Toronto: University of Toronto Press, 1973), 51 and 52.

6 David Riggs, *Ben Jonson, A Life* (Cambridge: Harvard University Press, 1989), 137–40. For exceptions, see also Paul Yachnin, *Stage-wrights: Shakespeare, Jonson, Middleton, and the Making of Theatrical Value* (Philadelphia: University of Pennsylvania Press, 1997), 49, and Jeffrey Knapp, "What Is a Co-Author?," *Representations* 89 (2005):1–10.

7 Robert Weimann, *Author's Pen and Actor's Voice: Playing and Writing in Shakespeare's Theatre* (Cambridge: Cambridge University Press, 2000), 30.

8 Doubt about whether Jonson is in the first quarto using calendar or alternatively old-style dating (in which case he would have actually written his epistle in February of 1608), troubled Brian Parker in his introduction to *Volpone* (8). Because if Jonson wrote the epistle in 1608, Parker speculates, he might have been thinking of the September 1607 visit by the King's Men to Oxford, instead of its performance in July, over a year earlier. It seems more probable, however, that these performances occurred in 1606. Based on strong internal evidence, Parker concluded that the comedy was probably completed sometime between 19 January and old-style New Year's Day, 25 March 1606 (7). That seems to account for why Jonson states on the title-page and colophon of the First Folio printing of *Volpone* that it was acted by "the K. MAIESTIES SERVANTS" in "the yeere 1605" [old style]. (See also Dutton, *Ben Jonson, Volpone, and the Gunpowder Plot*, 55–57, who supplements Parker's theory.) It is difficult consequently to believe that Jonson's "Epistle" would celebrate with such enthusiasm, in February of 1608, performances that took place so long after its premiere. It seems more likely that Jonson wrote the "Epistle" in 1607 to recall performances in 1606, when *Volpone* was still fresh. When the King's Men visited Cambridge in 1610, they also brought Jonson's latest hit *The Alchemist* (along with Shakespeare's warhorse *Othello*).

9 In *Cynthia's Revels*, 5.1.38, Jonson writes of exemplary courtiers whom "equal JOVE hath lov'd" (H&S, 4:132), and in *Volpone*, 3.2.14, Mosca tells Bonario that he is "unequal"-i.e. "unjust"-to him. Jonson repeats the word in the first line of the "Epistle".

10 In 1619, Jonson told William Drummond that "He was Master of Arts in both ye Universities by yr favour not his studie" (H&S, 1:139). Frederick Fleay, *A Biographical Chronicle of the English Drama, 1599–1642*, 2 Vols (London: Reeves and Turner, 1891) 1:351, speculated that Jonson's honorary degrees were a result of these performances, and C. H. Herford and Percy Simpson, *Ben Jonson*, 11 Vols (Oxford: Oxford University Press, 1925–1952), 1:5, note 83, hypothesized that the universities recognized Jonson, at least in part, as a response to his generous dedication. But this seems improbable. David Riggs, *Ben Jonson*, 262, states that the poet's Oxford degree was conferred on him through the recommendation of then Chancellor William Herbert, Lord Pembroke, between 1617 and 1619.

11 The most obvious venue for this performance, paid for by the municipal corporation, would have been the town hall. Frederick S. Boas, *Shakespeare at the Universities, and Other Studies in Elizabethan Drama* (Oxford: B. Blackwell, 1923), 33, notes that in February of 1579–80, the Oxford City Council ruled that "no players should be allowed to act in the Guild Hall, or the Lower Hall, or in the Guild Hall Court," but that an exception had already been made for the servants of the earl of Essex in May 1586. Appearances at town halls were sometimes supplemented by performances at local inns.

12 See *Records of Early English Drama, Cambridge*, 2 Vols, ed. Alan H. Nelson (Toronto: University of Toronto Press, 1989).

13 Although attitudes differed widely during different periods, Cambridge might have placed greater emphasis on controlling student behaviour. Scott McMillin and Sally-Beth MacLean, *The Queen's Men and Their Plays* (Cambridge: Cambridge

University Press, 1998), 67, based on payments by Cambridge University and the town (*REED, Cambridge* 1:369), conclude that in 1597 the Queen's Men "were welcomed by town and gown alike."

14   Nelson, *Records, Cambridge*, 1:395.

15   Nelson, *Records, Cambridge*, 1:404. See also, Alan H. Nelson, *Early Cambridge Theatres* (Cambridge: Cambridge University Press, 1994), 88. The following year, however, at Oxford, where the university was less restrictive, the town paid both Queen Anne's Men (on 14 August) and the King's Men (7 September) for performances.

16   Nelson, *Records, Cambridge*, 2 (Editorial Apparatus):985. Nelson also speculates, in this context, that the statement on the title-page of the 1603 *Hamlet* that the play was produced at Oxford and Cambridge is probably a "printer's groundless boast."

17   Boas, in his chapter on "*Volpone* at the Universities" in *Shakespeare at the Universities*, 261–66, remarks that "if ever there was an occasion on which the Vice-Chancellor and Proctors might be expected to turn a 'blind eye' upon the attendance of scholars at prohibited professional entertainments, it would be at a production of *Volpone*" (263).

18   The vice-chancellor sometimes overruled his superior. In 1580, Vice-Chancellor John Hatcher, who had previously refused to allow the earl of Leicester's players to perform, even turned down the request by Cecil's father, William Burghley, the university chancellor, to allow the earl of Oxford's players to spend four of five days at Cambridge. See *Records, Cambridge*, ed. Nelson, 2:724–25.

19   Richard Dutton, *Licensing, Censorship, and Authorship in Early Modern England* (Houndmills: Palgrave, 2000), 121–22, notes that the universities' "leading luminaries were key names in Jonson's history." Not only was Cecil the Chancellor of Cambridge, but its High Steward was Thomas Howard, Lord Chamberlain and earl of Suffolk, who seems to have been responsible, along with Cecil, for Jonson and Chapman's release from prison during the *Eastward Ho* affair. The Chancellor of Oxford was Thomas Sackville, earl of Dorset and Lord Treasurer, who had co-authored *Gorboduc* and who might also have intervened in securing Jonson's release. Dutton cites Jonson's recollection that "I laid the plot of my *Volpone*, and wrote most of it, after a present of ten dozen of palm sack from my very good Lord Treasurer" (quoted from H&S, 1:188). Dedicating *Volpone* to the universities, Dutton concludes, "was inevitably also a dedication to the power-brokers of the Privy Council" (122).

20   Riggs, *Ben Jonson*, 143. Grace Ioppolo, *Dramatists and their Manuscripts in the Age of Shakespeare, Jonson, Middleton, and Heywood* (London: Routledge, 2006), 59, notes that the extant "eight lines of the opening of Jonson's text in his own hand [. . .] contain three revisions in Cecil's hand," adding, "in a sense they were collaborators, and probably not for the first or last time."

21   Dutton, *Ben Jonson, Volpone, and the Gunpowder Plot*, 73–93.

22   See Nelson, *Records, Cambridge*, 2:797 and 725.

23   Joseph Loewenstein, *Ben Jonson and Possessive Authorship* (Cambridge: Cambridge University Press, 2002), 159.

24   Richard Helgerson, *Self-Crowned Laureates: Spenser, Jonson, Milton and the Literary System* (Berkeley: University of California Press, 1983), 145.

25   Riggs, *Ben Jonson*, 143.

26   Lukas Erne, *Shakespeare as Literary Dramatist* (Cambridge: Cambridge University Press, 2003), 145.

27   Ben Jonson, *Every Man Out of His Humour* (London, 1600), B3r.

28   *Hamlet* (2.2.399–400) in *The Riverside Shakespeare*, Second Edition (New York: Houghton Mifflin, 1997).

29   See Patrick Cheney, *Shakespeare, National Poet-Playwright* (Cambridge: Cambridge University Press, 2004), 17–28.

30   *Henslowe's Diary*, Second Edition, ed. R. A. Foakes (Cambridge: Cambridge University Press, 2002), 124, 203–04.

31   Cited from Ian Donaldson's notes in his edition of *Ben Jonson* (Oxford: Oxford University Press, 1985), 653.

32   Murray, *Theatrical Legitimation*, 49.

33   See the introduction to *Ben Jonson's Literary Criticism*, ed. James Redwine (Lincoln: University of Nebraska Press, 1970), xv. Dutton challenged Redwine's reading of the significance of the first quarto of *Volpone* in his discussion of "Poet and State" in *Ben Jonson: Authority: Criticism* (New York: St Martin's Press, 1996), 93–94, and in his chapter, "Jonson: the Epistle to *Volpone*," in *Licensing*, 125–27. One of Redwine's principal arguments is that a change in Jonson's approach to neoclassical criticism is evident in the difference between the poet's observation in *Every Man out of His Humour* (1599) that some of the ancient "laws" of comedy (including that of time) were "too nice observations" (Induction, line 237), and his new affirmation in *Volpone* of "the laws of time, place, persons." But in *Every Man Out* Jonson also demonstrates his neoclassical orientation when he mocks the choruses of Shakespeare's *Henry V* for failing to be plausibly bound by the laws of place and time. See James P. Bednarz, "When did Shakespeare Write the Choruses of *Henry V*?," *Notes and Queries* 251 (2006): 486–89. *Every Man Out*, like *Volpone*, engages in a critical dialectic of law and liberty that characterizes Jonson's criticism throughout his career.

34   Quoted from *Aristotle's Poetics*, trans. Leon Golden (Englewood Cliffs: Prentice-Hall, 1968), 10 and 9. For a more detailed study of Jonson's interpretation of the unity of "persons," see David Farley-Hills, "Jonson and the Neo-Classical Rules in *Sejanus* and *Volpone*," *The Review of English Studies* 46 (1955): 167–73.

35   Lodovico Castelvetro, *Poetica d'Aristotele vulgarizzata et sposta* (Basil, 1576), 109: "*in picciolo spatio di luogo, & in picciolo spatio di tempo.*" How Castelvetro added the law of "place" to those of "time" and "plot" is discussed by Joel E. Spingarn, *Literary Criticism in the Renaissance* (New York: Harcourt, Brace, & World, 1953), 56–63; Bernard Weinberg, *A History of Literary Criticism in the Italian Renaissance*, 2 Vols (Chicago: University of Chicago Press, 1963) 2:502–11; and Julie Peters, *The Book of the Theater* (Oxford: Oxford University Press, 2000), 166–80. All consider how Italian Renaissance literary theoreticians extrapolated rules from Aristotle's remarks in the *Poetics* that drama should have a unified plot and that tragedy was usually limited to a single day. To this Castelvetro added the law of place, based on an ancient preference.

36   Sir Philip Sidney, *An Apology for Poetry*, ed. Forrest G. Robertson (Indianapolis: Bobbs-Merrill, 1970), 75–76. The contradiction in Sidney's position as a general advocate of both restrictive dramatic law and imaginative freedom is explored by O. B. Hardison, Jr., "The Two Voices of Sidney's *Apology for Poetry*," in *Sidney in Retrospect*, ed. Arthur Kinney and the Editors of *ELR* (Amherst: The University of Massachusetts Press, 1988), 45–61.

37   Sidney, *An Apology for Poetry*, 76.

38   George Whetstone, "Dedication to William Fleetwoode, Recorder of London," in *English Renaissance Literary Criticism*, ed. Brian Vickers (Oxford: Oxford University Press, 1999), 173.

39   David M. Bergeron, *Textual Patronage in English Drama, 1570–1640* (Aldershot: Ashgate, 2006), 2. Bergeron however agrees with Loewenstein that the first quarto of *Volpone* is "counter-theatrical" (123).

40   Wendy Wall, *The Imprint of Gender: Authorship and Publication in the English Renaissance* (Ithaca: Cornell University Press, 1993), 89.

41   Kay, *Ben Jonson*, 87.

CHAPTER FIVE

New Directions: 'Live Free, ... Rob Churches, ... Lend me your Dwarf': What's Funny about *Volpone*?

Rick Bowers

According to academic critics of the 1950s, '60s, and '70s, the play is bestial at best. At worst, it is immoral, contemptible, and even blasphemous. In an article in the *Ben Jonson Journal* (2003), Murray Roston surveyed the distaste of past critics while limiting generic possibilities in the very question of his title, '*Volpone*: Comedy or Mordant Satire?' Herein, he observes the disparity between, on the one hand, stage performances full of laughter, delight and outrageously quirky possibilities; and, on the other hand, stern moral criticism that typically characterizes Volpone and Mosca as 'villains of the stuff of which tragedy makes use but without the dignity of that genre'. In his 1972 Casebook volume on *Volpone*, Jonas Barish commented on 'the surplus of moralizing in recent critical commentary'. Bruce Boehrer, in 1997, identified Volpone with the excesses of Deleuzian desire as Jonson's 'most successful villain'.[1] *Volpone*, however, shatters the assumptions of traditional moralizing criticism then and now, and it does so through manipulations of laughter in the theatre.

Ben Jonson's comic 'truth' is as vast as misunderstanding and as fast-paced as time spent out of control. Yet Jonson's sense of truth in comedy has only recently come out of the shadow of his moral truth as learned authority, masque artiste, defender of the 'plain style' or even arbiter of normative contemporary tastes. In 1998 Julie Sanders, with Kate Chedgzoy and Susan Wiseman, edited an important revaluation titled *Refashioning Ben Jonson* that deconstructed absolutist understandings of his work to stress multiplicity and pluralism in his various constructions of meaning. The following year, *Ben Jonson and Theatre*, edited by Richard Cave, Elizabeth Schafer and Brian Woolland, reconsidered Jonson's work from the standpoint of performance with special emphasis on energy, enthusiasm, comedy and risk. My chapter will place similar stress on Jonson's construction of comedy in *Volpone*. Consider the sense of glib profusion that Volpone himself voices early on in the play: 'What should I do | But cocker up my genius and live free | To all delights my fortune calls me to?' (1.1.70–72). He enjoys such rhetorical questions. Cocker up, live free and do it all – Volpone indeed has a 'fortune' that allows him to do so. Others may not be as lucky or as rich, but Volpone, like Jonson, represents a special case in terms of comic theory and practice.[2]

Critics have always expressed concern about the confusions, triviality and unseemly nature of laughter in comedy. It is an otherwise acceptable genre, one almost equal to tragedy if only the laughter would stop. Jonson, in full classical mode, even says as much:

> Nor is the movement of laughter alwaies the end of Comedy, that
> is rather a fowling for the peoples delight, or their fooling. For, as
> Aristotle saies rightly, the moving of laughter is a fault in Comedie, a kind of turpitude that depraves some part of a mans nature
> without a disease.[3]

And yet, even in his terminology Jonson cannot help himself: Volpone involves a lot of 'fowling' and 'fooling' wherein his turpitude may not be as operative as his depravity but there is no doubt about his diseased imagination. All comics are like that. Such a moralizing theory withers away throughout *Volpone* – just like the title character. Indeed at the level of theory, Jonson is as unsettling as he is unusual, as observed in Gantar's recent consideration of the ethics of laughter titled *The Pleasure of Fools*: 'Jonson may preach restraint when it comes to laughter, but the amount of humour he injects into his characters makes any attempt to reach his objective an exercise in masochism rather than an honest reception.'[4] Comedy, in *Volpone*, is more improvisational, less polite, always uncertain, out of control, open-ended, irresponsible and free in its credible absurdity and theatrical realization.

Volpone represents a character at once out of control in terms of moral intelligence, but radically in control of amoral situational intelligence. He asserts all the energies of the joker, grouch and scapegrace – a figure at once ethically void and yet constantly registering his ethical stance even as he is appalled by the unethical extremes of others. 'Good wits are greatest in extremities' (5.2.6), declares Volpone late in the play. This paradoxical and inflated sense of self-congratulation allows him to move rapidly and without conscience through modes of comic interaction in the moment-by-moment process of making sense (or nonsense) that effectively comprises all comedy. He may pause tactically for a moment, but the comic hero knows that every moment is subject to revision – if not reversal. *Volpone* contains, even as it asserts all the radical survivalist impulses pulled together in the Zany, the Spoil-Sport, the refusal of compromise and the promise of personal success subject always to ridiculous qualification.

In *Volpone* amorality is raised to a level of assertion that is forever empty of real consequences and full of useless information. But then, as Oscar Wilde affirmed in 'Phrases and Philosophies for the use of the Young' – especially relevant to a teenage octogenarian like Volpone – 'Nothing that actually occurs is of the smallest importance'.[5] That is, unless it happens to *you*. That is why audience and performance are so important to the comedy of this play. Like the breezy putative ironies pitched by Oscar Wilde, Volpone – along with his self-regarding intentions in the theatre – is forever 'out there,' 'on the edge,' 'over the top,' and 'too much,' in his excessive and constant manipulations of comedy. Jonson seems to have felt some moral discomfort in this regard. He even wrote an Epistle of explanation to the universities. But Volpone in action suffers from no such scruple. Neither do audiences – even when urged to do so by intrusive directorial intervention. (Such intrusion usually leads to audience resentment.) People don't usually leave a performance of *Volpone* feeling morally instructed. Instead, they feel theatrically exhausted, piqued and delighted.

I will return to Jonson's prefatory Epistle at the end of this essay. However, to address the laughable pleasures of the play, I will more necessarily rely on a measure of modified performance criticism. Herein, I adduce historical performances of *Volpone* not to indicate or justify by history. Rather, previous realizations of the play suggest possibilities and meanings in relation to the comedy and its presentist possibilities. In this way, I will attempt not to rob the humour by trying to explain the jokes. Instead, I will try to let the comedy speak its possibilities through suggestive performance and interpretation. From time to time, as in his moralistic Epistle, Jonson may try to explain matters. *Volpone* does no such thing. Great comedies such as *Volpone* insist on their own confusions.

Like the text itself for which he is named, Volpone opens up constantly to out-sized possibilities, to massive manipulations of meaning and creatively unfinished, ever-acting possibilities that are as ludicrous as they are overstated. He takes on the magnificently selfish and consumerist energies of the grotesque body in performance as identified by Bakhtin in *Rabelais and His World*:

> The distinctive character of this body is its open unfinished nature, its interaction with the world. These traits are most fully

and concretely revealed in the act of eating; the body transgresses here its own limits: it swallows, devours, rends the world apart, is enriched and grows at the world's expense [...] The limits between man and the world are erased, to man's advantage.[6]

Volpone attacks the worldly limitations of old age with all the certainty of a connoisseur, relentlessly using others and consuming them as nourishment toward his own ever-unfinished horizon of relief. Delighted early in the play that his deception has taken full hold of his rivals, Volpone fondles his treasure and proclaims his pleasure through joyful *non sequiturs*: 'Why, this is better than rob churches yet, | Or fat by eating, once a month, a man' (1.5.91–92). Disguised as a *commandatore* in two short scenes near the end of the play, he delights in the abuse hurled at him: 'varlet,' 'harlot,' 'rascal,' 'knave,' (5.6–7) – he loves being called these names, even as he sues nostalgically for his own 'handsome, pretty, customed bawdy-house' (5.7.12), the one 'at the end of your long row of houses | By the Piscaria' (5.7.9–10). In *The Performance of Pleasure in English Renaissance Drama*, Ronald Huebert shrewdly observes that Volpone mentions this place 'with the kind of affection you'd expect from a pimp who made a big enough killing to retire' (56)[7]. Huebert is as accurate on Volpone's character as he is on the nature of Volpone's social vision. After all, pimps and players want simply to get paid – and paid in accordance with their own significant self-image and self-willed performance. Because self-image is so inextricably linked to professional theatre, it is within the laughter-producing energies of theatre that the answers to the question posed in the title of this essay will begin.

Volpone's Breakfast

Other people have breakfast; Volpone has gold. Of course, Volpone is not a person, but then neither is he the Fox from Aesop's fables nor a moral allegory of Greed. He is an actor, and he constantly mediates a vexing tension between character and performance. Mosca does so too. The tension, within Volpone and between him and Mosca, generates a great deal of the comedy of the play. According to Parker, the great actor Donald Wolfit set the trend for modern interpretations: 'Wolfit saw the key to Volpone's character as life-greediness, an overweening virility, sexual in origin, which imposes itself relentlessly and cruelly on its surroundings but also has enormous *joie de vivre*'. A darker line, traced later by actors such as Ralph Richardson and William Hutt, stresses Volpone's aristocratic boredom, irony and contempt – often at the expense of the very comedy for which the play is so famous. Instead, as perceived by more recent performers such as Simon Russell Beale and

Michael Gambon in the mid-1990s, and reported by Richard Cave, actorly speed, pacing, truth-to-language and forward momentum combine to assert Jonson's peculiar and outrageously rich comedy.[8]

Paul Scofield launched the play with brisk superciliousness at the National Theatre Production in 1977. Signalling open production values immediately in terms of speed, finesse and glorious consumerism, he entered briskly through the centre doors, wide awake and exuberant in his exclamation: 'Good morning to the day; and next, my gold! | Open the shrine that I may see my saint' (1.1.1–2). Such pacing sets the tone for much of the boisterous self-parody to follow – both in Volpone and in Mosca. Literary critics of the last century stressed the immorality, even blasphemy, of Volpone's shrine to lucre, while Murray Roston updates the opprobrium by citing John Donne's 'The Relic' and arguing that to Protestant English audiences of the early Seventeenth Century, Volpone's imagining of gold as a saint's relic would have seemed 'an amusing burlesque of a despised practice'.[9] Maybe so. To an audience today, it certainly represents an obsessed principal character and an inedible breakfast. Moreover, then as now, when Volpone addresses his gold as his 'saint', he addresses his most appreciated girlfriend.

Volpone's 'girlfriend' however contains desirable androgynous traits that stimulate morning sexuality in wildly classical terms of admiration and consumption: 'O thou son of Sol, | But brighter than thy father, let me kiss, | With adoration, thee, and every relic | Of sacred treasure in this blessed room' (1.1.10–13). That suggests a lot of kissing and fondling and more: 'Thy looks when they to Venus did ascribe, | They should have giv'n her twenty thousand cupids, | Such are thy beauties and our loves!' (19–21). The multiple possibilities are almost unspeakable but they are lovingly centred on Volpone's tongue leading to delectable possibilities with his saint: 'Riches, the dumb god that givest all men tongues, | That canst do nought and yet makest men do all things' (22–23). She/he compels Volpone to do *everything*, inspiring delectable attributes that he itemizes with all the mounting fervour of orgasmic joy: 'Thou art virtue, fame, | Honour, and all things else! Who can get thee, | He shall be noble, valiant, honest, wise –' (25–27). Mosca intervenes at just this point to bring Volpone back to earth and sit him at his breakfast in terms of the ethical consumerism of not devouring 'soft prodigals' (41) and 'poor families' (44). Mosca reminds him of his acquisitive consumerist desire, a desire that indulges in courses of cunning purchase and glad possession, including heaps of corn, fine wines, sumptuous hangings and soft beds – leading all the way to his own mounting list of decidedly strange attributes, with which he strokes Volpone and compliments his largesse:

You know the use of riches, and dare give, now,
From that bright heap, to me, your poor observer,
Or to your dwarf, or your hermaphrodite,
Your eunuch, or what other household trifle
Your pleasure allows maintenance –

(1.1.62–66)

Volpone intervenes at just this point to take Mosca lovingly by the hand and bring him back to earth in terms of his own re-focused self regard. He fantasizes the exploitation of his victims in the manner of a tantalizing dessert, 'Letting the cherry knock against their lips, | And draw it by their mouths, and back again' (1.1.98–90). Volpone, of course, will play the tantalizer. Like everything else in this play, that sumptuous, beautiful, delectable, desirable gold of pleasure and satisfaction contains value only as it relates to Volpone himself.

Parker's stage history provides a full sense of the necessarily extra-textual, but credibly moral, sexual and farcical theatre possibilities further signalled at the opening of the play:

> Directors can also establish a critical context to match the way that Jonson has booby-trapped the fox's lines with self-condemnatory imagery; and this can be variously toned to represent the scene as a serious or comic blasphemy. For example, a certain comic degeneracy can be established in the way that Volpone is awakened. In the Ontario production [Stratford 1971] a whore slid out of bed as Mosca entered to wake his master, an effect made more luridly (but also more comically) at the New York Shakespeare Festival of 1967, when both a man and a woman were rousted out. More farcically, at Minneapolis [1964] Volpone was awakened by Mosca tickling his nose, then holding a drink beneath it which brought his master upright, still with closed eyes, following the liquor.[10]

Critical appraisals routinely ignore such comic byplay in performance, reducing the play to a single key of literary consideration. In doing so, such criticism routinely misses the comical vitality of the play or – perhaps worse – attempts to apologize for it. In a gesture towards performance criticism, Revels editor R. B. Parker mildly refers to 'Jonson's improprieties' as 'recurrent lapses from respectability that it is well to bear in mind in any evaluation of *Volpone*'.[11] I propose to bear them in mind more fully and assert them as the laughable centre of the play. Jonson might not agree, but Jonson as classicist was as abashed as his later followers of moral truth and plain style. Instead, as later critics have stressed (and even his contemporaries observed), Jonson is out of control. That prefatory Epistle to Oxford and Cambridge tried to run the fox to ground after the hunt had been called off. Instead, Volpone insists, enjoys, even insinuates himself into the future with unremitting histrionic demands on both audiences (implicit and explicit) and readers. Herein his mortality, like his morality, is insistently, inevitability, ridiculously delayed.

Paradox. Bickering. Metatheatre.

The opening scene launches into a fast forward clarity of exuberance, affirming rhetorical speed and one-upmanship through constant interruption. Volpone and Mosca repeatedly interrupt one another in mutual disregard. They constantly build and shatter tension, eliciting laughter through a variety of registers that loosen up and reorder consciousness in favour of new and different combinations, possibilities and expectations. Live, laugh, love (especially money and self) and therefore enjoy personal success. Volpone thinks he knows everything about success, but everything related to his blithe sense of certainty is radically uncertain. 'Nothing that is so is so' asserts the gag world of *Twelfth Night* wherein all the gags are related to some form of disguise or misconception ultimately sugared over in terms of moral romance. Malvolio might even be entreated 'to a peace' at the conclusion. But in *Volpone*, constant contradictions assert a larger compelling truth: Nothing matters *but* the contradictions, especially as asserted by the title-character who thrives as absurdist fall guy facing down death by faking his life. Faking death is merely an extrapolation. Having grasped the absurdity of the world long ago, he is at once too shallow and too complicated, miles beyond the simple contradiction of yes-and-no literalism and miles beyond the merry moral scorn usually reserved for old goats moving into ludicrous dotage.

Volpone is indeed a ludicrous fake, but one who asserts fraudulence in the manner of a confidence trickster, assuring everyone in attendance that they are suckers if they do not join in with all the other fakes out there. In effect, he achieves a postmodernist recurving of his personality as at once a survival strategy in a world where one would be crazy not to insist on any and all advantage, and as a shameless foregrounding of the cheating that takes place at all times across all societies with any form of social complexity. And destructive complexity is closer than even Volpone would allow. He demonstrates an almost limitless capacity for enjoyment, but Mosca is only in it for the money – and power. Indeed, Volpone performs the first part of the play as superior but unwitting stooge to Mosca's darker designs. Alone at last at the beginning of act three, Mosca levels with the audience even as he launches into his own orgy of self-regard. He reaches into audience consciousness in the form of an intimate hypothetical consideration, deftly describing himself as:

> Your fine, elegant rascal, that can rise
> And stoop almost together, like an arrow;
> Shoot through the air as nimbly as a star;
> Turn short as doth a swallow; and be here,
> And there, and here, and yonder, all at once;
> Present to any humour, all occasion;
> And change a visor swifter than a thought!
>
> (3.1.23–29)

Acrobatic, tactical, unpredictable, he engages with the audience even as he speaks by asserting adaptability and concord with everyone, crediting individual perceptions, and effectively performing the sort of wit and vitality that pleases both audience and Volpone.

Like a postmodern avatar, Volpone considers himself unconditionally sovereign. He is eighty years old but pretending to be near death, eliding the fact that he really is dying, in order to achieve advantage – material, physical, ethical, even tactile – over other characters and over himself. *Then*, he pretends to be dead. Throughout, he ludicrously misrepresents himself, forces many reversals and gesticulates energetically, pointing always toward a better future where he will enjoy further sovereignty. But the falsity really is the truth. In Volpone's world it is no pretence to be a fake. He does it for an audience, implicit, explicit and selfish. Years ago, Stephen Greenblatt observed that Volpone conditions his audience within a process of histrionic self-becoming crucially related to our own modern consciousness: 'Part of the contemporary fascination of Jonson's play is precisely that we feel ourselves present at the very fountainhead of modern consciousness, present just as the decisive, formative steps in the direction of our own minds are being taken [. . .] Volpone is consummately a man who has created his own identity, fashioned parts for himself which he proceeds to play with all the technical skill of a fine actor'. With time running out (although the play has only just begun), Volpone broadcasts the central rhetorical question of the play as a whole: 'What should I do | But cocker up my genius and live free | To all delights my fortune calls me to?' (1.1.70–72). The implicit answer is immediately understandable to a postmodern consciousness: everything; and nothing. Such action goes beyond farce to register itself as frenetic self-disclosure and awareness along the lines of Nietzsche's vaguely unsettling, oft-quoted observation that 'a joke [or witticism] is an epigram on the death of a feeling'. Through action, energy and purposeful absurdity, *Volpone* represents a massive joke enacted in multiple life directions.[12]

If anything, Volpone relates the hilarious mourning of a sense of youthful irresponsibility, durability, even peer-pressured participation. With Celia helplessly sprawled before him, Volpone, ever theatrical, disregards sex to brag about a significant stage credit from years before:

At recitation of our comedy
For entertainment of the great Valois,
I acted young Antinous, and attracted
The eyes and ears of all the ladies present,
T' admire each graceful gesture, note, and footing.

(3.7.160–64)

Then he launches into singing that famous, beautiful, oft-detached and recycled *carpe diem* lyric 'Come my Celia, let us prove, | While we can the sports of love' (165–66). Celia's reaction – nonplussed and horrified – 'No' elicits complex reactions of laughter and discomfort. It's not about sex; it's about art. Most pornographers affirm the same – with some regret. Volpone does so too, weaving frenetically eroticized fantasies through a list of classicized performance possibilities, from Ovid's *Metamorphoses* to the culinary delights of Roman orgies to the verses of Ben Jonson, including Europa, Jove, Mars and Venus, a proud Spanish beauty, quick Negro, cold Russian, Cretan wines, rope of pearl, brains of peacocks, tongues of nightingales, July-flowers, panthers' breath, milk of unicorns – and all to 'transfuse our wand'ring souls | Out at our lips and score up sums of pleasures' (3.7.233–34). That's a lot of pleasure. Volpone loves these pleasures (especially references to them), just as he loves his former (and current) virility. In fact, the older he gets, the better he *was*. To Mosca's suggestion that Volpone does not adequately savour his near-sex deception of the jealous husband Corvino, Volpone counters: 'O, more than if I had enjoyed the wench: | The pleasure of all womankind's not like it' (5.2.10–11). He really loves teasing out existence – his own and others'. He really loves intertextual joking in the form of constant exoticized deception. Whether played as bouncy bedroom farce or sadistic sexual force, this scene thrives on energy and timing undercut by Bonario's entry as would-be saviour. (This itself has been played as a farcically botched entry usually involving entangled bedclothes.) Is it rape or is it romp? In *Volpone* all data is dada.

Scoto. Performance. Parody.

Volpone is an inveterate 'player.' He collapses high and low culture in a 'performance' that is constantly out of Jonson's control. The play itself is like a series of outrageous high concept performance pitches along the lines of those satirized in the Robert Altman film *The Player*. Constantly subjective, objective and absurd, Volpone just as constantly contextualizes the performance arrangement of actors and situations, effectively dramatized in his performance of Scoto. Here, he handles his shifting character ontology especially well by quoting, performing, ventriloquizing a public huckster. He's a fake, playing a fake to fake out a girl, Celia, just noticeable offstage. It's all a matter of showing off, what people do who act professionally or who otherwise sell themselves – as every retail salesperson, popular entertainer, or Hollywood executive knows.

Hereby, *Volpone* satirizes people who act for a living and also, in Volpone's case, for a *dying*. The entire episode rather mirrors that moment in *The Player* when successfully devious producer Griffin Mill (played by Tim Robbins) is meeting with other Hollywood types on the patio of an upscale restaurant. Expressing some exasperation at the usual conversation he interjects with a disruptive Volpone-type rhetorical question, 'Can we talk about something other than Hollywood for a change? We're educated people.' The others acquiesce noncommittally and with some puzzlement for a brief moment until Mill bursts out in ironic laughter at the implicit answer to his own obviously rhetorical question.[13] It is all about 'cockering up' his genius and living free to all delights his fortune calls him to. As Scoto, Volpone is no less elegantly self-referential, manipulative and energetically articulated.

Indeed, Volpone plays Scoto on a whim and yet plays the part with genuine effectiveness. And why does he do it? For the golden experience of beholding the beauteous Celia, young wife of the greedy lawyer Corvino. But his motivation has nothing to do with romance. Mosca enthusiastically stimulates Volpone's interest in Celia in terms of commodity futures, soft porn and hard currency:

> The blazing star of Italy! a wench
> O' the first year! a beauty, ripe as harvest!
> Whose skin is whiter than a swan all over!
> Than silver, snow, or lilies! a soft lip,
> Would tempt you to an eternity of kissing!
> And flesh that melteth in the touch to blood!
> Bright as your gold! and lovely as your gold!
>
> (1.5.108–14)

Compared to gold, an 'eternity of kissing' swiftly loses staying power. Of course Volpone has already kissed or tried to kiss Mosca as conclusion to each of the previous scenes. Here, he seems coldly inquisitive: 'Why had not I known this before?' (115), until Mosca again makes the operative reference in form of a personal challenge: 'She's kept as warily as is your gold' (118). Indeed, Celia is gold. In the crazed play world of *Volpone*, it only makes sense to set up a mountebank's stage outside her window in the form of the *commedia dell' arte*, draw an inquisitive crowd and pitch the attributes of a miracle cosmetic until she, miraculously, comes to the window and Volpone can catch a glimpse of her beauty.

Volpone greatly enjoys playing Scoto. He creates the character in a moment-by-moment building of performance. His onslaught of unregulated prose, however, goes well beyond interrogating the implicit rhetoric of the marketplace as argued by stylistic and cultural critics alike. Notably, his performance takes place in what he himself identifies as 'an obscure nook of the Piazza' (2.2.38–39), an upscale neighbourhood 'removed from the clamours of the *canaglia*' (74) and his other competitors whom he scorns as 'turdy-facy-nasty-paty-lousy-fartical rogues' (61). He is on the offensive and he is loving it, creating reality with all the convincing possibilities of an enthusiastic teenager or a pathological liar. In doing so he relishes the fact that the usual parameters are sprung, facilitating his out-of-control rhetoric and behaviour. The scene is all about an inveterate actor's appetite, even compulsion, for performance. Recently, Sean McEvoy rather understates the episode when he observes that 'Volpone's verbal pyrotechnics entertain; salesmen's rhetoric may be meretricious but it can be fun. Venice is a place where bad language and bad behaviour entertain and engage.'[14] All true. But Volpone is beyond rhetoric here, moving rather into areas of performance manipulation, creation, absurd comedy and extroverted self-promotion. That's what salesmen do. Actors do so as well. That the process may be meretricious is not news. That it can be fun is a quality *lived* within the desperate absurdity of Volpone's performance – of pleasure, for pleasure – in the moment of audience perception and interaction.

Within such a comic performance zone *anything* is fair game even (perhaps especially) performance parody. McEvoy complains that Michael Gambon's 1995 'Tommy Cooper impression and ad-libbing in the same scene seemed awkward and meretricious' (73)[15]. But many stars have enjoyed particular license in the Scoto scene. It is an extended, openly-scripted role within. Besides, the retrograde stylization of Italian *commedia dell' arte*, on Jonson's stage, seems rather congruent with Tommy Cooper's passé red fez, one-liners and goofy magic tricks. Volpone himself is doing an extended parody of a known performer – whether within or without the play. Like a latter day Groucho Marx or Charlie Chaplin, Scoto of Mantua enjoyed an international reputation for comic performance in Ben Jonson's time. According to Parker's editorial note to the scene, the actual Scoto, an Italian actor, had performed in England in the 1570s and 80s and by 1605 'his name in England was synonymous with clever trickery'.[16] As argued by Robert N. Watson, in *Ben Jonson's Parodic Strategy* (1987), Jonson knew the performance power of cueing up an appropriate intertextual parody and directing it toward his audiences.

In *Volpone*, the play is definitely the thing. Herein, the possibilities of metatheatre easily trump ethical or economic considerations. Oliver Hennessey identifies Volpone's performance of Scoto as a 'display of skilled labor', and it certainly is that – but much more. Hennessey, however, adduces Tibor Scitovsky's 1976 study of consumer behaviour titled *The Joyless Economy* to probe the *real* motivations of *Volpone*, motivations whereby modern consumer behaviour is explicated as profoundly irrational and perverse, leading inevitably to boredom and pain. Yes, conscienceless Capitalism still performs a simple confidence trick on all of us. But Hennessey goes further to connect then and now as follows: 'For a society or socio-economic group that has been largely successful in eliminating basic want, such as twentieth-century America, or the moneyed classes of seventeenth-century Venice (as represented by an English playwright), the danger to subjective well-being is primarily one of boredom'.[17] Yes, Volpone is bored, and it stimulates ludicrous actions. His audiences, onstage and off, react in a variety of ways, but boredom is seldom one of them. Instead, the familiar, exoticized, eroticized and even eccentric extent of interaction in the play powers the ridiculously effective parody of this lengthy scene – then and now. To relate *Volpone* to the ennui of late market Capitalism makes about as much sense as relating *Carry On* movies to corporate tourism. *Volpone's* familiarity and its hilarity reach across time in performance to audiences, *both* as a now-classic work of English literature but also, and more comically, as a living experience of action in the theatre.

The Scoto scene provides a perfect opportunity to mesh onstage and offstage audience within an appreciative simultaneity. Here, the comedy of the play speaks for itself not as external interpretation but as metatheatrical experience in the *now*. That Volpone's complicated but entirely credible imposture as Scoto is performed ostensibly for an audience of *one*, namely Celia, is a matter of plot that pitches itself most effectively in terms of familiar cons and tricksters from contemporary culture. Parker relates how Wolfit 'delivered the spiel at great speed with the broad accent of a market huckster in the Newark of his youth, and invariably got a laugh by delivering the line 'let me tell you' (II.ii.40) in the Lancashire voice of 'Enoch,' a character in the BBC's variety show 'Hippodrome' at that time, whose entrance line it was'.[18] Groucho Marx, W. C. Fields, Tommy Cooper, the current Prime Minister – choose one and assert the caricature. Scoto's oil, literally and figuratively, revives Volpone's own interest in play. Nervously, delightedly, Volpone asks the actor's overwhelming question: 'But were they gulled | With a belief that I was Scoto?'(2.4.34–35). At once conventional and metadramatic, Mosca reaches outside the play in his response: 'Scoto himself could hardly have distinguished!' (36). Like Scoto, critical readers, and audiences collaborate as Volpone pimps his product and sells himself. His overwhelming irony of performance obliterates all literal consequences.

Interactive theatre, comedy, cultural studies and postmodern pastiche – all combine within *Volpone* in terms of unselfconscious parody and Menippean satire of brilliantly stupid ideas combined with irrefutable superficiality. In his readably witty critical intervention titled *After Theory*, Terry Eagleton characterizes the postmodern subject in terms that might readily apply to Volpone:

> The creature who emerges from postmodern thought is centreless, hedonistic, self-inventing, ceaselessly adaptive. He thus fares splendidly in the disco or supermarket, though not quite so well in the school, courtroom or chapel. He sounds more like a Los Angeles media executive than an Indonesian fisherman.[19]

Or, one might add, an actor always conscious of performance – like Volpone. William Slights describes such convincing actorly style in a performance at the Oxford Playhouse in 1980: 'Nigel Levaillant played Volpone with his legs in that unnaturally turned-out position characteristic of tight-rope walkers, ballet dancers and swordsmen. He tilted his head just so, as though posing for a vaguely inspirational portrait, and he caressed certain strategically placed words in Jonson's blank verse lines with richly operatic tones'.[20] Such physical, verbal and theatrical self-consciousness is central to Jonson's comically stylized sense of Volpone and Venice. Here, every place is a realized space of performance full of dense allusions, sharp ideas and comical associations: the miser's counting house, his boudoir, the humbug performance of Scoto, English tourists abroad, the judicial court of Venice – all imaginary performative spaces in which to do comedy.

Lend me your Dwarf

As will be apparent by now, there is something crazily valuable in all this comic complication, something physical and frenetic but also beautifully ludicrously deformed. The audience senses it from the outset of the play in Volpone's extravagant key of self assertion all-the-while undercut but also affirmed by Mosca's interjections. Nano, Castrone and Androgyno flutter through the play as Volpone's weird offspring, but they also – through their voices, actions and unusual/impossible appearances – unsettle any straightforwardness that the comedy might tend toward. The nominal subplot of the play does likewise, through the curious impostures of Sir Politic Would-be, his English interlocutor Peregrine and the sensualist bluestocking consciousness of Lady Politic Would-be. Clearly, Sir Pol has a great deal on his mind, but finds himself travelling in Venice at the behest of Lady Pol, as he complacently observes:

> A peculiar humour of my wife's,
> Laid for this height of Venice, to observe,
> To quote, to learn the language, and so forth –
>
> (2.1.11–13)

It all seems rather comfortable, self-improving, educational and so forth. But don't be fooled. In this world of theatrical assertion, no straight man (or woman) introduces anything like a credible ethical dimension. In *Volpone*, any straight character introduces an ethical *dementia* – one that is reinforced for laughs in the theatre rather than undercut by rational consciousness in the study.

In performance, rational reconsideration is for the little people, those in danger of being duped or disinherited – like Bonario and Celia, youthful innocents who play themselves and would never consider *playing* others. These are unrewarding roles in the world of *Volpone*, a world of amorality, paradox and absurd contrast that presents a new mobile self, one that is multiple, self aware and informed by total performance. Indeed, the character of Sir Politic Would-be, the most overtly rational figure in the play, is also one of the most ridiculous. In his *Text and Performance* study of the play, Arnold Hinchcliffe reports on Sir John Gielgud's remarkable 1977 portrayal at the National Theatre as

> carrying a camp stool and a tourist's shoulder-bag in which he was forever searching for this or that secret document. It was endearing, and it underlines what was happening. Here was one of the great actors of our time, famous for classic roles, turning in a cameo character part. Gielgud's Politick was officious, thick *but* kindly. Benedict Nightingale saw him as a character 'on day-release from a P. G. Wodehouse short story, forever inventing explanations for Venetian behaviour, finding spies and plots everywhere, and lecturing Peregrine on correct behaviour with

that upper-class assurance that addresses you at length without ever speaking to you.'[21]

One can almost hear the kindly condescension and metatheatrical consciousness with which Gielgud would deliver the line that opens Act 4: 'I told you, sir, it was a plot; you see' (4.1.1). One can readily imagine as well audience laughter responding to the earnestness of the line, teetering precariously as it does between inner and outer consciousness of play.

Much critical ink has been spilt in the name of structural unity by attempting to reconcile the Would-be subplot to the Volpone main plot. Watson, in his metatheatrical treatment of Jonson's parody, shrewdly observed: 'The Would-Be subplot is a would-be main plot.'[22] But, as an Englishman abroad full of important information and benign disinterest, Sir Politic seems as incapable of Venice-envy as Lady Would-be is consumed by it. Alexander Leggatt argues a unity-in-disunity relationship between Volpone and Sir Politic, resulting in 'a play blown apart by a centrifugal force that may be even more powerful and systematic in its operation than the centripetal force other critics have argued for, a force that makes response difficult and judgment impossible' (92).[23] That indefinable 'force' however is related to absurd performance farce in the theatre, a force operating outside Leggatt's rational distinction between Volpone's 'criminal behavior' and Sir Pol's 'harmless folly'. Any 'vision' of the world that Volpone might have is reducible to his whim, his bizarre 'crochets' and 'conundrums' as he says himself in a rare and belated moment of self-perception (5.11.16, 17). Characters such as Celia, Bonario and the others have no such interior life. Sir Politic, by contrast, enjoys a rather rich exterior life, benignly advising Peregrine: 'for your religion, profess none, | But wonder at the diversity of all' (4.1.22–23). Such patronizing grandiosity bears little resemblance to Volpone's ostensible worship of gold in the main plot. Rather, through such studied behaviour, Sir Pol, like a vaguely bemused cabinet minister in retirement, might very well gain a visiting professorship in the posthumanist academy.

The real Menippean academic of the play however is Lady Would-be. She is a figure of real energy that crosses over the plots most effectively in her unremitting assertions and insistences at Volpone's house. Through such behaviour, she unconsciously plays the opposite of the three crazily accommodating fortune hunters. Indeed, no one else in the play can actually annoy Volpone as Lady Would-be so obviously does every time she visits and familiarly accosts him, 'How does my Volp?' (3.4.39). Her unwilling host positively shrivels at the onslaught of her loud and condescending behaviour. He tries to patronize her by citing an unnamed classical poet who affirms 'your highest female grace is silence' and Lady Would-be immediately queries him:

> Which o' your poets? Petrarch? or Tasso' or Dante?
> Guarini? Ariosto? Aretine?
> Cieco di Hadria? I have read them all.
>
> (3.4.79–81)

For the first time in the play, Volpone finds himself playing a role which he does not enjoy, protesting privately, 'Before I feigned diseases, now I have one' (62). The audience, however, greatly enjoys Volpone's obvious distress as 'fall guy' to Lady Pol's assertions. She blithely complicates Volpone's desperation by referencing Aretine as 'a desperate wit, [. . .] | Only his pictures are a little obscene' (96–97) – but only just a little. What Volpone finds obscene is her incessant stealing of *his* scene.

Furthermore, and rather significantly, when Lady Pol arrives at Volpone's bedside, it is Nano the dwarf who sarcastically introduces her, 'It is the beauteous madam' (3.3.24). Nano can be easily overlooked (or cut in production) but bulks largely and conveniently to accompany Lady Would-be on her quest for her husband. Mosca interrupts her torment of Volpone by salaciously reporting that Sir Pol is 'Rowing upon the water in a gondola | With the most cunning courtesan in Venice' (3.5.19–20). Lady Pol exits and reenters in comic desperation intensified by the urgent request, 'I pray you, lend me your dwarf' and Mosca's equally urgent, if archly delivered, response, 'I pray you, take him' (29). David M. Bergeron sees all this as a matter of romance convention and satire related possibly to *The Faerie Queene* with its questing knights and reliable dwarfs. But the immediate physical comedy of large Lady Would-be, tiny Nano, and much bustling about on and offstage is more to the point. Bergeron reports that Lady Would-be's 'lend me your dwarf' evoked spontaneous applause in Stratford, Fall 1983.[24] The audience relishes visual, verbal and physical disjunction. Nano accompanies her because she needs direction to the gondola where she will confront her husband – and the man whom she mistakes as his courtesan – with even more gusto than that with which she so obliviously annoyed and tormented Volpone.

Playing Dead

Volpone knows (even if his audience does not) that nothing can escape derision. He also knows (as comic avatar of irrepressible vitality) that he alone, as title character, can escape death. Greenblatt suggestively observed that, at the beginning of act five, 'Volpone is in the surrealistic situation of a character who has somehow survived his play'.[25] Volpone is indeed a character in search of a performative ending. Hereby, the false ending that Greenblatt so sharply discerned takes on fuller meaning and possibility in light of other performer/audience engagements in the play. Note especially that early moment in act five when Mosca and Volpone seem to step out of their roles with some retrospective self consciousness concerning their performance – 'VOLPONE *is brought in as impotent*' (4.6.20 sd) – before the investigating Avocatori. Significantly, even as he admits to some performance discomfort, Volpone affirms that he never stopped acting:

> *Mosca.*   'T seemed to me you sweat, sir.
> *Volpone.* In troth, I did a little.
> *Mosca.*   But confess, sir,
>   Were you not daunted?
> *Volpone.* In good faith, I was
>   A little in a mist, but not dejected;
>   Never but still myself.
>
> (5.2.37–41)

He shared a similar momentary self-consciousness after his huckster performance as an Italian mountebank: 'But were they gulled | With a belief that I was Scoto?'(2.4.34–35). And he does so again even more pointedly at his death-in-life sentence in terms of generative complicity with the audience. After the witheringly lengthy statement of judgment by the court, Volpone exclaims, 'This is called mortifying of a fox' (5.12.125). The Revels editor lists many punning possibilities but Volpone is emphatically, publicly aghast, mortified at the way his performance has turned out he cannot help sharing his perspective with the audience. In a sense comically transferable to both his implicit and explicit audience, Volpone collapses performance.

He performs this collapse into mutual audience consciousness in a similar key at the epilogue. Greenblatt goes beyond a posited early modern rejection of God to reject performance itself as an ethical void at the conclusion of the play. He shrewdly argues that Jonson 'makes part of the meaning of the work the audience's exit from the playhouse. He directs the audience, as it were, to reject the theatrical principles of displacement, mask and metamorphosis'.[26] However, as noted previously, audiences do not usually exit performances of *Volpone* feeling dejected. Even Volpone's epilogue, while conventional, links self-consciousness with audience consciousness: 'He yet doth hope there is no suff'ring due | For any fact which he hath done 'gainst you' (3–4). Any audience is

probably still ringing with the ludicrous energy of Volpone's performances near the end: of his panic: 'To make a snare for mine own neck!
And run | My head into it willfully! with laughter!' (5.11.1–2); or his
exorcism of Corvino: "Twill out, 'twill out! Stand clear. See where it
flies | In the shape of a blue toad with a bat's wings!' (5.12.30–31); or
even Volpone's final spite as he rejects Mosca: 'My ruins shall not come
alone. Your match | I'll hinder sure; my substance shall not glue you, |
Nor screw you, into a family' (85–87). Unlike iconic comic heroes such
as Don Quixote or Falstaff or even Father Christmas – well-meaning,
life-affirming, even rather saintly although somewhat forbidding –
Volpone is anti-iconic. Like them, he will never die but he will always
battle death even as he teeters on the brink of it through energy, disguise and constant threat of exposure. This constant threat of exposure
in performance makes Volpone totally unsentimental. He is neither
saint nor sinner, nor even a person. As the Player in *Rosencrantz and
Guildenstern are Dead* affirms: 'We're actors – we're the opposite of
people!'. [27] As an old curmudgeon masking as a party-goer, Volpone
knows the feeling. He's out-of-control even as he tries to assert the
greatest control, like a middle-aged retrogressive look back at life
before chucking the whole thing. But Volpone would never assert such
closure. The 'God' of this play is performance itself and absurd laughter
is the hymn. Histrionics alone will live forever. Hence the false endings,
impossibility of closure and ironic palliative eternity of *Volpone* and its
title character.

As further paradox, Jonson's prefatory Epistle to the 'Most Equal
Sisters, The Two Famous Universities' of Oxford and Cambridge plays
its part at the conclusion. Recently, in *Ben Jonson and the Politics of
Genre*, Richard Dutton reads this Epistle strictly in terms of biography.[28]
But his earlier work, published in *Refashioning Ben Jonson*, took a more
open approach to credit powerful irony near the end of the play: The
invocation of the 'equal sisters' as 'arbitresses' in literary matters should
perhaps be put alongside the performance of the Court of Avocatori
within *Volpone* itself. Herein, as Dutton observes, 'the "justice" meted
out is hard to distinguish from the revenge of a self-seeking, hood-
winked court.'[29] Or, one might add, the judgements – good, bad, indif-
ferent, ridiculous and otherwise – of generations of theatre audiences.
The Avocatori are routinely condemned as incompetent at best, and not
to be taken any more seriously than the Keystone Cops, Dogberry or
Elbow. In relation to the theatre, Jonson's oft-quoted dedicatory letter to
Oxford and Cambridge, although morally serious and somewhat pedantic, is rather exterior to the play in terms of performance comedy – as if
Oscar Wilde wrote similar letters declaring that Algernon's Oxford
degree really was genuine, or Evelyn Waugh solemnly affirming that his

fictionalized Bollinger Club had nothing whatsoever to do with more recent out-of-control Bullingdon Club dinners.

I return to Jonson's Epistle because it accomplishes at the outset what *Volpone* does throughout: appeals to the subjective even as it tries to be objective. But it does not relate so much to literal exposure of a scorned satirical target such as Robert Cecil or Sir Thomas Sutton, or to the grand objectivity of remote classical authority. Rather, it prefixes (without fixing) multifarious subjectivities and responses of comedy – the collective laughter that binds (momentarily) the many idiosyncrasies of reproach and delight. So, what's funny about *Volpone*? Everything. And none of it is completely innocent even though, in the theatre, it is crucially permissible. Volpone's technologies of greed might manifest themselves today as computer spyware and internet scams. Sir Politic Would-be would be fascinated and fleeced – but not us as audience. Or would we? To search *Volpone* for moral renovation or even for a darkly coherent satirical plot is to reduce the comic power of the play in performance. This justly notorious play is more complicated in equal measures of painful self-awareness and painless other-deprecation. Volpone *is* guilty. We all are. But, as comic hero, he admits it. He lives it irresponsibly throughout. And will do so again in performance somewhere tomorrow. That is part of the reason why *Volpone* will always be a guilty pleasure, but a pleasure nevertheless (and perhaps more) for being so thoughtfully, entertainingly and laughably guilty.

Notes

1   Murray Roston, '*Volpone*: Comedy or Mordant Satire?' *Ben Jonson Journal* 10 (2003): 1–21, qtn. from 1; Jonas A., Barish, ed. *Jonson:* Volpone, *A Casebook* (London: Macmillan, 1972), 19; Bruce Thomas Boehrer, *The Fury of Men's Gullets: Ben Jonson and the Digestive Canal* (Philadelphia: U of Pennsylvania P, 1997), 104.

2   Julie Sanders, Kate Chedgzoy and Susan Wiseman, eds. *Refashioning Ben Jonson* (London: Macmillan, 1998); Richard Cave, Elizabeth Schafer and Brian Woolland, eds *Ben Jonson and Theatre: Performance, Practice and Theory* (London: Routledge, 1999).

3   Jonson, 'Discoveries', 643, cited from Volume 8 of Ben Jonson, *Ben Jonson*, ed. C. H. Herford and Percy and Evelyn Simpson, 11 Vols (Oxford: Clarendon Press, 1925–1952).

4   Jure Gantar, *The Pleasure of Fools: Essays in the Ethics of Laughter* (Montreal and Kingston: McGill-Queen's UP, 2005), 21.

5   Oscar Wilde, *Complete Works* ed. Vyvyan Holland (London: Collins, 1966), 1205.

6   Mikhail Bakhtin, *Rabelais and His World*. Trans. Helene Iswolsky (Bloomington: Indiana UP, 1984) 281.

7   Ronald Huebert, *The Performance of Pleasure in English Renaissance Drama* (Basingstoke: Palgrave Macmillan, 2003), 56.

8   R. B. Parker, '*Volpone* in Performance 1921–1972.' *Renaissance Drama* 9 (1978): 147–73, qtn. from 154; Cave, Schafer, and Woolland, eds, *Ben Jonson and Theatre*, 64–65.

9   Roston, '*Volpone*: Comedy or Mordant Satire?', 9.

10 Parker, '*Volpone* in performance', 166.

11 Parker, 'Introduction' to Ben Jonson, *Volpone* ed. R. B. Parker (Manchester: Manchester UP, 1983), 10.

12 Stephen Greenblatt, 'The False Ending in *Volpone*.' *Journal of English and Germanic Philology* 75 (1976): 90–104, qtn. from 95; Friedrich Nietzsche, *Human, All Too Human: A Book for Free Spirits* trans. R. J. Hollingdale (Cambridge: Cambridge UP, 1986), 261.

13 Robert Altman, dir. *The Player*. Fine Line Features, 1992.

14 Sean McEvoy, *Ben Jonson, Renaissance Dramatist* (Edinburgh: Edinburgh UP, 2008), 60.

15 McEvoy, *Ben Jonson*, 73.

16 Jonson, *Volpone*, ed. Parker, 149.

17 Oliver Hennessey, 'Jonson's Joyless Economy: Theorizing Motivation and Pleasure in *Volpone*' *ELR* 38.1 (Feb. 2008): 83–105, qtns from 92–93.

18 Parker, '*Volpone* in performance', 168.

19 Terry Eagleton, *After Theory* (London: Allen Lane, 2003), 190.

20 William W. E. Slights, *Ben Jonson and the Art of Secrecy* (Toronto: U of Toronto P, 1994), 58.

21 Arnold P. Hinchcliffe, *Volpone: Text and Performance* (London: Macmillan, 1985), 79.

22 Robert N. Watson, *Ben Jonson's Parodic Strategy* (Cambridge: Harvard UP, 1987), 94.

23 Alexander Leggatt, "*Volpone*: The Double Plot Revisited." *New Perspectives on Ben Jonson*, ed. James Hirsh (London Associated UP, 1997), 89–105, qtn from 92.

24 David M. Bergeron, '"Lend me your dwarf": Romance in *Volpone*' *Medieval and Renaissance Drama in England* 3 (1986): 99–113, qtn. from 100.

25 Greenblatt, 'The False Ending in *Volpone*', 100.

26 Greenblatt, 'The False Ending in *Volpone*', 102–03.

27 Tom Stoppard, *Rosencrantz and Guildenstern are Dead* (London: Faber, 1968), 46.

28 Richard Dutton, 'Jonson's Metempsychosis Revisited: Patronage and Religious Controversy.' *Ben Jonson and the Politics of Genre*, ed. A. D. Cousins and Alison V. Scott. (Cambridge: Cambridge UP, 2009), 134–61.

29 Richard Dutton, 'The Lone Wolf: Jonson's Epistle to *Volpone*.' *Refashioning Ben Jonson*. ed. Julie Sanders et al. London: Macmillan, 1998. 114–33, qtns from 122, 125.

CHAPTER SIX

New Directions: Ben Jonson and Imprisonment

Frances Teague

Jonson and the 'Knotty Laws'

Ben Jonson was a recidivist, a repeat offender. As a quick look at his arrest record (see Table One) shows, he was in and out of trouble all his life, especially before 1606. David Riggs remarks, 'Had [Jonson] disappeared after *Eastward Ho!*, he would be remembered today as a shadowy outlaw poet who squandered his chances.'[1] The most serious of his offenses is murder, for which he was sentenced to death. Jonson is the only canonical author to have read his neck verse, using a medieval loophole in English common law that allowed a condemned man to save himself from execution by demonstrating literacy and pleading benefit of clergy. Most of the items on his arrest record are not serious: there are occasional cases of debt or brawls and complaints about his work from those who felt themselves mocked. But three serious cases do exist. He went to prison in 1597 for his involvement as one of the authors of seditious *The Isle of Dogs*, in 1598 for murdering the actor Gabriel Spencer, and in 1604 for co-authoring *Eastward Ho!*

Table One: Ben Jonson (1573–1637): His Arrest Record[2]

1597: Jonson and Thomas Nashe write *The Isle of Dogs*. Privy Council closes all London theatres (28 July) and charges that the play contains sedition, lewdness and slander. Nashe flees to Yarmouth. Jonson imprisoned with two actors, Robert Shaw and Gabriel Spencer, 15 August. Interrogated by Richard Topcliffe. Spies observe him. Released 8 October from Marshalsea Prison without a conviction.

1598: 22 September, Jonson kills Gabriel Spencer. Jonson claims it was a duel and self-defence. Pleads guilty to murder on 6 October. Jonson reads neck verse and thumb branded with Tyburn T. While in Newgate prison, Jonson converts to Roman Catholicism, probably by imprisoned priest, Father Thomas Wright. (Imprisoned at the Clink at this time, Wright seems to have had some freedom to move about).

1599: Jonson imprisoned at Marshalsea for debt at suit of Robert Brown. Judgment given for Brown, and after payment of debt, Jonson freed January 1598/99.

1599–1601: 'War of the Theaters,' during which Jonson beats John Marston and takes away his pistol. Complaint filed with Chief Justice Popham about Jonson's play *Poetaster*, but attorney Richard Martin intercedes and no action taken.

1603: 23 April, Jonson beats an attendant to Lord Henry Howard. Jonson summoned before Privy Council (probably in December, possibly later), charged with Popery and treason for his play *Sejanus* by Lord Henry Howard (soon to be Earl of Northampton). Found innocent.

1604: 6 January, Jonson and Sir John Roe cause disturbance at court during masque by Samuel Daniel and 'thrust out'.

1605: Jonson, George Chapman, and John Marston charged with libel by Sir James Murray and with failure to get Lord Chamberlain's approval for *Eastward Ho!* Marston flees. Jonson and Chapman imprisoned (probably some time after 4 September) and told that if they are found guilty, they will have their ears and noses slit. They write to many powerful men pleading their innocence and are freed in the fall. Jonson gives a party for his friends. His mother attends and shows a packet of poison to company, declares that had he been found guilty, she would have killed him and committed suicide.

1605: In October, Jonson attends a dinner given by Robert Catesby and others involved in the Gunpowder Plot. The Privy Council moves against the Gunpowder Plot conspirators on 4 November. On 7 November issues a warrant to Jonson to bring in a certain priest. He says he cannot do so on 8 November. Guy Fawkes tortured for the last time on 9 November to provide information. Father Thomas Wright brought in to hear his confession and tells Privy Council that it agrees with what Fawkes has said under torture.

1606: Jonson indicted as recusant Catholic on 10 January. Interrogated again on 26 April. Sentenced to a course of religious instruction.

Of the three most serious charges, the 1598 charge of murder is startling. Although Jonson told William Drummond that Spencer had instigated the duel and that he killed in self-defence, he nevertheless pleaded guilty to murder. Perhaps because Spencer had killed a man before, which lends some credence to Jonson's claim of self-defence, the judge chose to allow Jonson benefit of clergy, a generosity that was not always the case, so Jonson read his neck verse, and was released after he had been branded with the Tyburn T. An indication of how serious his situation was may be found in his conversion to Roman Catholicism during his imprisonment, probably by another prisoner, Father Thomas Wright, a captured priest.[3] Clearly Jonson was thinking about his soul while he waited to learn whether he would die or read.

Nor were the two other cases trivial. In the *Isle of Dogs* case, the authorities considered the play that Jonson and Thomas Nashe had written so damaging that they did not simply shut down that production, but all of London theatre. In the *Eastward Ho!* case a few years later, a conviction would have meant judicial mutilation, the slitting of Jonson's ears and nose. His mother's pledge to murder her son and commit suicide also indicates how devastating that outcome would have been. It is worth noting that after this dramatic escape from punishment, Jonson was quickly embroiled with those who planned treason, although no one knows whether his involvement was instigated by the plotters, by Jonson himself or by the government using Jonson as a cat's paw. One can understand why scholars like Barbara de Luna or Paul Durst have suggested that while Jonson was in prison for the *Eastward Ho!* case, he was recruited as a secret agent to spy on the Gunpowder Plotters.[4] Unfortunately, no proof exists that he was recruited, so one cannot be sure what exactly was going on.

Around October 9, Jonson attended a supper party at the Irish Boy Inn in the Strand with a group of Catholics. The supper was given by Robert Catesby, who lodged at the Irish Boy and was completing his plans to blow up King James, Prince Henry and others at the opening of Parliament; most of the guests at the supper party – Francis Tresham, Thomas Winter, Lord Mordaunt – had roles in this plot. On November 4, the plot failed when Guy Fawkes was discovered guarding the gunpowder they had stored under Parliament. Initially, Fawkes refused to provide any useful information about the men with whom he had plotted. On November 6, therefore, King James had ordered that 'the gentler Tortures are to be first used unto him *et sic per gradus ad ima tenditur,*' yet Fawkes continued uncooperative. Because of Fawkes' silence, the Privy Council recruited Jonson as a special agent, probably at the instigation of Robert Cecil, Earl of Salisbury, one of the men to whom Jonson had appealed for release from prison. On November 7, Jonson agreed to work for Privy Council by searching out a 'certaine priest' and offering that priest a warrant from the Privy Council guaranteeing his safety for his cooperation. Jonson wrote Salisbury on November 8 about his lack of success, but promised to continue his search.[5] Scholars have thought that Jonson's involvement ended there in failure, but a contemporary's account suggests that he did succeed.

After torture, Fawkes began to confess late on November 7 and made two more confessions on November 8 and 9. Afterwards Father Thomas Wright was brought to Fawkes, and a contemporary describes what happened:

> [. . .] the Lords of the Councel, requested that a Priest should be appoynted to perswade and assure Fauxe (a chiefe agent in it) that he was bound in conscience to vtter what he could of that conspiracie, and M. Tho. Write a learned Priest did hereupon come to the councell, and offer his best seruice herein, and had a warrant to that purpose subsigned with 12.priuie Councellors hands, which he shewed vnto me, and I am witnesse of his hauing such a warrant. But as he said, Faux had confessed all they could wish before he could come vnto him [. . .][6]

Father Wright's warrant sounds remarkably like that issued to Jonson on 7 November: it bears a guarantee of safe conduct to which the Privy Councillors had sworn upon their honours. Since 'Faux had confessed all they could wish,' Father Wright must have seen the prisoner after he had made his third confession on 9 November 1605. Jonson's letter to Salisbury, saying he had not yet located the priest, was written on 8 November 1605, so Jonson may well have succeeded after he had written the letter.

As the investigation proceeded, the various conspirators died or were arrested; also arrested were innocent people who nonetheless fell under suspicion. The official trial began in January, although as Fraser points out,

> The decision was never in doubt. The mere fact that these men were on trial for high treason meant that they would inevitably be found guilty, and equally inevitably be sentenced to death. Refinements such as a defending counsel were unknown. In the nineteenth century, Lord Macauley would describe the process as 'merely a murder preceded by the uttering of certain gibberish and the performance of certain mummeries.' Yet one should be wary of too much anachronistic indignation. These were the rules of a treason trial at the time, proceedings which were quite literally

intended as a show trial. [. . .] The real trial had already taken
place in the form of interrogations before the Privy Council.

(218–19)

Sir Edward Coke prosecuted the case, and all of the defendants
were indeed found guilty, based on the evidence gathered by the Privy
Council's interrogations. It seems likely that Jonson, as a recusant
Catholic who was acquainted with Catesby and his circle, was one of
those interrogated between November and January when the trial began.
Nevertheless, he was in good odour with government officials, which
indirectly supports the argument that he did succeed in helping the Privy
Council. The Earl of Suffolk, the Lord Chamberlain, commissioned
Hymenaei from Jonson for his daughter's wedding; the masque was
performed 6 January 1606, about three weeks before the trial began.

Riggs argues that Jonson and his wife had reconciled, probably in
late October, and began attending Anglican services (without taking
communion) soon after the Gunpowder Plot revelations. Despite
attending the Anglican services, Jonson continued as a recusant Roman
Catholic when the inevitable backlash against Catholics occurred in the
early months of 1606; his punishment for remaining in that faith, however, was relatively light. This rush of events – Jonson's imprisonment
for *Eastward Ho!*, his supper meeting with the Gunpowder Plotters, his
service to the Privy Council against the conspiracy, and his investigation as a Roman Catholic – not only occurred before and during Jonson's
composition of *Volpone*, but also marked several months when he was
simultaneously within the law and outside it, a hunter and a fox.

The London public generally responded with horror and anger to
the news that certain Catholics had sought to blow up the King, the
royal family, and many members of Parliament. Thus, when King James
spoke to Parliament about the plot, he explicitly warned his people
against the persecution of Catholics in retribution for the Gunpowder
Plot, since the vast majority of recusants were innocent. Providence had
intervened, James said, and a divine miracle had preserved the state. In
passing he referred to the Monteagle letter, the now infamous anonymous missive that warned Lord Monteagle to stay away from the opening of Parliament on November 5 lest he be blown up. Lord Monteagle
took this letter to the government, and it may have contributed to the
discovery of Guy Fawkes. The letter is a problem because to this day no
one knows its source: it may have come from one of the conspirators;
Monteagle himself may have been a conspirator who had developed
cold feet; or the letter may have been a plant from the government,
specifically from Salisbury, who may have had men serving as *agents
provocateurs* to entrap the conspirators.

Nor is the Monteagle letter the only disturbing part of the Gunpowder Plot investigation. When the plot was discovered, men were tortured to extract confessions; the various confessions conflicted and could not be reconciled. Moreover, confession took on a particularly unsavoury connotation because the government said that a priest had known in advance about the plan to blow up Parliament but remained silent because he had been told of it under the seal of the confessional. The argument that it was acceptable for a priest to equivocate rather than to break the seal of the confessional was treated by the London public with especial scorn.[7] Finally there was the execution of the men who were convicted of treason. Their deaths were horrible: first they were dragged through the streets tied to hurdles; then each was hanged, cut down alive, drawn, and quartered. After they were dead and the executioners had burned the organs of their bodies removed during the drawing, pitch was poured over what was left of their quartered corpses to preserve the remains for public display.

Jonson's role in the plot and its investigation is obscure, but his concern with the Gunpowder Plot is manifest from the poems he wrote about the events. His poem praising William, Lord Monteagle, suggests that whether or not he accepted the story of the letter as genuine, Jonson felt Monteagle's warning had helped to save the country (Epigram 60). He was greatly relieved by the survival of the king (Epigram 51). His poem to Sir Edward Coke, who prosecuted the case against the Gunpowder plotters, provides a useful index to Jonson's attitude toward the law at this point in his life and suggests that the case of the Gunpowder Plot had helped to alter his outlook. Coke, he declares, has the sort of eloquence that 'Stood up thy nation's fame, her crown's defence.' As Lord Chief Justice, Coke was 'like Solon's self,' in the way that he 'explait'st the knotty laws | With endless labors' (*Underwood* 46: 14, 17). Now in conjunction with Epigrams 51 and 60, the poem on Coke is obviously a poem praising him, yet the phrase 'knotty laws' is just as obviously a play on words that suggests Jonson thinks some of the laws being enforced are 'naughty'. A Catholic forced to worship outside the law, Jonson disapproves of some laws; a man witnessing a horrible act of attempted treason, he is deeply grateful for laws that protect the state.

As an aggressive and often angry man, Jonson got into trouble with the law when he was violent. As a playwright, he was subject to constant scrutiny from the Lord Chamberlain's office lest his work prove offensive. As a convert to Catholicism, he was also at odds with the law, for under the 1559 Act of Uniformity, he was forbidden to practise his faith. The pressure of his position as a Catholic intensified after the revelations of the Gunpowder Plot, but the affair may have also suggested the rewards available to one who served powerful men. It is frustrating, to be sure, that even in a history so well-documented as is Jonson's, so many questions remain.

Yet what I find most striking about Ben Jonson's record of imprisonment is how flexible the early modern system of justice was. While the threatened punishments, the intolerance for dissent and religion, or the toleration for informers and torture dismay us, other aspects strike me as progressive. Convicted of murder, Jonson was allowed to go free, not because he was literate, but because the judge decided that there were enough extenuating circumstances to allow him benefit of clergy. Imprisoned for his plays, Jonson did not hesitate to lobby for his release to the highest men in the government whether he knew them or not: what seems more surprising today is that his letters were taken seriously. In his case, at least, being a poor commoner did not mean being passive or ignored. Given his arrest record, one might expect a discreet reticence about the law, but he published his opinions, often scathingly, and scripted satire against bad laws badly enforced. When his Catholicism was investigated during the very same time that the Gunpowder Plotters are on trial, he was told to go and study religion. Would that twenty-first century governments were so enlightened.

History and *Volpone*

The play most likely to have been affected by the Gunpowder Plot is *Volpone*, which was written immediately in the aftermath of the investigation. Not only does the titular hero, the fox, echo the name of Guy Fawkes, as William Sessions has pointed out, but the play features a bungled investigation, an unjust trial, and the providential discovery of truth despite legal corruption and incompetence. Moreover, the play concerns itself with the confinement of Celia in her husband's house and of Volpone in his bedroom: Celia is an unwilling prisoner, while Volpone is a prisoner by choice because of his secret identity. One can, if such speculation pleases, note parallels to Jonson's life. More to the point, however, the play's concern with imprisonment and its effect on identity is consistent and pervasive.

One cannot argue that Jonson's changing attitudes toward the legal system stemmed solely from his experiences concerning the Gunpowder Plot. He had used legal scenes to mock the legal system in his plays before 1605–1606, and he would do so repeatedly throughout his career. In several earlier poems about members of the legal system, he addresses lawyers and judges not involved in the Gunpowder Plot. Thus in the Chevril epigrams or in the epigram 'On Spies' (Epigrams 37, 54, 59), he shows open contempt for corrupt lawyers or for the practice of setting spies to gather evidence. In 'An Epigram to the Counsellor that Pleaded and Carried the Case,' Jonson describes lawyers as 'hirelings, wranglers, stitchers-to of strife,' | Hook-handed harpies, gownèd vultures [. . .]' (*Underwood* 33: 8–9). He admits in this poem, however, that one exceptional attorney (almost certainly Sir Anthony Benn) has made him 'conceive a lawyer new' so that 'Thy sincere practice breeds not thee a fame | Alone, but all thy rank a reverend name' (38: 14, 39–40). Similarly in the second epigram to Thomas, Lord Ellesmere, Jonson speaks of how the judge's good example repairs the bad impression left by 'great foes, | Both armed with wealth and slander to oppose' (Underwood 32: 7–8). Neither Benn nor Ellesmere is a figure concerned in the Gunpowder Plot trial. The point of these examples is that Jonson's concern with or shifting view of the legal system, while it was quite certainly affected by the events of the Gunpowder Plot, was not affected solely by these events. The law was a topic of continuing concern for Jonson, which makes sense if one considers his own changing identity.

One can easily imagine that Jonson as a young man was wild, having seen violence when he served in the army and when he entered the playhouse world. In his later years, he bragged to William Drummond:

> In his service in the Low Countries he had, in the face of both the camps, killed an enemy and taken 'opima spolia' from him; and since his coming to England, being appealed to the fields, he had killed his adversary, who had hurt him in the arm, and whose sword was 10 inches longer than his; for the which he was imprisoned, and almost at the gallows. Then took he his religion by trust, of a priest, who visited him in prison. Thereafter he was twelve years a Papist.

As Jonson began to enjoy success and as he realized the cost of that violence in civilian life, he began to exercise greater control over his temper. At the same time that he settled down, however, his conversion to Catholicism meant he was automatically outside the law of England. Ironically, his life as a recusant was sufficiently respectable that he began to gain entrée and patrons in aristocratic circles. Thus, his life as an outlaw introduced him to the inner circles of power.

In his work, Jonson generally preserved a discreet silence on religion, reserving his open criticism for corrupt lawyers and judges or for judicial practices he considered unethical (like spying on the accused). While reticent about theology, he did, along with most of his audience, have a deep-seated belief in providential intervention in human affairs. He was also deeply interested in the practice of rhetoric by attorneys and judges, although he recognized that their skill in using language might be employed to a bad end. Finally, he was taken with the potential absurdities of a hearing in which various accounts of an event were given and then reconciled, to judge from his repeated use of that device in his comedies. In the rest of this essay, I want to examine the aspects of *Volpone* that this historical background illuminates: the nature of imprisonment, providence and injustice, and the way that we can understand the play's concern with these issues.

One might ask how the play's ideas about imprisonment, injustice and providence alter during its course, particularly given the sentences that the Avocatori hand down. Most analyses of imprisonment depend in some way on the monumental work by Michel Foucault *Discipline and Punish*, which shows how an institution like a prison is a way for a society to exercise systematic control over the population. An analysis of *Volpone*, however, can take a different approach. Rather than simply consider the way that the system of imprisonment illuminates the society, one can examine how a former prisoner imagines imprisonment. Frank Kermode's discussion of Christopher Burney's memoir *Solitary Confinement* in *The Sense of an Ending* offers a model for such a discussion. Jonson had been a prisoner, and we might expect the play to show some traces of his experience, of what happens to someone who is locked up, unable to see or speak with people, spied upon.

Imprisonment in the Play

In *Volpone* Celia is the most virtuous character. When she first appears, however, the audience may not realize her modesty. Mosca's description praises her beauty in sensual terms that suggest she is sexually available to any man that is in her presence:

> Oh, sir, the wonder,
> The blazing star of Italy! A wench
> O' the first year! A beauty, ripe as harvest!
> Whose skin is whiter than a swan, all over,
> Than silver, snow, or lilies! A soft lip,
> Would tempt you to eternity of kissing!
> And flesh that melteth in the touch to blood!
> Bright as your gold, and lovely as your gold!
>
> (1.5.107–14)

A man who is with Celia will kiss her, touch her, melt into her: she is an object to be handled like a golden ornament. When Volpone asks for more information, Mosca speaks of how 'warily' she is kept within Corvino's household where every servant is a guard. He says nothing about her character. Thus, when she first appears in 2.2 at her window and lets fall her handkerchief, the audience may well presume she is amenable to anyone's advances.

In 2.5 the audience hears Celia and for the first time realizes that she is not an object, but a subject, a person who has her own ideas about things. Those ideas are distinctly at odds with both Mosca's initial description and her husband's treatment. Corvino rails at her, calling her a whore, greedy for trinkets, and she replies by telling him to have patience, meeting his violent language with restraint. As the dialogue proceeds, we learn that looking out the window is her sole amusement, for she never leaves the house save to go to church. Because she is a prisoner within her own home, however, her words go unregarded. In the world of the play, a prisoner is less than human in the eyes of her jailer. Corvino takes the opportunity to threaten Celia with corporal punishment: he will limit her more stringently, beat her, force her to wear a chastity belt, and dissect her corpse. For Celia being a prisoner is humiliating. She is disregarded, spoken of and treated with contempt. Spied on and browbeaten, she says little and that little is ignored. After Mosca's visit, Corvino changes his tune. Approached by Mosca to prostitute his wife, Corvino eagerly acquiesces, assuring her that he now trusts her, although he is careful to tell her nothing of the plan until the last moment.

First Corvino must bring his wife to Volpone's house for the exigencies of Volpone's scheme mean that he too is imprisoned, isolated within his bedroom. To be sure, his imprisonment is filled with such delights as the luxuries of his life and the constant visits by legacy hunters. Leaving his prison is also easy, since he simply disguises himself as a mountebank to achieve release, although such release depends upon his servants making all the arrangements. Since the world comes to him and he can visit it in disguise, his condition seems to have little in common with that of Celia. Yet his behaviour, like hers, is under surveillance, both by the legacy-hunters and by Mosca; his privacy, like hers, nonexistent; and those outside his household regard him as less than human, a nuisance who might be murdered with little trouble. Corbaccio even brings poison to that end, while Corvino and Mosca discuss smothering him as he lies there, reduced to a humiliated object. We soon realize that those threats are empty, just as Corvino's threats are empty.

Forced to bring Celia to Volpone, Corvino begins by trying to persuade her to have sex with the invalid. She first thinks he is testing her again, but then is appalled, referring to heaven and the saints as she refuses. Next he proceeds to threats, the ugliest in the play:

> Be damned!
> Heart! I will drag thee hence home by the hair,
> Cry thee a strumpet through the streets, rip up
> Thy mouth unto thy ears, and slit thy nose,
> Like a raw rochet! – Do not tempt me; come,
> Yield; I am loath – Death! I will buy some slave
> Whom I will kill, and bind thee to him, alive,
> And at my window hang you forth, devising
> Some monstrous crime, which I, in capital letters,
> Will eat into thy flesh with aquafortis
> And burning cor'sives, on this stubborn breast.
> Now by the blood thou hast incensed, I'll do it!
>
> (3.7.95–106)

His threats are three. First he plans her public humiliation, dragging her through the city and proclaiming that she is a whore. Next he threatens mutilation, cutting her mouth and nose to disfigure her (much as the authorities threatened to mutilate Jonson and George Chapman in 1605). Finally, he will buy and murder a slave, use acid on her breast to accuse her of a crime, tie her to the corpse, and hang his wife and victim from a window for all to see and loathe. The result of this horrific speech is that Celia calls his bluff. 'Sir, what you please, you may; I am your martyr,' she tells him, and his language immediately shifts from threats to wheedling. Celia may be his prisoner, may be disregarded or treated as less than human, but, finally, she has some power over her jailor. She has almost none, however, over another prisoner.

Celia has recourse to religion when she is left by herself with the seeming invalid: her speech may be an expostulation or a prayer, but she certainly uses religious language when she says, 'O, God and his good angels!' A moment later Volpone cheerfully embarks on his seduction and, like Corvino, ignores what she says and does. Announcing himself in love with her, he welcomes Celia to his bedroom; she immediately moves away, eliciting his line, 'Nay, fly me not,' and a renewed declaration that includes a song. She calls on heaven to destroy her beauty, and he shows her his shrine and its concealed treasure. She appeals to his conscience, and he appeals to her appetite for sensual delights. Finally she refuses, invoking the 'holy saints – or heaven' and offering to kneel and pray for him if he will 'let [her] scape.' He declares his intention of raping her: 'Yield, or I'll force thee.'

Imprisoned in the bedroom, neither can communicate with the other. When Volpone is imprisoned in his bedroom, he either performs for the legacy hunters or does as he pleases, while Celia deals with her imprisonment by putting up with Corvino's abuse to a point and then balking. Thus Volpone continues his seduction long after it has proven to be useless because he pays no attention to Celia. His performance is largely for himself, it seems, since he persists blithely despite her initial response: 'Some serene blast me, or dire lightning strike | This my offending face,' a line that would discourage anyone else. Nor is she any more able to listen to him: her obliviousness to his catalogue of delights can be seen when she commences praying for his soul while kneeling before his blasphemous shrine to wealth. The scene is arguably not dialogue, but dueling monologues. How their inability to understand one another might have developed is unresolved. Volpone claims in 1.1.52 that he loathes violence and brutality, so would he have raped Celia? As a prisoner, she has always maintained her autonomy by trusting in her faith and, Lucrece-like, preferring death to disobeying God, as she tells both Corvino and Volpone (3.7.93–94, 3.7.243). Could she have resisted the rape he offers and won him over with tears and protests? One cannot tell because as prisoners, they are under surveillance by Bonario, who intervenes and carries Celia away to the courts where they charge Volpone with a crime. A prisoner has no privacy.

Providence and Injustice

The trial scenes in Acts IV and V of *Volpone* are often read as demonstrations of injustice, and the Avocatori are generally considered corrupt.[8] Yet if one looks at the trial scenes analytically, the Avocatori actually seem to be reasonable in their judgments. When they enter in 4.5, the Avocatori are predisposed in favour of Celia and Bonario, speaking of their virtuous reputations. When Bonario and Celia defend themselves, while Voltore, a professional advocate, speaks for Volpone, the case quickly turns against them. Bonario and Celia have no witnesses, while Voltore has several, one of whom, Lady Pol, seems disinterested. Corbaccio's testimony silences his son Bonario, while Celia is unable to speak more than a line or two before she swoons. In addition to the witnesses, Voltore has the physical evidence of Mosca's wound, as well as the woebegone appearance of Volpone who seems to be a comatose invalid. The Avocatori decide the case, inevitably, for Volpone and order Celia and Bonario to prison. Celia's freedom has been short-lived.

The court appearance also imprisons Volpone in his role. When he next appears, he speaks of the misery he has endured:

> Well, I am here, and all this brunt is passed.
> I ne'er was in dislike with my disguise
> Till this fled moment. Here'twas good, in private;
> But in your public – *cavé* whilst I breathe.
> 'Fore God, my left leg'gan to have the cramp,

And I appre'nded straight away some power had struck me
With a dead palsy. [. . .]

(5.1.1–7)

The pain and his inability to speak have ended his acceptance of his imprisonment within his bedroom. No more will he be content to have his freedom restricted or to be silent. The experience in court leads him to gain his freedom by declaring himself dead and reinventing himself as a spy on the actions of others. His choice also leads him into disaster: his control over his servants is gone and Mosca acts to seize the fortune.

When Celia and Bonario come once again before the Avocatori, they enter as prisoners, not plaintiffs. Because of Volpone's final trick, however, the disillusioned Voltore begins the hearing by confessing his malpractice: providence seems to intervene on behalf of the prisoners, as Celia notes when she exclaims, 'O heav'n, how just thou art!' The opposition of Corvino and Corbaccio, who contradict Voltore, quickly brings the matter to an impasse. When Volpone secretly reveals his identity to Voltore, persuading the lawyer to perjury again, providence seems to have lost out to greed. Once more, the trial seems to swing against the innocents because of Voltore's clever performance (this time as a man possessed of a demon, 'In shape of a blue toad with a bat's wings') and the eager perjury that supports his claims. Yet the trial ends with a providential release from imprisonment. Just when all seems darkest, the newly freed Volpone reveals himself rather than lose his fortune to Mosca. The first Avocatore declares, 'The knot is now undone by miracle!' Outraged by the abuse of the courts, the Avocatori hand down a series of alarmingly harsh punishments, after rebuking Celia for daring to mention mercy. As 'a fellow of no birth or blood,' Mosca is publicly whipped and sent to life as a galley slave, the dupes undergo humiliating and painful punishments, and Volpone is 'to lie in prison, cramped with irons | Till thou be'st sick and lame indeed.' Celia is returned to her father's house with three times her dowry. While she is likely to enjoy more freedom there than she did in her father's house, she will be in an uncomfortable social position, neither married nor marriageable, which are the two possibilities open to her. Volpone, like Celia, has enjoyed a brief freedom with disastrous results, and his punishment, though milder than Mosca's, is nonetheless harsh.

Understanding Imprisonment

To this point, my reading imagines the play as one that concentrates on a prisoner's identity and circumstances because of Jonson's experiences in the months before he wrote *Volpone*. He had been imprisoned for his part in *Eastward Ho!* and threatened with mutilation (much as Corvino threatens Celia in 3.7). While isolated, he had written in desperation to powerful men who could help him and declared the injustice of the charges. The humiliation of his position is suggested by his mother's vow to poison him if he were convicted. Immediately after his release, however, he was involved, although how deeply we cannot be sure, with the Gunpowder plotters and men that he knew were condemned to horrible executions. He declared that the revelation of that plot was providential. Humiliation, isolation and physical violence turn up in his description of the prisoners in *Volpone*; moreover the play suggests that justice is found through providence more often than through human investigation. Whether Jonson meant to produce such an account of imprisonment or whether he was unconscious of what he had created, the play does have parallels to the playwright's experience.

By using that tight focus, however, I have deformed the play in important ways: its comedy is gone, the protagonist has become a victim of his circumstances instead of a clever Overreacher, and Celia has attained more subjectivity than most critics would allow her. Such a reading does not invalidate other interpretations, of course, and it does underscore the traditional ideas that the play creates a dark world, that this comedy is less comic than most, and finally that Jonson's own experiences are relevant to his plays. Specifically, my reading reminds us that while there are different kinds of incarceration, the end result for the prisoner is humiliation and limitation. Furthermore, prisons breed spies, as Jonson knew from his own experience, and the threat of violence is always present. The surveillance that a prisoner must always imagine is taking place, the inability to reach people who could help, the way that a prisoner is regarded as an object unworthy of attention – all these impediments restrict the prisoner's ability to communicate, to become a speaking subject. Nevertheless, a prisoner can maintain some autonomy. Jonson wrote letters to the powerful, Volpone invents private entertainments, and Celia insists upon her own integrity.

One should also consider such a reading within a cultural and critical context. As I suggested earlier, two possible works seem to me particularly suited for this process. Michel Foucault's *Discipline and Punish: The Birth of the Prison* affords an historical excavation into how prisons have existed, although the bulk of his work concentrates on the practices of the eighteenth and nineteenth centuries.[9] The other work is Frank Kermode's *The Sense of an Ending: Studies in the Theory of Fiction*, a work that includes a chapter about one prisoner's experiences as Kermode tries to describe the importance that time has in narrative works.[10] Both are influential works, though both have been contested. In this instance, however, I shall use them pragmatically as ways to make sense of what happens when the play describes prisons and punishments: what do these critical works suggest about Jonson and *Volpone,* and what might Jonson and *Volpone* suggest about them?

The earlier sections of Foucault's book are of particular interest because he uses those to offer an account of how punishment and prisons worked before the eighteenth and nineteenth centuries, which brought the introduction of 'the almost universal adoption of the jury system, the definition of the essentially corrective character of the penalty and the tendency, which has become increasingly marked since the nineteenth century, to adapt punishment to the individual offender' (7–8). In contrast, incarceration during the early modern period was principally for those (like Jonson) who were awaiting trial or who needed to settle a debt before being released. Prison was not so widely used for punishment as were corporal punishments that marked the guilty prisoner's crime upon his body. One might consider the brand that Jonson had received as punishment for killing Gabriel Spencer in his 1598 duel or the 1605 threat to slit his ears and nose that so appalled his mother. The thumb brand meant the Jonson lived the rest of his life, quite literally, as a marked man. Because Jonson and Chapman were charged with putting on a play that mutilated the state's reputation, they would themselves be mutilated. In Jonson's own life, the prisoner's body provides proof of the crime with each moment of his existence.

Foucault also argues that torture used in interrogation is also part of the ceremony that leads to the public punishment of the prisoner's body. Thus the torture inflicted on Guy Fawkes was not extraordinary, but a part of a standard investigation procedure necessary to produce the confession that would lead to the punishment for treason. When Fawkes and his confederates were punished by being hanged, drawn, and quartered, the punishment was considered equivalent to their crime. They had attempted to destroy the state, so in turn their bodies were destroyed, torn to bits. Yet when one turns to *Volpone* the principal character threatened with mutilation is Celia. Today we find Corvino's threats distasteful and hyperbolic, so we are amused by Celia when she calls his bluff and tells him to go ahead and act. If Foucault is correct, however, the point of that scene may be that Corvino has assumed the role of the state: his threats are not hyperbolic. Celia's defiance is less a dismissal of him as a blowhard than an expression of her certainty that she is innocent. The concluding punishments that strike us as unduly harsh also make more sense in Foucault's terms since they attempt to replicate the men's crimes on their bodies. Volpone tried to cheat people by pretending to be old and crippled, so the state will see to it that he actually becomes crippled. Mosca tried to take away people's freedom, so he is enslaved.

Just as important as marking the prisoner's body, Foucault suggests, was the public nature of punishment: punishment was a sort of ceremony in which the public saw the power of the ruler and the ruler's government. In later systems, that public punishment becomes replaced by incarceration and surveillance. Because Foucault is particularly interested in the way that power operates in social relationships, he also notes that these early modern displays of punishments were in significant ways like a performance in a theatre. After all, the audience's interpretation of that performance might be different from what the government intended. Rather than having the public watch the state's power and loathe those who broke the state's laws, such public performances might actually stir up sympathy for the criminal and hostility to the state. Yet Corvino is sure of how the audience will react to his public exposure as a wittol, a man who seeks to prostitute his own wife: they will pelt his eyes out with stinking fish. In Jonson's case, the threat of having his ears and nose slit was a proclamation of his guilt to the public The horror of that proposed punishment led his mother to consider killing her son and committing suicide because her son's slit nose and ears would forever testify to his guilt, although he always insisted on his innocence.

While acknowledging that Foucault's analysis of how torture and mutilation operate fits well with the play, one might also question Foucault's analysis of surveillance. He argues that it is a feature of prisons (and indeed of all carceral establishments, including hospitals and schools) after the eighteenth century. Jonson's bitter denunciation of prison spies and *Volpone*'s emphasis on how the characters are watched suggests that surveillance was also a feature of the seventeenth-century world. One might argue, however, that the people most aware of surveillance were those like Jonson who had undergone imprisonment. While the later culture may have institutionalized the practice of surveillance in carceral settings, *Volpone* shows clearly that for a prisoner there is never a sense of privacy. The play also suggests a feature of the prisoner's existence about which Foucault says little: a prisoner who believes himself innocent must trust in providence because human error is the reason that he is imprisoned in the first place. In short, when one wants to investigate how imprisonment alters a person's identity, Foucault's emphasis on the system offers relatively little help.

The final chapter in Kermode's *The Sense of an Ending* is useful and suggestive when one considers the way that the experience of imprisonment alters a human being, whether it be Ben Jonson, the fictional Volpone and Celia, or the subject of Kermode's essay: a British officer who was a prisoner of war. The book is a collection of lectures that Kermode gave in which he speculates about fiction-making and time.

In it he argues, 'It is not expected of critics as it is of poets that they should help us to make sense of our lives; they are bound only to attempt the lesser feat of making sense of the ways we try to make sense of our lives'(3). For Kermode, that process involves a study of how individuals use language to make fictions that help us handle the sense of an ending, both of our own mortality and of the world's apocalypse. Having established that the condition of humanity is a bleak one, he remarks: 'To be alone and poor is, in a sense, everyone's fate; but some people have been alone and poor in a very literal sense, as most of us have not; and in solitary confinement some of them have tested the gaiety of language as a means of projecting their humanity on a hostile environment' (156). He then explores the experience of Christopher Burney who was held in solitary confinement when he was captured in France by the Nazis. As Burney sat alone, his situation altered his understanding of the world. For example, 'the man in the next cell tried to communicate by knocking on the wall' (157), but Burney rejected him. Instead he preferred his own thoughts, for 'In prison he found himself, paradoxically free, within the limits set by hunger and 'the animal lust to roam' [...] to impose his humanity on the world' (157). Much of his time was spent considering the universe and his position in it: Kermode characterizes this contemplation as fiction-making, but adds that Burney made a second sort of fiction for Gestapo interrogators, who might beat him. His contemplation took him through the texts he had studied in school, family tales, and the Biblical passages that he knew: he considered death, humanity, and God. Among the fictions that Burney invents for himself is the sense of an ending. To carry out his contemplations, as Kermode points out, Burney made a sort of clock to measure the passage of time. He resolves that "One thing is out of the question. I cannot still be here at Christmas [...]. This was an axiom" (161), but when Christmas came, he began his calculations anew with a new 'definite' ending.

When prisoners write about imprisonment from experience, what they (Burney and Jonson) produce is not always what one might expect. Imprisonment highlights the pleasures of language, the fictions that one knows and the fictions that one makes. Jonson was a fine playwright before imprisonment, but it was after his third serious brush with the law that he produced his greatest plays. The pleasures of communicating with another person were, for Burney, less exhilarating than the pleasure of managing his thoughts, although awareness of surveillance may have much to do with his decision to shun the person who knocked on his wall. Imprisonment is attended by physical suffering and surveillance, whether by the spies who were set on Jonson or the interrogators who beat Burney. The prisoner's account of the world must make allowance for fictions created to please these spies. Time is a constant presence, and if time keeping is impossible, one invents a clock. Finally, one must make room for providence, for the belief that one will be home by Christmas or that a great man might listen to a bricklayer turned actor turned playwright.

In the play *Volpone,* traces of these concerns remain. The play's structure is tightly built to fit in a single day, for in this play, as in all of Jonson's major works, time is a constant concern. Both Volpone and Celia endure being watched and both face pain. Both withdraw from others, Celia into her belief in the necessity of her own virtue and Volpone into his pretence of death. Volpone spins out his isolation in speeches of wonderfully hyperbolic verse, while Celia enjoys the rodomontade of the mountebank and speaks for herself with language that is eloquent, if brief. The chief difference would seem to be what each character thinks of providence. For Volpone, the man who chooses imprisonment, providence is a force to be evaded. For Celia, like Burney, like Jonson, providence is the sole hope of escape.

The point of investigating imprisonment in *Volpone* is not to see how it might have been affected by Jonson's experiences, of course, nor to generalize about how the experience alters one's perception of the world. It is simply, as Kermode suggests, 'a way of making sense of the ways we try to make sense of our lives.' We make up a fiction about the making up of fiction. Whether one prefers Foucault to Kermode or Jonson's biography or the text of the play itself, the important part of the process is not to answer questions for others, but to raise them for ourselves, because in this activity we find a way into the text that allows each of us to make some part of it our own.

Notes

1   David Riggs, *Ben Jonson: A Life* (Cambridge, Mass.: Harvard University Press, 1989), 141; a similar argument is made in W. David Kay's *Ben Jonson: A Literary Life* (London: Macmillan, 1995). The basic standard is, of course, Herford and the Simpsons' *Collected Works* (Oxford: Clarendon, 1925–1952), cited as H&S. Riggs and Kay have excellent and accessible biographies that incorporate research done after H&S.

2   My source for the arrest record is principally Herford and the Simpsons. Jonson's further encounters with authority included:

> 1610: 8 February, the Venetian Ambassador reports that Jonson's new play *Epicoene* has been suppressed because it mocks Lady Arbella Stuart.
> 1616: 2 February, James I awards Jonson a royal pension of 100 marks per annum, for life, "divers good considerations us att this present especially moving."
> 1623: January, trouble at court over Jonson's satire of George Wither in *Time Vindicated.*
> 1624: January, Jonson's *Neptune's Triumph* cancelled lest it offend Spanish Ambassador.

1626: Robert Clarke files charges against Jonson for debt.

1627: Nathanaell Field (probably not the actor) files charges against Jonson for debt.

1628: 26 October, Privy Council questions Jonson about Buckingham's death and certain verses in praise of the assassin. Jonson denies writing the verses, which were by Zouch Townley, but says he had given Townley a dagger.

1629: 15 January, Peter Johnson files charges against Jonson for debt.

1630: 17 May, Richard Milward files charges against Jonson for debt.

1633: 7 May, Jonson is told his play *Tale of a Tub* cannot be licensed unless he removes attack on Inigo Jones. He agrees, but actually changes little, infuriating Jones.

3   David Kay points out that no evidence exists that Wright converted Jonson, although Wright is the only priest that Jonson certainly knew since he gave Wright a dedicatory poem for Wright's book *The Passions of the Mind*.

4   I would disagree with both Paul Durst and Barbara de Luna in their analyses of Jonson's role in the Gunpowder Plot simply because I do not think Jonson was a long-time agent or that De Luna's reading of *Catiline* effectively explains events. For accounts of the Gunpowder Plot, there is an embarrassment of riches. The official government account is *The King's Book* (London, 1605) and the standard history is S. R. Gardiner's account, both in *The History of England* (1883) and in *What the Gunpowder Plot Was* (1897); all of these are firmly anti-Catholic. A corrective to Gardiner is John Gerard's *What Was the Gunpowder Plot?* (1897), which is deeply sympathetic to the conspirators. The best lay histories that I have found are Paul Durst, *Intended Treason* (pro-Gardiner, but suspicious of Robert Cecil's role), Antonia Fraser, *Faith and Treason* (very detailed, sympathetic to the conspirators). Finally, anyone concerned with Jonson's attitude toward the Gunpowder Plot owes a debt to Barbara de Luna's *Jonson's Romish Plot*, although I interpret the evidence very differently. Of some use, also, is Eric Linklater's *Ben Jonson and King James* (London and New York: Jonathan Cape, 1931), especially chapter eight, 144–58.

5   See my article, 'Jonson and the Gunpowder Plot.' *Ben Jonson Journal* 5 (1999): 249–52. My essay in *Solon and Thespis,* ed. Dennis Kezar (South Bend, Ind.: Notre Dame Press, 2007), develops a reading of the play as a response to the Gunpowder Plot.

6   Richard Broughton's *English Protestants Plea and Petition for English Preists [sic] and Papists* (1621, STC 3895.5 and 3895.7), 59. To the best of my knowledge, no one has previously argued that Jonson was ultimately successful in his efforts to locate the unnamed priest.

7   It is allusions to "equivocation" that allow scholars to date *Macbeth* after 1606. See Kenneth Muir's Arden edition of *Macbeth*, xv–xviii for an account of Shakespeare and the Gunpowder Plot.

8   My essay in *Solon and Thespis* discusses the Avocatori at length.

9   Michel Foucault, *Discipline and Punish*, trans. Alan Sheridan (New York: Pantheon Books, 1977). This edition is the first English translation of *Surveiller et punir* (Paris: Gallimard, 1975); Vintage issued a paperback edition in 1977 and a second edition in 1995.

10 Frank Kermode, *The Sense of an Ending: Studies in the Theory of Fiction* (New York: Oxford University Press, 1967). Published in both hardback and paperback, the work was re-issued by Oxford in 2000.

CHAPTER SEVEN

New Directions: Age and Ageing in *Volpone*

Stella Achilleos

Corbaccio. *Excellent, excellent; sure I shall outlast him!*
This makes me young again, a score of years.
(Volpone, I.iv.55–56)¹

In the lines that immediately precede the words quoted above, Mosca
assures Corbaccio that bed-ridden Volpone has reached the final stage
of a fatal apoplexy, asserting that he 'Hath lost his feeling, and hath left
to snort; | You hardly can perceive him that he breathes' (I.iv.53–54).
The fantasy of rejuvenation, expressed in the lines so gleefully spoken
by Corbaccio in response to Mosca's words, points to an intriguing
preoccupation with age and ageing that pervades Jonson's play at many
different levels. The theme is no doubt most prominently found in
Volpone's impersonation of the role of the wealthy but childless old
man – a key feature in the trick devised by him and his parasite Mosca
in order to trap the three dupes who aspire to his fortune – but the play
contains various other points of reference associated with senescence.
As I would like to argue in this chapter, drawing from a large store of
images and perceptions of old age found in classical literature as well as
in early modern culture, *Volpone* provides an exploration of senescence
that engages with a much broader set of social and cultural anxieties
concerning age and ageing in the early modern period. Concentrating
in particular on the characters of Volpone and Corbaccio, this discussion
aims to bring Jonson's play into dialogue with his culture's assumptions
about senescence and to point to the ways in which the study of this
theme allows us to find a new set of insights, both into the play itself
as well as into that broader set of assumptions.

Rather surprisingly, despite the apparent centrality of age and ageing in *Volpone*, Jonson's exploration of this theme has so far been largely

overlooked.[2] This can perhaps be seen as a symptom of a more general neglect of this category that has only recently begun to receive sustained consideration by scholars. The last few years have indeed witnessed an explosion in the amount of research on the social, cultural and political implications of old age, with scholars from various disciplines within the humanities as well as the social sciences drawing attention to how 'age' functions as a social and cultural, rather than a simply biological category, and pointing to the ways in which it participates in a much broader system of cultural values and representations that are intricately intertwined with the formation of subjectivity.[3] Yet, for many years in the past the study of this topic had remained at the margins of critical concerns.[4] Kathleen Woodward, among others, has addressed this issue as symptomatic of a much wider set of social and cultural attitudes towards old age and ageing in the West that reflect a largely persistent gerontophobia. Analysing people's frequently silent response to her own scholarly preoccupation with ageing, she comments that 'this silence all too often speaks of a suspicion that the subject of aging is, simply, morbid.'[5] The inadequate attention previously paid to this subject has thus been read as a sign of a broader discomfort with senescence that appears to have characterized Western societies, and a tendency to deny and repress its consideration. 'Old age is a time in our lives about which many of us feel anxiety and fear', Woodward points out, to add that 'the symptoms of these feelings of apprehension are denial and repression of the very subject of aging and old age.' But, she further observes, far from being a strictly personal issue, the fear of old age is deeply interlinked with the discursive ways in which that experience has often been constructed through various forms of representation. 'Our culture's representations of aging are predominantly negative and thus are inextricably linked to our personal anxieties – for ourselves and for others.'[6]

Indeed, representations of old age in Western culture have been largely embedded in an overwhelmingly negative set of stereotypes, while age, just like various other categories (most notably gender, race and class), seems to have undergone a process of hierarchical organization whereby youth has been valorized at the expense of senescence. Far from being a modern phenomenon of course, the privileging of youth over age appears to have been long-ingrained in the culture of the West. In his *History of Old Age*, George Minois traces in early modern representations of old age in art and literature a 'cult of youth' that often countenanced senescence with horror and disgust. 'The Renaissance,' he comments,

> like every time of renewal and rebirth, celebrated youth, the fullness of life, beauty and novelty. It abhorred everything that

presaged decline, decrepitude and death . . . The unprecedented
violence of attacks against old age in the sixteenth century was
derived from the impotent rage of a generation which worshipped
youth and beauty.[7]

Yet, while pointing to the persistent vilification of senescence in various
forms of representation, Minois also addresses a certain paradox in the
role ascribed to the old in the early modern world: by 'flagrant contradiction' to this negative conception of old age, old people were often
found in various places of authority in society and politics, as well as the
arts. 'The Renaissance,' he argues, 'proclaimed its execration of the old
through its humanists, while simultaneously giving them even greater
responsibility and conferring the highest honours on them.'[8]

More recent scholarship has paid considerable attention to this
ambiguity, suggesting how the early modern period in fact reveals a
bewilderingly varied and often contradictory set of perceptions about
old age and ageing. On the one hand, various accounts provide a fairly
positive image of senescence that often reproduces the figure found in
classical literature of the wise *senex*, who maintains his intellectual
capacities despite any physical decline, and is placed in a position of
esteemed authority for his experience and wisdom. Cicero's widely-
disseminated *De Senectute*, a text that valorizes the benefits of old age,
highlighting the useful role men of advanced years may have in state
affairs, offered the *locus classicus* for such treatments. On the other hand
though, a great number of texts focus on a fairly grim image of old age
as a period of physical, as well as mental decline, infirmity and power-
lessness. Evoking the narrative of inevitable degradation and decay
drawn in the Ages of Man schema (found in classical sources like
Hippocrates and Aristotle, but also in numerous reconfigurations of the
topos in the Middle Ages and the Renaissance), Jacques's dreary description of old age in Shakespeare's *As You Like It* as 'a second childishness
and mere oblivion, | *Sans* teeth, *sans* eyes, *sans* taste, *sans* everything'
(II.vii.166–67)[9] reflects the more widespread belief that senescence brought
one back to a condition of complete helplessness and dependency.

As I would like to argue in this chapter, Jonson's play appropriates
and transforms a number of the negative stereotypes associated with
age and ageing in the early modern period. Indeed, drawing on a
bewilderingly wide range of sources, senility is presented in all its
dreaded aspects, and the processes of ageing in many ways provide the
object of ridicule and satiric laughter in *Volpone*. Yet, at the same time as
it burlesques senescence, the text, I suggest, provides an exploration of
the fears and anxieties related with that condition. At many different
levels, Jonson's play may be said to reflect his culture's obsession with

youth and its anxiety concerning the ravages of time on human nature. The desire for rejuvenation may no doubt be found in various references or allusions made in the text to alchemy and the philosopher's stone, that is evoked not only in its purported capacity to turn base metals into gold but also in terms of its alleged ability to function as an elixir of life that could be used to restore youth and achieve immortality. This concept is clearly called up during Volpone's performance as Scoto of Mantua in the second Act, where his advertisement of his 'precious liquor' (II.ii.79) as a 'blessed *unguento*, [a] rare | extraction, that hath only power to disperse all malignant | humours that proceed either of hot, cold, moist, or windy | causes' (II. ii. 97–100), evokes descriptions of the philosopher's stone found in texts like Paracelsus's *De Lapide Philosophorum* and *De Tinctura Physicorum*:

> . . . it is a medicine blessed by God, which is not revealed to everyone. For it is far superior to the stinking medicines which a sluggish Doctor keeps in his toga and filters through a double hat band or a dunce's cap [. . .] Indeed, this blessed medicine is three times stronger and better for any illness, whatever its name, than all the drugs you have ever seen.[10]

Scoto likewise praises his 'precious liquor' as a universal medicine, the capacity of which in fact supersedes all previous attempts to find a definitive cure for diseases, while further promising – as one of the songs delivered by Nano suggests, inviting those who 'would last long, list to my song, | Make no more coil, but buy of this oil' (II.ii.197–98) – to restore not only health, but also beauty, youth and virility:

> Would you ever be fair? and young?
> Stout of teeth? and strong of tongue?
> Tart of palate? quick of ear?
> Sharp of sight? of nostril clear?
> Moist of hand? and light of foot?
> Or I will come nearer to't,
> Would you live free from all diseases?
> Do the act your mistress pleases,
> Yet fright all aches from your bones?
> Here's a med'cine from the nones.

(II.ii.199–208)

The philosopher's stone – in its double capacity to transmute base metals into gold and old age into youth – provides a trope that registers a fascinating link between the desire for gold and the desire for rejuvenation that is compellingly explored by Jonson in the character of Corbaccio. Corbaccio, who like the other two principal dupes, Voltore and Corvino, visits Volpone with the hope of becoming his heir, is ironically a decrepit old man himself. Spoken with a fair amount of contempt and disgust, the lines used by Mosca to make reference to Corbaccio immediately before his first entrance in Act I Scene iv, prepare the audience for the extent of his decrepitude:

> [...] Now shall we see
> A wretch who is indeed more impotent
> Than this can feign to be, yet hopes to hop
> Over his grave.
>
> (2–5)

The infirmity of Corbaccio's condition is emphasized in this scene by his deafness. This element produces an immensely comic effect as Corbaccio becomes alarmed, mishearing Mosca's words and thinking that Volpone may have recovered from his illness:

> *Corbaccio.*　　　　　　How does our patron?
> *Mosca.* Troth, as he did, sir; no amends.
> *Corbaccio.* [*Mishearing*] What! mends he?
> *Mosca.* [*Loudly*] No, sir: he is rather worse.
>
> (I.iv.6–8)

The desire of such a frail old man to become Volpone's heir is of course at best ludicrous, and has been read as a sign of the character's overarching avarice. Like Voltore and Corvino, Corbaccio has been read within the context of Jonson's deriding satire of human folly and, in particular, of the vices of greed and hypocrisy. Indeed, the three dupes seem to be very much alike in this respect as to a great extent they all seem to be drawn to the trap set up for them by Volpone and Mosca, due to their avaricious desire to inherit his wealth. Volpone's comment following Corbaccio's exit in Act I, Scene iv, 'What a rare punishment | Is avarice to itself!' (I.iv.142–43), properly reflects on the situation of all three of them. In David Bevington's words, 'These three craven worldlings clearly deserve what they get. Their names – Voltore the vulture, Corbaccio the crow, Corvino the raven – all point to their being carrion birds, disgusting in their alacrity to feed on decaying human flesh.'[11]

Yet, while the predatory drive of these characters is undeniable, the tendency to read them merely as satirical butts whose actions are all dominated by the same avaricious impulse often served in the past to reduce them to the level of caricatures, or mere vehicles for Jonson to instruct his audience and rebuke moral depravity. In a reading that offers, according to Anne Barton, 'a long overdue corrective to the view that Jonson was a man only capable, even in his greatest comedies, of caricature',[12] John Creaser suggests that while greed may be the most apparent force governing the actions of Jonson's characters in *Volpone*, they may in fact be attributed with a much greater degree of individual complexity than previously granted to them. Corvino's avaricious impulse, for instance, may be seen as 'just part of a complex tormented nature', while the source of his torments may be found in 'a feeling of insecurity and inferiority' that results in an 'unstable mixture of aggressiveness and timidity' and extreme apprehension of public mortification.[13]

Likewise, Jonson's exploration of the elements of age and ageing, I suggest, provides an element that allows us to look beyond the strictly moralizing strain of *Volpone* and invest the character of Corbaccio, as well as Volpone, with a greater sense of individual complexity that looks beyond their predatory subjectivities. Indeed, Corbaccio's ludicrous desire to become Volpone's heir seems to be triggered not simply by greed, but by a desperate attempt to recapture youth. His tenacious hope to inherit Volpone gives him a strangely powerful hold on life. The thrilled excitement expressed in the remark that 'sure I shall outlast him! | This makes me young again, a score of years' (I.iv.55–56), suggests that the mere fantasy of outliving Volpone and inheriting his fortune functions for Corbaccio as an elixir of life, an alchemical essence the attributes of which make him feel rejuvenated, just as the 'bag of bright *chequins*' (I.iv.69) brought by Corbaccio as a gift is said by Mosca to have the ability to recover Volpone:

> Mosca. [*Taking the bag.*]   Yea, marry, sir!
>   This is true physic, this your sacred medicine;
>   No talk of opiates to this great elixir.

> (I.iv.70–72)

The attempt to invert the natural course of time and recapture youth seems to be at least as important to Corbaccio as the desire to acquire Volpone's wealth. Indeed, the two projects seem to be intricately intertwined, and Corbaccio's quest for Volpone's fortune may be seen not simply as an end in itself, but as a means to rejuvenation, the earnest desire for which is reiterated by Corbaccio before his exit in this scene: 'I may ha' my youth restored to me, why not?' (I.iv.129).

Absurd as it may be, Corbaccio's structural position as Volpone's heir acquires a special significance in light of this regressive attempt to recapture youth. In his assumption of the role of the heir, Corbaccio seems to displace his own fears of ageing and death on Volpone, as the structural relation formed between the two characters is largely based on the supposition that Volpone is going to die first. Mosca's proposal that Corbaccio disinherit his biological son and 'frame a will whereto you shall inscribe | My master your sole heir' (I.iv.94–95), so as to ingratiate himself with Volpone who 'cannot be so stupid, or stone dead', in Mosca's words, 'But out of conscience and mere gratitude' (I.iv.107–08) will in return pronounce Corbaccio his own heir, is similarly based on the old man's conviction that Volpone is going to die first. Mosca, a truly acute reader of those around him, appears to be fully aware of Corbaccio's earnest desire to deny his own senile condition and outlive Volpone, and skilfully touches upon this chord in order to convince him to proceed with the plan:

> *Mosca.* Which, when he hath done, sir–
> *Corbaccio.*   Published me his heir?
> *Mosca.* And you so certain to survive him–
> *Corbaccio.*   Ay.
> *Mosca.* Being so lusty a man–
> *Corbaccio.*   'Tis true.
> *Mosca.*   Yes, sir–
>
>   (I.iv.112–14)

Mosca's heavily ironic reference to Corbaccio as a 'lusty man' who will surely outlive Volpone clearly manipulates the old man's desire to see himself as young and vigorous.

Corbaccio's instant affirmation of this description of himself highlights his denial of his old age and his indulgence in a self-aggrandizing fantasy of youthful vigour and creative energy. This is further emphasized by his equally illusory belief in the generative powers of his intellect, as he insists in claiming that each of the ideas presented by Mosca are in fact his own 'inventions':

> *Corbaccio.*   This plot
>   Did I think on before.
> *Mosca.*   I do believe it.
> *Corbaccio.* Do you not believe it?
> *Mosca.*   Yes, sir.
> *Corbaccio.*   Mine own project.
>
>   (I.iv.109–11)

Corbaccio's self-enhancing fantasies of youthful vigour are contemptuously satirized by Volpone who comments on the futility of the old man's attempt to rejuvenate himself. Finding in the classical myth of Aeson – Jason's father who had his youth restored through the use of magic by Medea, Jason's wife – a template that only serves to foster delusions, Volpone launches a tirade against Corbaccio's attempt to deny his old age and recapture youth. Pointing to a split between myth and reality, this treatment of the story of Aeson lays emphasis on the actual irreversibility of the process of ageing:

> [. . .] Nay, here was one
> Is now gone home, that wishes to live longer!
> Feels not his gout, nor palsy; feigns himself
> Younger by scores of years; flatters his age
> With confident belying it; hopes he may
> With charms, like Aeson, have his youth restored;
> And with these thoughts so battens, as if fate
> Would be as easily cheated on as he,
> And all turns air!
>
> (I.iv.151–59)

In the lines that precede this contemptuous outburst against Corbaccio, Volpone reflects on old age as a loathsome condition, full of suffering and degradation. Burdened by physical and mental decline, senescence according to Volpone's description renders life so insufferable that it is ultimately not worth living. From this perspective, death is seen as welcome release from a condition of intolerable misery that is countenanced by Volpone with an equal amount of contempt and disgust:

> So many cares, so many maladies,
> So many fears attending on old age;
> Yea, death so often called on, as no wish
> Can be more frequent with 'em. Their limbs faint,
> Their senses dull, their seeing, hearing, going,
> All dead before them; yea, their very teeth,
> Their instruments of eating, failing them:
> Yet this reckoned life! [. . .]
>
> (I.iv.144–51)

It has been noted that this description makes a close allusion to Juvenal's *Satire* X and its remark on the unending miseries of senescence, but also to those words of Pliny the Elder in his *Naturalis Historia* that make reference to the dreadful wretchedness of old age as a condition that renders a short life a clearly much more preferable course:

> [Old age] remains to be tormented, [with] all the kinds of dangers, all the diseases, all the fears, all the anxieties, with death so often invoked that this is the commonest of prayers [. . .] The senses

grow dull, the limbs are numb, sight, hearing, gait, even the teeth and ailment organs die before we do, and yet this period is reckoned a portion of life!'.(Book VII, 167–69)[14]

At the same time though, Volpone's treatment of old age evokes a much larger tradition of classical texts that typified senescence as a progressively incurable disease. An example may be found in the writings of the fifth-century BC Greek physician Hippocrates, who is credited with the introduction of the theory of humours. According to this theory, physical as well as mental health depended on the right mixture of the four bodily fluids, or humours (blood, phlegm, yellow bile and black bile), which corresponded to the four cosmic elements: air (hot and moist), water (cold and moist), fire (hot and dry) and earth (cold and dry). An imbalance in the combination of the humours, caused, for instance, by the predominance or deficit of one of them, was accordingly considered to lead to disease.

Ageing was defined as a gradually debilitating process caused by the irreversible cooling of the body and the loss of that heat that was thought to be essential for the balanced mixture of the humours. 'By implication,' Karen Cokayne notes, 'old age would therefore be classified as an illness, and indeed a number of people in antiquity considered old age to be a chronic, incurable and progressive disease, from Aristotle (fourth century BC) [. . .] to Seneca (first century AD).'[15] This illness is often described in the Hippocratic corpus in terms of various symptoms that mark the gradual enervation of the body. An impressively large store of symptoms, for instance, is provided in the *Aphorisms*:

> Old men suffer from difficulty of breathing, cararrh accompanied by coughing, strangury, difficult micturition, pains at the joints, kidney disease, dizziness, apoplexy, cachexia, pruritus of the whole body, sleeplessness, watery discharges from bowels, eyes, and nostrils, dullness of sight, cataract, hardness of hearing.[16]

In *De Morbis*, also, Hippocrates makes reference to a pain that suddenly hits the head, whereby the person's 'voice is cut off [. . .], and he snores [. . .], and his mouth gapes wide open [. . .]: and if someone calls him, or moves him, he only sighs, but is not aware of anything.'[17] Such symptoms would point to the final stage in Hippocrates's scheme of the seven Ages of Man, appropriated among various others by Shakespeare in Jacques's speech on the seven ages of man in *As You Like It* that I cited earlier in this essay.

Volpone demonstrates his familiarity with the theory of humours in Act II Scene ii where, as Scoto of Mantua, he advertises his oil's capacity to cure 'all malignant humours that proceed either hot, cold, moist, or windy causes' (98–99). Indeed, the long list of diseases he enumerates there might well have been borrowed from such medical treatises as those found in the Hippocratic corpus or in the writings of the second-century AD Greek physician Galen, who further developed the theory of humours and who is set in Nano's song side by side with Hippocrates. In its characteristically exaggerated praise of the purportedly miraculous effects of Scoto's medicinal art, the song lauds the mountebank's unguent as a medicinal triumph that supersedes by far both of the Greek physicians' laborious attempts to find cures for diseases:

> Had old Hippocrates, or Galen,
> That to their books put med'cines all in,
> But known this secret, they had never
> (Of which they will be guilty ever)
> Been murderers of so much paper,
> Or wasted many a hurtles taper;

(II.ii.123–28)

Volpone's prolonged performance as Scoto of Mantua may no doubt be said to burlesque cure, just like his impersonation of the dying old man earlier in the play – a performance that also makes use of numerous elements from his knowledge of classical medical treatises – may be said to burlesque the symptoms of disease. His trick can only be successful if all would-be inheritors, 'Vulture, kite, | Raven, and gorcrow, all my birds of prey' (I.ii.88–89), as he says, 'think me turning carcass' (I.ii.90), and his performance of the role is very much based on the successful enactment of various symptoms of illness. In lines that parody the conventional invocation to gods or the muses, he thus prepares for the visit of the first dupe, Voltore, by calling upon:

> . . . my feigned cough, my phthisic, and my gout,
> My apoplexy, palsy, and catarrhs,
> Help, with your forced functions, this my posture,
> Wherein this three year I have milked their hopes.
> He comes; I hear him [*He coughs*] Uh! uh! uh!
> uh! O–

(I.ii.125–29)

Volpone's symptoms are also described by Mosca in Act I Scene iv, where he provides a detailed report of Volpone's condition to the eagerly-awaiting Corbaccio. As Brian Parker points out, each of the symptoms described here is often burlesqued in productions of the play:[18]

> *Corbaccio.* [. . .] How does his apoplex?
> Is that strong on him still?
> *Mosca.*   Most violent.
> His speech is broken, and his eyes are set,
> His face drawn longer than 'twas wont.
>
> > (I.iv.36–39)

This is followed by a description of Volpone's mouth as 'ever gaping, and his eyelids hang' (42). Further, 'A freezing numbness stiffens all his joints, | And makes the colour of his flesh like lead' (43–44), while 'His pulse beats slow and dull' (45). Mosca finally assures Corbaccio that from Volpone's brain 'Flows a cold sweat, with a continual rheum | Forth the resolved corners of his eyes' (I.iv.48–49), while his head is 'past the scotomy' (I.iv.52). If not from classical sources, Jonson's audience would no doubt have been familiar with such long lists of symptoms as signs of a diseased man's upcoming death from similar kinds of catalogues that appeared in various English sources from the Middle Ages onwards, such as that found in *Fasciculus Morum*, a fourteenth-century preacher's handbook, that describes the upcoming end as a moment,

> when my eye mists and my hearing fails and my nose goes cold and my tongue curls back and my face falls in and my lips blacken and my mouth gapes and my spittle runs and my hair stands on end and my heart trembles and my hands shake and my feet go stiff.[19]

Rosemary Horrox notes that such lists would be used for medical purposes in order to identify the approach of death (since diseases, at least in the Middle Ages, were hardly defined as identifiable entities), but also, as the list in *Fasciculus Morum* probably indicates, for moralizing purposes to prompt the sinner to contemplate on death and thus to make the appropriate spiritual preparation before the arrival of that moment – the extract quoted above from *Fasciculus Morum* notably ends with a warning that it may be too late to attempt to make that spiritual preparation if the symptoms described have already arrived: 'All too late, all too late | When the bier is at the gate'.[20] Nina Taunton also notes that the early modern period saw 'a deluge of printed matter on the need for the old to sublimate the weakening of the physical self by strengthening the mind and spirit'.[21]

It is no doubt part of the element of farce in the play, to find that, while Volpone merely counterfeits many of the symptoms of illness and upcoming death, Corbaccio who visits him desiring to be his heir has some of the symptoms for real. This is emphasized by his characteristic deafness, an element clearly identified both in Hippocrates's *Aphorisms* as well as in *Fasciculus Morum* as one of the warning symptoms. A further example may be found in Act I Scene iv:

> *Mosca.*   Sir,
>   He has no faith in physic.
> *Corbaccio.*   Say you? Say you?
> *Mosca.*   He has no faith in physic. He does think
>   Most of your doctors are the greater danger,
>   And worse disease t'escape. I often have
>   Heard him protest that your physician
>   Should never be his heir.
> *Corbaccio.*   Not I his heir?
>
> (I.iv.18–24)

This follows Corbaccio's suggestion that Volpone take the opiate he has brought, purportedly 'but to make him sleep' (I.iv.17). Far from embarking on any kind of spiritual preparation as prescribed in texts like *Fasciculus Morum*, Corbaccio seems to be prepared to go as far as murder in order to satisfy his ambitions. Ridiculously ineffective as his attempt may be, this design renders him particularly appalling. His readiness to disinherit his son and absurdly install Volpone as his heir may be said to further contribute to this appreciation of the character.

Bringing a disruption of the parental and filial bond, Corbaccio's disinheritance of Bonario may be said to point to a broader theme in the play, namely an 'unnatural' breaking of family relations, that has largely been put down to the characters' overwhelming tenacity of greed. 'Gold in Venice "unnaturally" breaks bonds,' Brian Parker points out, as all families in the play 'are distorted by greed [...] In such a society, the very word "family" degenerates from its primary meaning of a blood bond to the secondary one of economic household.'[22] 'I know not how to lend it any thought,' Bonario comments, 'My father should be so unnatural' (III.ii.53–54). Quite importantly, Corbaccio's 'unnatural' repudiation of his son may further be said to disrupt the intergenerational cycle of mutual duty and care-giving that was prescribed time and again in various early modern sources as essential for the preservation of a harmonious bond in parental and filial relations – indeed, the idea that by installing Volpone as his heir, Corbaccio 'multiplie[s]' (I.iv.118) the good on his son ultimately parodies the model provided in this prescriptive literature. As this example from Castiglione's *The Book of the Courtier* suggests, this model, that in many ways involved issues of material exchange and inheritance, defined the bond between parents and children in terms of a reciprocation of benefits:

> [T]hrough the meanes of this felowship of male and female [nature] bringeth furth children, that restore the received benifites in their childhood to their fathers in their olde dayes, in that they nourishe them [...] whereby nature (as it were) tourning her about in a circle, fulfilleth an everlastingnesse, and in this wise geveth an immortalitie to mortall men.[23]

In another example from Geoffrey Whitney's 1586 emblem *Gratiam referendam*, discussed by Philip D. Collington alongside this extract from Castiglione, parents are prompted 'to imitate the stork that diligently feeds its young.'[24] By the same token, children were expected to respect and obey the authority of parents, and to repay those benefits received by supporting and caring for them in their old age.

While Corbaccio's repudiation of Bonario provides an example where the father parodically disrupts this intergenerational cycle of reciprocity, the literature of this period very often points to the flip side as well, where disruption of this model is caused by children that challenge the authority of senescent parents and fail or refuse to provide the expected respect, obedience and support. As Nina Taunton comments, even though numerous early modern manuals prescribed that the authority of the elderly should be respected,

> their manifestation in fiction and sometimes non-fiction is much more complex and fraught with ambiguity. Sometimes they appear as weakened in mind and body, lacking the respect of the younger generation, either humiliatingly dependent on their children or ridiculed for attempting to hide their age and weakness, sometimes as blocking figures (in drama particularly), unbending and formidable bastions of authority who must be challenged by the young.[25]

Shakespeare's *King Lear*, a text that has received considerable attention in recent years for its representation of old age,[26] is a source that provides a powerful dramatization of both sides of this issue. Having undeservedly repudiated and disinherited Cordelia for what he perceived to be a disruption of her filial duty towards him, Lear is after his transfer of land and property to Goneril and Regan, ironically met with the ingratitude of the two elder daughters. No longer in possession of property, Lear ultimately comes to depend entirely on the mercy of his two daughters who refuse, however, to acknowledge his subsequent claims to authority.[27] As Nina Taunton further points out, in the prescriptive literature of the period 'those who had property were urged not to transfer it to their children in their lifetime in order to avoid dependency upon them and their kindness, since there is nothing as hard and as miserable as poverty in old age.' Versions of the Lear story were, according to Taunton, to be found in numerous sermons that circulated from the Middle Ages onwards, 'as a warning not to dispose of inheritance without first making provision for oneself and as a censure to ungrateful offspring who drove the suffering aged out of house and home.'[28] Indeed, the literature of the period abounds in examples of elderly fathers who are, like Lear, ultimately reduced from a position of power and authority, to a state of complete dependency, vulnerability, marginalization and loss.

Quite intriguingly, Volpone's assumption of the role of the decrepit but childless old man provides a powerful inversion of that narrative. *Volpone* may be seen to stand, in Andrew Gurr's words, 'as a comic contrary, unnatural children and all, to its stable-mate [. . .] *King Lear*.'[29] Both plays were notably produced by Shakespeare's playing company, the King's Men, at about the same period of time in, or about, 1605,[30] and they share, as Sidney Musgrove has noted, a number of thematic links, especially in their use of images of monstrosity to refer to the fracture of 'natural' bonds between parents and children.[31] Another scholar has further remarked that it is possible that *Volpone* was written shortly after *King Lear*, with Jonson 'in part responding to Shakespeare's great tragedy.'[32] That possibility is no doubt tempting to consider since, as I will also be pointing out further down, Jonson's play seems to provide a parodic version that, in certain ways, ironically inverts the story of Shakespeare's ageing monarch who is driven out by children that behave in an 'unnatural' way. In Jonson's plot, it is exactly the old man's childlessness that enables him to maintain the central position denied to figures like Lear by ungrateful children.

Several of Jonson's contemporaries suspected that Jonson found inspiration for the character of Volpone in the figure of Captain Thomas Sutton (1532–1611), a wealthy but childless old financier who was apparently courted by many who wanted to lay hands on his fortune. This suggestion is preserved in John Aubrey's *Brief Lives* that makes reference to Sutton as one who 'fed severall with hopes of being his Heire. 'Twas from him, that B. Jonson tooke his hint of the Fox; and by Seigneor Volpone is meant Sutton.' According to Aubrey, Sutton, who had accumulated near the end of his life 'so many chests full of money, that his chamber was ready to grone under it', was courted by the Earl of Dorset who hoped to be named his heir, 'and so did severall other great persons.'[33] Other seventeenth-century sources, brought to the fore by Robert C. Evans, also suggest that the idea that Sutton provided the model for Volpone was widely discussed in the years that followed the play's first production and the possibility of personal satire was accepted by many of Jonson's contemporaries. These documents have been overlooked, Evans points out, by a range of modern commentators who have generally discounted this possibility.[34] Brian Parker, for instance, has argued that besides the fact that Sutton was rich and indeed gathered around him a number of people who aspired to gain his legacy, further parallel with the figure of Volpone is rather thin. This man, who eventually left his legacy for the foundation of the Charterhouse hospital, was, in Parker's words, 'a rather admirable person, with no other resemblance to Volpone's character or situation.'[35] This tendency to dismiss the idea that Jonson aimed to satirize Sutton may be attributed, according to Evans, to the fact that 'until recently, much of the biographical commentary on Sutton had an almost hagiographic tone,' that cast this figure 'as a model of Protestant benefaction.'[36]

But, without discounting the possibility that Volpone might have been, at least partly, based on Sutton, it is once more to Jonson's reading that we can more safely turn in order to find his sources of influence. In particular, Jonson appears to have found inspiration in a rich tradition of legacy-hunting in classical literature that places the figure of the wealthy but childless old man at the centre of attention for various *captatores*, grasping legacy-hunters who are attacked in various classical texts, especially by the Roman satirists. An example may be found in Horace's *Satires* 11.5, where in a parody of the encounter between the two figures in Book XI of the *Odyssey*, Tiresias advises Ulysses how to regain his fortune by turning to legacy-hunting: 'Fish craftily in all waters for old men's wills, and though one or two shrewd ones escape your wiles after nibbling off the bait, do not give up hope,' and then 'If some day a case be contested in the Forum, whichever of the parties is rich and childless, villain though he be [. . .] do you become his advocate.'[37] Also, Petronius's description of Croton in *The Satyricon* makes reference to a society that is largely constituted by two categories of people, money-hunters and those they hunt on; a society that completely marginalizes those who have families, elevating those who lack relatives and direct heirs to positions of authority. As mentioned by the bailiff who is met at Croton by Encolpius and the elderly poet Eumolpus during their journey there, 'in this city no one brings up children, for if a man has his own heirs, this disqualifies him from dinners and public entertainments. He gets none of the perks, and lives unknown as a social leper.' In contrast, the bailiff comments, 'those who have never married and have no relatives not only attain the top positions, but are regarded as the only men of true valour and integrity. You are approaching a town,' he warns Encolpius and Eumolpus, 'that is a plague-ridden expanse, populated by nothing but corpses being pecked to pieces, and the crows at work pecking them.'[38] Like Eumolpus, who finds in Croton a very good opportunity to make profit, Volpone makes use of his condition to attract the attention of would-be heirs. As in those classical sources Jonson draws upon, Volpone's trick is largely based on his lack of children and other family relations:

> I have no wife, no parent, child, ally,
> To give my substance to; but whom I make
> Must be my heir: and this makes men observe me.
> This draws new clients, daily, to my house,
> Women and men, of every sex and age,
> That bring me presents, send me plate, coin, jewels,
> With hope that when I die (which they expect
> Each greedy minute) it shall then return
> Tenfold upon them; [...]
>
> (I.ii.73–81)

Jonson's plot of legacy-hunting is also highly reminiscent of those stories in Lucian's *Dialogues of the Dead* 15–19, about the rich old men Eucrates, Theocritus, Ptoeodorus, Hermolaus and Polystratus. Polystratus, having died at the age of 98, describes to Simylus how he enjoyed 'an exceedingly pleasant life' in his last thirty years as 'good things came pouring in from others [...] at the crack of dawn crowds of fold would start flocking to my doors, and later in the day all kinds of choice gifts from every corner of the earth would arrive,' to add that, 'I had thousands of lovers [...] indeed the noblest lovers in the city. Though I was old and bald, as you see, yes, and blear-eyed and sniveling too, they were delighted to court me, and anyone of them I favoured with a mere glance thought himself in heaven.' Explaining how he came to be 'the desire of all,' Polystratus then comments that 'this great love of rich, childless old men is there for all to see.'[39] Simylus, who initially listens to the story with incredulity, notably raises the question whether Polystratus managed to attract so much attention and benefits by acquiring the position of tyrant.

Quite importantly, far from leading to marginalization, the figure of the childless old man is used in these examples in order to acquire a central position of power and influence. While childlessness and the lack of any family network might otherwise be considered as an element that could contribute to the vulnerability of the old man, here it is in fact manipulated so as to gain control over would-be heirs and reap the benefits of their attention. The schema, as Polystratus points out, would lead to struggles of rivalry among his legacy-hunters who 'would vie with each other in their zeal for my affection.'[40] This rivalry is powerfully dramatized by Jonson, as Volpone sees his 'clients' who would 'engross me whole, | [. . .] counterwork the one unto the other, | Contend in gifts, as they would seem in love' (82–84) – a compellingly parodic form of the rhetorical contest initiated by King Lear in Shakespeare's play when he invites his daughters to say which 'doth love us most, | That we our largest bounty may extend | Where nature doth with merit challenge' (I.i.51–53).[41] Indeed, as I have already mentioned, *Volpone* may be said to provide an ironic inversion of the narrative of *King Lear*. While Lear calls upon his daughters' 'natural' affection in order to receive validation of his power and authority, Volpone exults in having no natural ties and finds himself empowered in a household that provides a parody of a family, with Nano, Castrone and Androgyno, but also the broader circle of would-be heirs, as his 'children' (I.i.72–74).

It is perhaps one of Jonson's major departures from the tradition of legacy-plots found in his classical sources that Volpone merely impersonates old age – or, rather, the symptoms of disease associated with old age. His satirical tirade against Corbaccio's desire for rejuvenation in Act I Scene iv seems to be launched from the safe distance of a man who is very far from that situation himself. As has been noted, his repeated use of the words 'their' and 'them' in his speech on the loathsome condition of old age discussed earlier in this essay – '*Their* limbs faint, | *their* senses dull, *their* seeing, hearing, going, | All dead before *them*; yea, *their* very teeth, | *Their* instruments of eating, failing *them*' (I.iv.147–50; italics my emphasis) – points to Volpone's attempt to disassociate himself from the emphasis paid in the original source to the inevitability of that condition for all men.[42] Yet, rather ironically, Volpone's insistent attempt to distance himself from the horrors of senility seems to point to his own fear of old age. As Brian Parker notes, commenting on the character's 'method of dealing with the reminders of disease, age, and death which so plentifully bestrew the play,' Volpone may attempt to 'control the mortal threat of which these are reminders by burlesquing both disease and cure, but uneasiness keeps surfacing through his mockery.'[43] Indeed, in a certain sense, Volpone's satirical outburst of indignant contempt against Corbaccio may be said to point to a displacement of his own anxiety about old age.

Much as his object of satirical indignation, Volpone himself may in fact be said to have a certain obsession with the preservation of youth.

His allusion to the mythical Golden Age in his opening speech in worship of gold is one that evokes the idea of everlasting youth. 'The basis of the myth of a Golden Age,' Brian Parker points out, 'is that it constituted the reign of Saturn (Cronos), god of time, and it was not until Saturn was deposed that the world became subject to mortality. Thus, all paradisal visions take place in a time that is out of time, an everlasting Spring of unending youth.'[44] It is in the seduction scene though where Volpone compellingly turns to this idea of prolonged youth. 'I am, now, as fresh, | As hot, as high, and in as jovial plight' (III. vii.157–58), he tells Celia,

> As when in that so celebrated scene
> At recitation of our comedy
> For entertainment of the great Valois,
> I acted young Antinöus, and attracted
> The eyes and ears of all the ladies present,
> T'admire each graceful gesture, note, and footing.
>
> (III.vii.159–64)

Perhaps due to his numerous transformations during the play, Volpone's actual age range seems to remain fairly elusive. Yet, despite his earnest desire in this scene to present himself as youthful and vigorous as the character of Antinöus that he impersonated for the entertainment of Henry of Valois, his reference to this event that took place in 1574, thirty-two years before *Volpone* was first performed,[45] in fact reveals that Volpone would not exactly have been, as Brian Gibbons mentions, 'in the prime of life'[46] – especially if one takes into consideration that the standard-life expectancy of the early modern period would have been much shorter than nowadays.

While Jonson's debt to Catullus in the seduction scene has been well-documented by scholars, it may perhaps further be argued that in fashioning Volpone's character here Jonson may also have had in mind the figure of the old and physically unattractive lover in the *Anacreontea*, whose attempts to find erotic gratification are only met with rejection.[47] Indeed, Volpone seems to cast himself in the role of the anacreontic lover when he makes an allusion to this corpus upon his return to his house in Act II Scene iv, following his venture outside as a mountebank. Having just seen Celia for the first time, he here makes reference to 'angry Cupid' that

> [. . .] bolting from her eyes,
> Hath shot himself into me like a flame;

Where now he flings about his burning heat,
As in a furnace an ambitious fire
Whose vent is stopped. The fight is all within me.

(II.iv.3–7)

The lines here recall various moments in the anacreontic corpus, such as that in *Anacreontea* 26, where the speaker tells of how he was captured by a 'strange kind of army, striking me with its eyes,' or *Anacreontea* 11, where he refers to how he was set on fire by Love. In another instance in *Anacreontea* 13, he describes how he was challenged to a fight by Love, who 'hurled himself for a javelin, pierced the middle of my heart and loosened my limbs. My shield (and spears and corslet),' he laments, 'are useless: why hurl weapons from me when the fight is within me?'[48]

Volpone's erotic advances toward Celia in the seduction scene are notably as unsuccessful as those of the old man toward potential lovers in the *Anacreontea*. Further, his attempt to confirm his potency and virility by seducing Celia in that scene is in many ways reminiscent of those endless fantasies of rejuvenation in the anacreontic texts, where the old man imagines himself transcending the restrictions imposed upon him by senility and joining youthful recreations, like a 'youth among the youths' as he mentions in *Anacreontea* 53. Ironically, it is also strikingly reminiscent of those self-aggrandizing fantasies of youthful vigour that Volpone so bitterly satirizes in Corbaccio. Volpone ultimately seems to share Corbaccio's anxiety of old age, and it is perhaps no coincidence, given Mosca's acute insight into other characters, that in one of his exaggerated attempts to flatter Volpone, he tries to assure him that 'when I am lost in blended dust, | And hundred such as I am in succession, | [. . .] You shall live | Still to delude these harpies' (I.ii.119–20, 121–22). As John Creaser astutely observes, Volpone is eventually shocked into the realization of his own impotence and fear, after having to suffer his public appearance at the court in Act IV:

'Fore God, my left leg 'gan to have the cramp,
And I appre'nded straight some power had struck me
With a dead palsy.

(V.i.5–7)

'As his world turns topsy-turvy,' Creaser comments, Volpone 'has found himself physically *becoming* through fear one of the parts he has enjoyed playing,'[49] and his sense of freedom from the wretchedness of old age proves as illusory as Corbaccio's self-enhancing fantasies of rejuvenation.

Jonson's burlesquing of old age in *Volpone* ultimately provides an intriguing exploration of the fears and anxieties associated with that condition. In this light, it should perhaps come as no surprise that Corvino, a character who, unlike Volpone and Corbaccio, may perhaps be identified as a younger man – as may be suggested by Mosca's reference to him as 'our spruce merchant' (I.iv.161)[50] – compares himself to the figure of '*Pantalone di Besogniosi*' (II.iii.8), the miserly old husband of the *commedia dell'arte*, as soon as he finds Volpone-as-mountebank outside his house.[51] Seeing himself threatened with cuckoldry, Corvino furiously beats away the mountebank, comparing him to '*Signor Flamineo*' (II.iii.3) – the name given in the *commedia* to the young lover.[52] Of course, ironically, little does Corvino know that the '*Signor Flamineo*' he feels so threatened by is no one else but Volpone, the old man he had visited earlier on, supposedly on his death-bed.

All in all, the association of old age with the anxiety over the loss of power and virility pervades the play at many different levels, providing a persistent undercurrent of unease to the element of parody. In years to come, the anxiety of old age would acquire for Jonson himself a personally much more poignant edge as his attempts to return to the writing of plays for the public stage in the late 1620s – after a period of withdrawal from 1616, when *The Devil is an Ass* was performed, to 1626, when *The Staple of News* was put on stage – would be met by various voices of scorn and disapproval, that depicted Jonson as an author who had lost his former abilities in playwriting, having declined into senility and drinking.[53] At that point, as I have argued elsewhere, the anacreontic model of the old man, so finely evoked by the title character in *Volpone*, would become for Jonson himself a compelling mode of self-presentation.[54]

Notes

1   Quotations are from the Revels Plays edition of *Volpone, or The Fox*, ed. Brian Parker (Manchester and New York: Manchester University Press, rev. ed. 1999).

2   An exception may be found in an essay by Brian Gibbons, that does not, however, concentrate solely on *Volpone*. See his chapter, 'The Representation of Ageing in Shakespeare and Jonson,' in *Old Age and Ageing in British and American Culture and Literature*, ed. Christa Jansohn (Münster: Lit Verlag, 2004), 39–49.

3   See Sara Munson Deats and Lagretta Tallent Lenker, eds, *Aging and Identity: A Humanities Perspective* (Westport, CT: Praeger, 1999); Alan Walker and Gerhard Naegele, eds., *The Politics of Old Age in Europe* (Buckingham and Philadelphia: Open University Press, 1999); Lynn Bothello and Pat Thane, eds., *Women and Ageing in British Society Since 1500*, Women and Men in History (Harlow, London, New York, et al.: Pearson Education, 2001); Brian Worsford, Maria O'Neill, and Llena Zamorano, eds., *The Aesthetics of Ageing: Critical Approaches to Literary Representations of the Ageing Process* (Lleida: University of Lleida, 2002); Christa Jansohn, ed., *Old Age and Ageing in British and American Culture and Literature* (Münster: Lit Verlag, 2004); Erin Campbell, ed., *Growing Old in Early Modern Europe: Cultural Representations*

(Aldershot: Ashgate, 2006); Oliver Davis, *Age Rage and Going Gently: Stories of the Senescent Subject in Twentieth-Century French Writing* (Amsterdam: Rodopi, 2006); Nina Taunton, *Fictions of Old Age in Early Modern Literature and Culture* (New York and London: Routledge, 2007); Albrecht Classen, ed., *Old Age in the Middle Ages and the Renaissance*.

4   The publication in 1970 of Simone de Beauvoir's provocative study of old age marked a largely uncharted territory. Originally published in French under the title *La Vieillesse*, de Beauvoir's book was also made available in English two years later in a translation by Patrick O'Brian. See *The Coming of Age*, trans. Patrick O'Brian (New York: G. P. Putnam's Sons, 1972). Further exploration of the topic was only taken up by a handful of scholars in the two decades that followed, though the period witnessed certain important attempts by scholars across different disciplines. See, for instance, Stuart F. Spicker, Kathleen M. Woodward and David D. Van Tassel, eds., *Aging and the Elderly: Humanistic Perspectives in Gerontology* (Atlantic Highlands, NJ: Humanities Press, 1978); Laurel Porter and Laurence M. Porter, eds., *Aging in Literature* (Troy, MI: International Book Publishers, 1984); Kathleen Woodward and Murray M. Schwartz, eds., *Memory and Desire: Aging – Literature – Psychoanalysis* (Bloomington: Indiana University Press, 1986); Thomas M. Falkner and Judith de Luce, eds., *Old Age in Greek and Latin Literature* (New York: State University of New York Press, 1989); Georges Minois, *History of Old Age: from Antiquity to the Renaissance*, trans. Sarah Hanbury Tension (Cambridge: Polity Press, 1989); Barbara Frey Waxman, *From the Hearth to the Open Road: A Feminist Study of Aging in Contemporary Literature* (New York: Greenwood Press, 1990).

5   Kathleen Woodward, *Aging and its Discontents: Freud and other Fictions* (Bloomington and Indianapolis: Indiana University Press, 1991), 21.

6   Woodward, *Aging and its Discontents*, 4.

7   Minois, *History of Old Age*, 249.

8   Ibid., 288.

9   Cited from William Shakespeare, *As You Like It*, ed. Juliet Dusinberre, The Arden Shakespeare (London: Thomson Learning, 2006).

10   Quoted from Parker's notes in his edition of *Volpone*, 146 (note to line 97).

11   See David Bevington, 'The Major Comedies', in *The Cambridge Companion to Ben Jonson*, ed. Richard Harp and Stanley Stewart (Cambridge: Cambridge University Press, 2000), 75.

12   Anne Barton, *Ben Jonson, Dramatist* (Cambridge: Cambridge University Press, 1984; repr. 1986), 108.

13   See Creaser's introduction in his edition of *Volpone, or The Fox*, The London Medieval and Renaissance Series (London: Hodder and Stoughton, 1978), 9–10.

14   H. Rackham, trans., *Pliny, the Elder: Natural History*, Loeb Classical Library, 10 vols. (Cambridge, MA: Harvard University Press, 1942), Vol. 2, 619; here cited from Brian Parker's notes in his edition of *Volpone*, 120.

15   Karen Cokayne, *Experiencing Old Age in Ancient Rome* (London: Routledge, 2003), 35.

16   W. H. W. Jones, trans., *Hippocrates, Volume IV : The Nature of Man*, Loeb Classical Library (London: Heinemann, 1931), 133,135; here quoted from Parker, *Volpone*, 114 (note to lines 37–54).

17   Ibid.

18   See Parker, *Volpone*, 114 (note to lines 37–54).

19   See *Fasciculus Morum: A Fourteenth-Century Preacher's Handbook*, ed. Siegfried Wenzel (University Park: Pennsylvania State University Press, 1989), 718–21. The relevant extract is quoted and modernized by Rosemary Horrox in 'Purgatory, Prayer

and Plague: 1150–1380,' in *Death in England: An Illustrated History*, ed. Peter C. Jupp and Clare Gittings (Manchester: Manchester University Press, 1999), 92.

20   Horrox, 'Purgatory, Prayer and Plague,' 92.

21   Nina Taunton, *Fictions of Old Age in Early Modern Literature and Culture* (New York and London: Routledge, 2007), 1.

22   Parker, *Volpone*, 25, 30.

23   Count Baldassare Castiglione, *The Book of the Courtier*, trans. Sir Thomas Hoby, ed. Virginia Cox (London: Everyman – J. M. Dent, 1994), 223–24.

24   Both of these examples are discussed by Philip D. Collington in his chapter 'Sans Wife: Sexual Anxiety and the Old Man in Shakespeare,' in *Growing Old in Early Modern Europe*, 185.

25   Taunton, *Fictions of Old Age*, 3–4.

26   In various recent examinations of old age in this text, King Lear is often read side by side with Prospero from Shakespeare's *The Tempest*, who is used as more positive model of ageing. See, for instance, Sara Munson Deats, 'The Dialectic of Aging in Shakespeare's *King Lear* and *The Tempest*,' and Kirk Combe and Kenneth Schmader, 'Shakespeare Teaching Geriatrics: Lear and Prospero as Case Studies in Aged Heterogeneity,' in *Aging and Identity*, 23–32 and 33–46 respectively.

27   It has of course often been pointed out that the issue of inheritance has much broader political implications in *King Lear* as it concerns the division of the kingdom. As Sara Munson Deats points out in a reading that otherwise concentrates on Lear as an old man who 'wishes to retire and yet not retire' rather than the political dimensions of that action, 'Lear's decision to divide his kingdom and abdicate from the throne would doubtlessly have been viewed as egregiously irresponsible by a Jacobean audience.' See 'The Dialectic of Aging in Shakespeare's *King Lear* and *The Tempest*,' 25–26.

28   Taunton, *Fictions of Old Age*, 52–53.

29   Andrew Gurr, *The Shakespearian Playing Companies* (Oxford: Clarendon Press, 1996), 300.

30   The title-page of the 1616 folio edition of Jonson's *Works* in which *Volpone* appeared indicates that the play was performed by the King's Men in 1605. However, as Brian Parker notes, this is 'a dating that in the old-style legal calendar could extend to 25 March 1606.' As Parker further argues, on the basis of various allusions made in the text, the play was probably composed in late February to early March 1606, and first acted before 25 March of that year. See Parker, *Volpone*, 9–10. The first recorded performance of *King Lear* was before James I at Whitehall during the Christmas season of 1606, but, as Jay L. Halio notes, the play was probably first performed at an earlier date at the Globe and its composition had probably started by spring or summer 1605, if not sooner. See his introduction in his edition of *King Lear*, The New Cambridge Shakespeare (Cambridge: Cambridge University Press, 1992; updated 2005), 1–2. R. A. Foakes also remarks that, although evidence is relatively thin, the date of composition and first performance of the play may probably be placed in 1605–6. See, his introduction in his edition of *King Lear*, The Arden Shakespeare (Walton-on-Thames: Thomas Nelson and Sons, 1997), 89–92.

31   Sydney Musgrove, *Shakespeare and Jonson: The Macmillan Brown Lectures 1957*, Auckland University College English Series No. 9, Bulletin No. 51 (Philadelphia: Pilgrim Press, 1957), 21–39. Making the case that the thematic correspondences between *King Lear* and *Volpone* point to a close professional relationship between Shakespeare and Jonson, Musgrove suggests that the two dramatists may have seen each other's work in rehearsal, as well as in performance, or perhaps read it in manuscript (32). 'If this reading of the facts is correct,' he notes in his concluding remarks,

'the minds of Shakespeare and Jonson came into closer rapport about the year 1605 than ever they had done before, or were to do again' (38–39).

32   James Tulip, 'The Intertextualities of Ben Jonson's *Volpone*,' *Sydney Studies in English* 20 (1994): 20–35 (28). Tulip also suggests that Jonson might have written *Volpone* with Shakespeare's group of actors in mind. His article further lays out various parallels between *Volpone* and other plays produced by Shakespeare about this period, especially *Othello*. The parodic overtones of *Othello* in *Volpone* are also set out by Brian F. Tyson in his article 'Ben Jonson's Black Comedy: A Connection Between *Othello* and *Volpone*,' *Shakespeare Quarterly* 29.1 (1978): 60–66.

33   John Aubrey, *Brief Lives*, ed. Andrew Clark, 2 Vols (Oxford: Clarendon Press, 1898), Vol. 2, 246.

34   See Chapter 3, 'Thomas Sutton: Jonson's Volpone?,' in Robert C. Evans, *Jonson and the Contexts of His Time* (Lewisburg: Bucknell University Press; London and Toronto: Associated University Presses, 1994), 45–61.

35   Parker, *Volpone*, 11. One cannot help but notice of course that Volpone's wealth, just like that of Sutton, eventually goes to the foundation of a hospital, 'the hospital of the *Incurabili*' (V.xii.120). Robert C. Evans notes that, although it calls in question the possibility of personal satire, Parker's Revels Plays edition provides an exception, since in the majority of modern editions of the play the idea is altogether silenced. See Evans, *Jonson and the Contexts of His Time*, 45 and 191, note 1.

36   Evans, *Jonson and the Contexts of His Time*, 46.

37   H. Rushton Fairclough, trans., *Horace: Satires, Epistles and Ars Poetica*, Loeb Classical Library (New York: Heinemann, 1926), 199.

38   P. G. Walsh, trans., *Petronius: The Satyricon* (Oxford: Clarendon Press, 1996), Section 116, 110.

39   M. D. MacLeod, trans., *Lucian*, Loeb Classical Library, 8 Vols (London: Heinemann; Cambridge, MA: Harvard University Press, 1969), vol. 7, 97–99. For a comprehensive study of Lucian's influence on the Jonsonian canon, see Douglas Duncan, *Ben Jonson and the Lucianic Tradition* (Cambridge: Cambridge University Press, 1979).

40   MacLeod, trans., *Lucian*, 99.

41   Here cited from R. A. Foakes, *King Lear*.

42   See Creaser's commentary on these lines in his edition of *Volpone*, 223. As Creaser notes, 'by inserting the words 'their' or 'them' eight times in four lines [Volpone] insists on his freedom from the wretchedness of the aged.'

43   Parker, *Volpone*, 34.

44   Ibid. For a more comprehensive discussion of the appropriation of this myth in the early modern period, see Harry Levin, *The Myth of the Golden Age in the Renaissance* (London: Faber and Faber, 1969).

45   Brian Parker notes that Jonson probably read about the entertainment of Henry of Valois that took place in Venice in 1574 'in the appendix from Sansovino's *Venetia* (1581) in Lewkenor's translation of Contarini, and in Florio's *Worlde of Wordes*.' Parker, *Volpone*, 197 (note to line 161).

46   Gibbons, 'The Representation of Ageing in Shakespeare and Jonson,' 43.

47   The anacreontic corpus notably contains a number of instances where the old man is rejected by potential lovers due to his waning looks and physical decline. See, for example, *Anacreontea* 7, where a group of women point out to Anacreon that he is old, asking him to take a look at his declining appearance in the mirror.

48   Translations are here quoted from David A. Campbell, ed. and trans., *Greek Lyric II: Anacreon, Anacreontea, Choral Lyric from Olympus to Alcman*, Loeb Classical Library (Cambridge, MA and London: Harvard University Press, 1988).

49   Creaser, *Volpone*, 30.

50 The two meanings given to the word 'spruce' in the *OED* are 'trim, neat, dapper; smart in appearance,' and 'brisk, smart, lively.' The term may therefore be said to indicate Corvino's elegant apparel, but possibly his age range as well. As John Creaser also notes, 'the word suggests that Corvino is a youngish man, not a *senex amans* (or that he tries to behave like a young man).' See, Creaser, *Volpone*, 223. If this is so, Corvino's entrance in Act I Scene v creates a sharp contrast, as it follows the exit of old Corbaccio in the immediately preceding scene.

51 As has been noted, Volpone himself may be said to have an even greater resemblance with the character of 'Pantalone.' Indeed, the indication that Volpone is a 'Magnifico' of Venice evokes that association, since 'the Magnifico' is an alternative name for 'Pantalone' in the *commedia dell'arte*. See Parker, *Volpone*, 22–23.

52 In this scene, Corvino also compares Celia to 'Franciscina,' the lusty serving wench of the *commedia*.

53 The decline of Jonson's theatrical career was marked by the failure of *The New Inn* in 1629. An anonymous poem written in response to this play under the title 'The Cuntrys Censure on Ben Johnsons New Inn', asks 'decaying Ben' (line 1) to 'Listen [...] and Counsell heare, / Witts have their date and strength of braines may weare, / Age steept In sacke, hath quencht thy Enthean fier' (lines 1–3). Noting that 'Wee pittye now, whom once, wee did Admire' (line 4), the poem therefore prompts Jonson to 'Surrender then thy right to th' stage' (line 5). From Bodleian MS. Ashmole 38, 79–80; here quoted from C. H. Herford, Percy Simpson and Evelyn Simpson, eds., *Ben Jonson*, 11 vols. (Oxford: Clarendon Press, 1925–1952), 11: 344–46.

54 See my chapter, 'Youth, Old Age, and Male Self-Fashioning: The Appropriation of the Anacreontic Figure of the Old Man by Jonson and his "Sons"', in *Growing Old in Early Modern Europe*, 39–53.

CHAPTER EIGHT

Resources for Teaching and Studying *Volpone*

Matthew C. Hansen

Just as this volume as a whole examines Jonson in relationship to Shakespeare, and reads *Volpone* both as a specimen of literature and as a text for performance, this essay surveys various strategies for self-study or teaching *Volpone* that are comparative in nature and that examine the play as both literary text and script for performance. I begin by locating *Volpone* on the syllabus or course reading list, and I discuss some of the course contexts in which *Volpone* is frequently read and studied and offer some ideas for alternative configurations. Next, I survey editions of the play with a focus on affordable editions readily available for classroom use. A brief discussion of strategies for making the most of an initial reading of the play precedes a longer, detailed discussion of possible thematic, contextual, performative and interpretive issues in the play and suggestions on how to supply relevant background for, and frame conversations of, those issues. I identify and offer suggestions for locating texts – both primary and secondary – as supplemental reading and then offer possible discussion questions or ideas for in-class activities that explore the connections between the play text and its contexts. For those interested in exposing their students (or themselves) to different theoretical approaches to the play I likewise identify ways for thinking about the play from different critical-theoretical perspectives. I then turn to a list of possible projects that students could undertake in order to explore the play in-depth on their own terms. Finally, I conclude with a brief filmography providing resources for teaching or thinking about the play and the issues surrounding it.

Locating *Volpone* on the Syllabus

Volpone is a fixture in several courses ranging from surveys of British Literature, surveys of Dramatic Literature, or more focused period courses dealing with Elizabethan and Jacobean literature (generally) or drama (specifically). The last may well split its focus on Shakespearean and non-Shakespearean drama although it is far more common to see Shakespeare taught in a stand-alone course (or courses, with either a chronological or a generic division) while Shakespeare's contemporaries vie for representation in a course that samples highlights of dramatic work by Jonson, Marlowe, Middleton, Massinger, Dekker, Heywood, Webster, Ford and others. Such is the case in my institution, where I offer an upper-division undergraduate course on Elizabethan and Jacobean drama every other year. I tend to alter the reading list somewhat each time I offer the course, but at least one Jonson play (typically either *Volpone* or *The Alchemist*) is included on the syllabus and we spend two weeks studying the play. I ask students to perform scenes in class and read selected supplemental essays to focus discussion for particular sessions, usually as a means of exploring broader themes and concerns across a number of plays.

Among the Shakespeare plays with which *Volpone* readily combines for comparative study are *The Merchant of Venice* and *Othello*. The most obvious and immediate link for these three texts is their shared Venetian setting. As Ann Rosalind Jones has observed, Italy, in Renaissance England, signified not just 'another country, [but] a country of others, constructed through a lens of voyeuristic curiosity through which writers and their audiences explored what was forbidden in their own culture.'[1] This notion of watching the foreign and forbidden is certainly a rich thematic connection fruitful for seminar exploration. Suggested readings on *Volpone*'s Venetian settings can be found below. Questions of genre can also be explored through the comparative study of these three plays. What makes Corvino's jealousy and fear of cuckoldry (including its threats of violence in Act 2, scene 5) comical in *Volpone* while the same emotions and fear turn tragic in *Othello*? How do Shakespeare and Jonson's visions of comedy compare? The two courtroom scenes in *Volpone* and *The Merchant of Venice* likewise invite comparison and contrast: do the two scenes represent a unified or a disparate vision of Venetian justice? How do these two playwrights use the courtroom as analogous to the theatre?

If the course focus extends beyond England to include European drama, Moliere's *Imaginary Invalid* (1673) offers a text rich in opportunities for a comparative approach. The two plays' shared concern with the performance of feigned illness, metadramatic levels of performance and playful exploration of the morality of deceit and feigned death make them ripe for comparison. The suggested readings that help cast light on *Volpone*'s satiric treatment of seventeenth-century medical theory and practice below compliment a comparative discussion of these two plays. Among the contemporary non-dramatic literature with which *Volpone* invites comparison are Erasmus's *Praise of Folly* and Robert Greene's cony-catching pamphlets. I offer suggestions for locating useable texts of and incorporating the latter below.

Volpone also might reside in a course focused exclusively on Jacobean City Comedy. Indeed a comparative study of several of Jonson's plays alone – *Volpone, The Alchemist, Epicene* or *The Silent Woman, Bartholomew Fair, The Staple of News* – leads to exciting discussions of Jonson's treatment of the metropolis. A clear sense of Jonson's view of the city emerges; such a discussion can be supplemented by readings from or lectures based upon James D. Mardock's *Our Scene is London: Ben Jonson's City and the Space of the Author* (Routledge, 2008), Gail Kern Paster's *The Idea of the City in the Age of Shakespeare* (University of Georgia, 1985) and Laurence Manley's two very useful books on this topic: *Literature and Culture in Early Modern London* (Cambridge, 2005; rpt. 2008) and *London in the Age of Shakespeare: An Anthology* (Pennsylvania State University Press, 1986). We can complicate and build upon this picture by studying other plays in which the urban setting (and often, as in the case for the plays above apart from *Volpone*, specifically London setting) plays a shaping role such as Thomas Dekker's *The Shoemaker's Holiday,* Thomas Middleton and Dekker's *The Roaring Girl,* or plays by Jonson's protégé Richard Brome. An invaluable resource for this theme is Francis C. Chalfant's *Ben Jonson's London: A Jacobean Place-Name Dictionary* (University of Georgia, 1985; rpt. 2008). What does Jonson have to say about urban sophistication? What are the positive aspects that come from the growth of cities? What are the downsides Jonson calls into question?

Volpone is also an excellent choice for a course concerned more largely with the use and appropriation of beast fables and animal lore. Putting Jonson's foxy morality play in conversation with Aesop's fables, Chaucer's *Parliament of Fowls*, Orwell's *Animal Farm*, Ionesco's *Rhinoceros,* Art Spiegelmann's graphic novel *Maus* – perhaps also with some consideration of non-mainstream Western culture's significant use of animal lore such as Native American legends (especially the trickster figure of Coyote in the legends of several tribes) and/or Joel Chandler Harris's Uncle Remus (Brer Rabbit) tales – could lead to fascinating discussion, writing and research.

Editions

That *Volpone* frequently appears on the reading list for the early portion of surveys of British Literature likely has a great deal to do with the play's inclusion in two major anthologies: *The Norton Anthology of English Literature* (eighth edition, 2006) and McGraw-Hill's *Literature: Approaches to Fiction, Poetry, and Drama* (2003). Other anthology sources for the play include *English Renaissance Drama: A Norton Anthology* (Norton, 2002), edited by David M. Bevington, Lars Engle, Katharine Eisaman Maus and Eric Rasmussen; and *The Duchess of Malfi: Eight Masterpieces of Jacobean Drama,* edited by Frank Kermode (Modern Library, 2005).

A number of selected works of Jonson are also available. G. A. Wilkes's edition of *Five Plays* (Oxford, 1999) – *Every Man in his Humour, Sejanus, Volpone, The Alchemist and Bartholomew Fair* – in the Oxford World Classics series is shortly to be superseded by the same collection of plays edited by Gordon Campbell and re-titled *The Alchemist and Other Plays* (Oxford, 2009). Penguin has a three play collection, *Volpone and Other Plays* (*The Alchemist* and *Bartholomew Fair*) (Penguin, 2004) edited by Michael Jamieson. The Longman Annotated Texts series includes *Volpone* along with *Epicene, The Alchemist* and *Bartholomew Fair* edited by Helen Ostovich in *Ben Jonson Four Comedies* (Longman, 1997). Cambridge University Press includes *Volpone* in Volume 1 (of 2) of *The Selected Plays of Ben Jonson,* edited by Johanna Procter with an Introduction by Martin Butler (Cambridge, 1989).

Three single-volume editions of the play are also widely available: R. B. Parker has edited both the Revels Plays edition of *Volpone* (Manchester, 1983; revised edn, 1999), by far the most comprehensive, single-volume scholarly edition of the play, and, with David Bevington, The Revels Student edition (Manchester, 1999). The New Mermaids series second edition of the play is edited by Robert N. Watson (Methuen, 2007).

The standard scholarly edition at the time of this writing remains the 11-volume edition of Jonson's works by C. H. Herford, Percy Simpson and Evelyn Simpson (Oxford, 1925–1952). We continue to await the long-anticipated *Cambridge Edition of the Works of Ben Jonson.*

Initial Reading

Published materials on the study or teaching of Jonson's plays universally begin with a note of caution concerning the difficulty students face coming to terms with Jonson's language.[2] While the same cautionary note often also informs guides to reading and studying Shakespeare, the immediate remedy offered is to see the play in performance either on the stage or the screen. That same advice is likewise proffered as a strategy for better understanding Shakespeare's contemporaries, including Jonson; however, the chances of finding a current stage production of *Volpone* to attend when one sits down to study the play are slim. Even available film adaptations (see filmography below) or filmed stage productions of the play are difficult to locate. In a similar vein, readers are presented with a choice among possible audio-book versions of Shakespeare's plays but no such comparable library exists for Shakespeare's contemporaries. The first-time reader of Jonson's *Volpone* has to do more to create their own opportunities for hearing or experiencing the text in a performance-oriented vein. Few resources are in fact necessary to accomplish this end, however. Taking a page out of theatrical practise, students (or instructors) can easily coordinate a group read-through or table reading of the play.[3] If an instructor – or more advanced student already familiar with the play – can be present, then a table reading session can go a long way towards laying a firm foundation of understanding the play text in its most general terms: who's who and what happens.[4] Some of the usual suspects in the commercial academic marketplace (for example, SparkNotes, Gradesaver) intended to aid with this sort of knowledge acquisition do exist for *Volpone* and offer a number of helpful resources for *supplementing* and helping to clarify students' understanding of the play.[5] Once students have a firm grasp of Jonson's plot and characters, they are better positioned to achieve success discussing and writing about the more nuanced aspects of theme, symbolism, source study, historical context and correspondence offered below.

In-depth topic: Jonson's sources

In the Introduction to his Revels Plays edition of *Volpone,* R. B. Parker provides a superb overview of Jonson's likely sources, convincingly demonstrating that the play derives not from a single source but from a 'vast amount of contradictory influences'.[6] These include Classical sources and analogues as well as Medieval influences; bestiary, beast fables and emblems; and the city of Venice – the setting of the play – and its own artistic and cultural traditions. The latter – the role and significance of Venice – will be discussed in more detail below. Immediately, however, it is useful to consider ways that an examination of some of Jonson's Classical and Medieval sources, especially those related to the play's animalism, might be explored. Parker collects brief excerpts of source materials and publishes them as 'Appendix B' (pp. 299–320) and demonstrates the central role that beast fables, and the beast epic of

Reynard the Fox played in Jonson's creation of Volpone (the fox), Mosca (the parasite or fly) and the majority of the other characters in the play who, as is frequently noted, are given names emblematic of an animal nature that to varying degrees the characters demonstrate: Voltore (vulture), Corvino (crow), Corbaccio (raven), Sir Politic and Lady Would-Be (parrots), Peregrine (falcon or hawk).

Read Parker's overview of Jonson's use of sources (Introduction pp. 10–24) and the source excerpts he reprints in 'Appendix B'. Consider also Robert Shaughnessy's essay 'Twentieth-Century Fox: Volpone's Metamorphosis', *Theatre Research International* 27.1 (2002) pp. 37–48.

Questions to Consider

Consider the sources that Parker discusses and excerpts in his edition of *Volpone*. How successful do you feel Jonson is in blending this wide array of materials? Should we praise Jonson or condemn him for picking bits and pieces – parasite- or carrion-bird-like – from multiple corpses or texts? How does that praise or condemnation then affect our views of his characters?

How significant is Jonson's debt to the Italian *commedia dell'arte* and its use of exaggerated character types and emblematic costumes and masks? For useful illustrations of the masked *commedia* characters see Jacques Callot's 1621 *Balli di Sfessania*. A number of the images can be viewed at *http://www.spamula.net/blog/archives/000330.html*. Callot's drawings of the masks have an especially bird-like quality to them, with exaggerated noses that look like beaks.

Do you understand Jonson's characters to be essentially human, infused with certain animal characteristics as indicated by their names, or do you see them as 'talking animals'? What is the fundamental tension at work between these two readings? How does this tension relate to larger notions of hierarchy and order in the early modern period? Which dynamic – animalistic humans or humanistic animals – is more threatening?

How central should the animalism be to a performance of *Volpone*? (See Shaughnessy's 'Twentieth-Century Fox.') What could modern film technology do for a performance of the play that fully embraced the suggestion that the characters in this play are animals that behave like humans? Some characters are not linked to animal types: Celia, Bonario, Nano, Castrano Androgyno, the Avocatori. If you were to imagine the play as a fable populated by talking animals, what animal types would you assign to these characters? Defend the animal type that you assign them by analysing the specific details of what these characters say and do in the play and how that is consistent with the fabled reception of a particular animal.

Because beast-fable has a long tradition of serving as social or political commentary, we may want to consider Jonson's beast fable *Volpone*
as likewise concerned with recent events. Two major scholars have
recently re-examined the play's links to the Gunpowder Plot: Richard
Dutton, in *Jonson*, Volpone *and the Gunpowder Plot* (Cambridge, 2008)
and Frances Teague in both her contribution to this volume and 'Ben
Jonson and London Courtrooms' in *Solon and Thespis: Law and Theater
in the English Renaissance*, ed. Denis Kezar (University of Notre Dame,
2007): 64–77. While they agree on some points there are also important
points of interpretive disagreement between Dutton and Teague. Whose
work do you find more convincing? Why?

In-depth topic: Jonson's Venice
Accounts of English travellers in Italy can provide rich context for
thinking about Jonson's vision of Venice in *Volpone*. Particularly valuable materials supplying the broad brushstrokes of early-modern
Englishmen and women's likely perceptions of Italy, Venice and
Venetians can be found in Fynes Moryson's *Itinerary* (1617) and
Thomas Coryate's *Coryats Crudities* (1611). Although the publication
of both of these texts post-date Jonson's play, they provide useful
background for accessing and assessing early modern English representations of Italy, Italians and Italian culture. Relevant modern,
edited excerpts of both these and other writers can be found in the
Bedford/St. Martin's Text and Context series editions of Shakespeare's
The Merchant of Venice (see pp. 125–53, 167–72) and *Othello* (see pp.
234–47).[7] Readers with institutional access to Early English Books
Online (EEBO) can access digitized versions of the original printed
books that the Bedford editors excerpt (Reel Positions 996:18 [Mory-
son] and 1063:01 [Coryate]). Internet Archive (*http://www.archive.
org*) has available the 1903 (first) edition of Charles Hughes's *Shakespeare's Europe, A Survey of the Condition of Europe at the end of the
16*th *century, being unpublished chapters of Fynes Moryson's Itinerary*
(1617) (*http://www.archive.org/details/shakespeareseuro00moryuoft*).
The most immediately relevant material on Venice and Jonson's *Volpone* can be found on pages 163–65 in which Moryson discusses the
law in Venice and 'England's desired and actual affinity with Venice' in
the city-state's representation as a maiden (that is never conquered)
city. Also available at Internet Archive is the 1905 reprint of the 1611
edition of *Coryat's Crudities* (*http://www.archive.org/details/coryat-
scrudities01coryuoft*). Coryate's observations on Venice constitute the
book's final chapter, pages 301–428. While reading the whole of
Coryate's 'Observations of Venice' yields many delights it is perhaps an
unwieldy supplemental assignment to reading Jonson's play. Arguably
most potentially illuminating and stimulating for discussion would be

pages 397–412 in which Coryate observes and comments upon Venetian dress and customs (of men and women), Courtesans and Mountebanks. In the United States, both of these books are also accessible through Google Books (*http://books.google.com*).

The available evidence suggests that Jonson never travelled to Italy nor did he speak Italian. His knowledge of Venice therefore most likely comes from books. A text that Jonson did have access to and more than likely drew upon in writing *Volpone* is Gasparino Contarini's *De Magistratibus et Republica Venetorum* (1589) translated into English in 1599 by Lewis Lewkenor. In Act 4, scene 1, Sir Politic Would-be mentions this book as the source of his own knowledge of Venice: 'I had read Contarine [...]' (4.1.40). The 1599 edition of this book is available on EEBO (Reel Position: 205:04). The Schoenberg Centre for Text and Image at the University of Pennsylvania has a photographed reproduction that can be viewed on its website: *http://dewey.library.upenn.edu/SCETI/ PrintedBooksNew/index.cfm?TextID=contarini&PagePosition=1*.

Questions to Consider

How does Jonson's portrayal of the two principal female characters in *Volpone*, Celia and Lady Politic Would-Be, relate to the presentation of female characteristics in the city of Venice itself (virgin/whore)?

How are we to take Jonson's treatment of women more generally in this play? Celia is a largely pliant and acquiescent puppet who is referred to frequently in language that suggests she is little more than an object to be possessed. True to her parrot-like name, Lady Pol chatters at length (see 3.4) but says little of substance. How are we to react to what would appear to be unveiled misogyny on Jonson's part?

How do the relative constraints and freedom that Celia and Lady Pol experience relate to the Venetian setting, a city famed in part for its courtesans?

Is there a conflict between praise for Venice as a city with just laws and equal financial opportunity for all and criticism for such openness inviting greed and excess in *Volpone*? On which side of the debate do you believe Jonson's sympathies lie?

How uniquely Venetian do you find Jonson's Venice to be? Is Venice here really just London in disguise?

To what extent is the significance of the play's Venetian setting an issue of reading the play versus seeing the play in performance?

Read aloud – or prepare a short performance of – Act 2, scene 5. In what ways are the tropes of virgin and whore explored in this exchange between the jealous merchant Corvino and his wife, Celia? What is the significance of his desire to 'keep [Celia] backwards' (2.5.58–61)?

Read aloud – or prepare a short performance of – Act 3, scene 7. Can attempted rape be funny? What conditions must exist to keep this scene

in the realm of comedy and not tragedy? How seriously – or threaten-
ingly – should the scene be portrayed? How does this scene relate to
Jonson's overarching treatment of women in the play?

Read aloud – or prepare a short performance of – Act 5, scene 12.
What does this scene and its deliberately meta-dramatic character have
to say about Justice and the *performance* of Justice in Venice? How does
it relate to the other play-within-a-play scenes in *Volpone* (Volpone's
performance as Scoto of Mantua; Volpone's feigned death; the performance by Nano, Castrone and Androgyno in 1.1)? Consider Theresa
DiPasquale's questions from her on-line study guide: 'How does the
courtroom play-within-a-play relate to the play *Volpone* itself? That is,
how do the performances in the courtroom (directed toward the judges)
comment on that of the play *Volpone* (directed toward the theatre
audience)?'[8]

Is a feminist reading of the play possible? Read and discuss Peter
Parolin's essay, 'A Strange Fury Entered My House: Italian Actresses and
Female Performance in *Volpone*' *Renaissance Drama* 29 (1998): 107–35.

In-depth topic: Usury and *Volpone*
Peter Womack has observed that the play's exploration of the 'opposition between natural and unnatural increase is a trace, parodically
glamorized, of a contemporary debate about usury' (188).[9] The play
therefore might be usefully considered in light of early modern debates
about usury, the practise of charging interest on loans of money. The
Bedford / St. Martin's edition of *The Merchant of Venice* offers a useful
survey of this contentious issue (see 'Finance' pp. 187–89 and 192–211)
with excerpts from texts that discuss usury in England in general terms
and with reference to the debate over a specific usury bill introduced in
Parliament in 1571. An EEBO keyword search of the term 'usury' in
texts from 1550 to 1625 yields 45 records that students could usefully
survey and report on to gain a feel for the sentiments for and against
usury. Perhaps still more manageable as an assignment for classroom
discussion would be to have students read the two sermons on usury
available from The Schoenberg Centre for Text and Image at the
University of Pennsylvania: Miles Mosse's 'Arraignment of Usury'(1595)
and Henry Smith's 'Examination of Usury' (1591; reprint 1751). To
locate these materials, use the advanced search engine with keyword
'usury': *http://dewey.library.upenn.edu/sceti/AdvancedSearch.cfm*.

Questions to Consider
Does Jonson demonize or valorize Volpone's attempts to use money
to make money? How do the presence of his curious servants Nano,
Castrone and Androgyno and his own childless state (the reason he is in

search of an heir) relate to the terms of the usury debate regarding natural and unnatural increase?

Does wealth and the accumulation of wealth have a positive effect on any character in this play? Are there any characters who are 'untainted' by greed and acquisitiveness?

Read aloud – or prepare a short performance of – Act 1, scene 1. Analyse the language Volpone uses in reference to his gold: how are we to react to his characterization of the cabinet that contains it as a 'shrine' and the gold itself as 'my saint' (1.1.2)? Look closely at Volpone's description of how he gains – or rather the catalogue of means by which he did not gain – his wealth and the discussion of that with Mosca which follows (lines 30 and following): what kind of opposition between natural and unnatural increase is Jonson setting up here? How does this relate to the debate on usury?

Volpone specifically states that his wealth does not come from usury: 'I turn no moneys, in the public bank; | Nor usure private' (1.1.39–40). How then has he gained his wealth? Does this in fact relate to the near-contemporary debate in England concerning usury?

Oliver Hennesey, relating *Volpone* to contemporary restrictions of usury, notes,

> Money, so this argument went, should not reproduce itself. But this of course is exactly what is happening in *Volpone*. The magnifico's wealth is not static, hoarded; it reproduces itself through the mechanism of his 'crotchets' [(5.9.16)]. The rhetoric of wealth and status in Volpone's household – bullionist, feudal, display-related – belies the reality of the wealth production at work before our eyes. Volpone's wealth is put to work for itself, luring its suitors and promising them a massive return. Of course, Volpone must mediate for this to happen, and the return on his own capital investment comes with the application of skilled labour, the learned ability to manipulate the various tropes and figures of trade as well as those of a sumptuous aristocratic ethos of display.[10]

To what extent then is the play about money increasing itself as opposed to the accumulation of wealth through certain kinds of labour? Are Volpone and Mosca less reprehensible because they seek to work – however dishonestly or immorally – to increase Volpone's wealth when compared with Voltore, Corbaccio and Corvino who desire to passively inherit Volpone's wealth?

To what extent are Volpone's financial scams and schemes universally morally repugnant? How might current events influence readers or audiences of these plays? In other words, do we judge Volpone and

Mosca more harshly in light of the global economic crisis of 2009, a crisis brought on by efforts to manipulate credit and debt in sophisticated ways ultimately far removed from earlier concepts of labour, capital and compensation?

Considerations of economics, labour and capital place one on the verge of a Marxist reading of the play. For a fascinating reading of the play that builds on the tenets of Marxist criticism, read and discuss Oliver Hennesey's essay, 'Jonson's Joyless Economy'.[11]

In-depth topic: Medicine and Mountebanks in *Volpone*
Jonson wanted his arrival as a writer of dramatic poetry to be associated with his comedies of humours – *Every Man in His Humour* (1598) and *Every Man out of His Humour* (1599). While he likely wrote earlier apprentice pieces, he appears to have self-consciously crafted his authorial persona by presenting *Every Man in His Humour* as the earliest play included in his 1616 Folio *Works*. These plays develop a dramatic analogue to the prevailing theory of medicine in the late sixteenth century, that the human body is composed of four humours (Latin *umor*: liquid): blood (hot + wet), phlegm (cold + wet), yellow bile or choler (cold + dry) and black bile or melancholy (cold + dry). When in proper balance, the result is a healthy mind and body. This medical theory provides the backdrop for Jonson's theory of character, which he explains in the Induction to *Every Man Out of His Humour*:

> As when some one peculiar quality
> Doth so possess a man, that it doth draw
> All his affects, his spirits, and his powers,
> In their confluctions, all to run one way,
> This may be truly said to be a Humour.

> (Ind. 105–09)

Because Jonson's characters usually represent one humour and are therefore unbalanced, they are effectively caricatures rather than fully three-dimensional characters. While Jonson's comedy of humours relates to earlier vernacular drama, including the morality play tradition and its allegorical characters, Jonson's aim is clearly to imitate the classical comedy of Plautus and Terence and to offer a challenge to the kind of romantic comedy that Shakespeare popularized. Its satiric bite is sharpened by its realism, an aspect that Jonson develops in *Volpone* and subsequent comedies.

Appropriately satire, and especially Renaissance English satire, frequently employs images and metaphors that are medical in nature – and also violent, because blood-letting was such a widespread cure to bring about humoural balance. Mary Clare Randolph observes, 'To the Renaissance critic and satirist, satire is a scourge, a whip, a surgeon's scalpel, a cauterizing iron, a strong cathartic – all in one; its mission is to flay, to cut, to burn, to blister and to purge; its object is now a culprit, a victim, a criminal and now an ailing, submissive patient, a sick person bursting with contagion; and the satirist himself is a whipper, a scourger, a barber-surgeon, an executioner, a 'doctour of physic'.[12]

Although many critics see Volpone as 'the play that marks the transition from [Jonson's] moderately successful comedies of humours [. . .] to his great middle comedies,' Jonson's view of comedy remains fundamentally satiric and the importance of medical thinking prevails.[13] Indeed, *Volpone* is rife with images of illness and explores hypochondria and quack medicine as forms of theatrical performance. Curiously, Volpone himself thinks about the life of his cons as analogous to a human body. When, late in the play, the entire scheme teeters on the verge of dissolution he notes that Mosca must play the surgeon: 'He must now | Help to sear up this vein, or we bleed dead.' (5.11.6–7).

In Act 2 scene 2 Volpone ventures forth from home in a disguise that likewise references early modern medicine, and, intriguingly, metadramatic performance. Volpone's turn as Scoto of Mantua, a supposedly famous Mountebank, allows Jonson to play with the idea of a play within a play: Peregrine and Sir Politic Would-be frame and comment upon Volpone's performance. The scene likewise celebrates the play's Venetian setting. That inveterate traveller Thomas Coryate, mentioned above in the suggested readings related to Venice, offers an extended comment on Venetian Mountebanks (see pages 409–12).

Questions to Consider

Read aloud – or prepare a short performance of – Act 1, scene 4, lines 1–92. What critique of sixteenth-century medical practice and knowledge is raised in this exchange? How can the distrust of physicians that Mosca claims Volpone has, be related to larger themes of performance and fakery in the play?

Read aloud – or prepare a short performance of – Act 2, scene 2: Volpone's performance as the Mountebank Scoto of Mantua. What role do Peregrine and Sir Politic Would-be play in the scene?

Read closely Nano's second song that is part of the overall 'marketing effort' at work in the mountebank scene (Act 2, scene 2, lines 197–208). What does the song suggest is the promise of Scoto's miraculous oil? Relate the relative claims of this pharmaceutical wonder to contemporary prescription drugs and their advertisements. In the allure of perpetual youth, freedom from disease or decay and sexual perform-ance, do we not see many of the same obsessions and desires to which twenty-first century pharmaceutical companies pitch their wares?

Read and discuss Tanya Pollard's essay "No Faith in Physic': Masquerades of Medicine onstage and off' in Stephanie Moss and Kaara L. Peterson, eds., *Disease, Diagnosis, and Cure on the Early Modern Stage* (Ashgate, 2004) pp. 29–42.[14]

In-depth topic: Volpone's Confidence Games

Volpone dramatizes an elaborate confidence scheme and therefore the play can be usefully considered in comparison with other literature about con games, tricksters and frauds. The most colourful material of this nature from the early modern period is, of course, Robert Greene's cony-catching pamphlets. Four of Greene's cony-catching pamphlets (*A Notable Discouery of Coosnage* [1591], *The second and last part of Conny-catching* [1592], *The third and last part of Conny-catching* [1592] and *A Dispvtation Betweene a Hee Conny-catcher and a Shee Conny-catcher* [1592]), have been transcribed by Risa Bear and are available as free electronic texts as part of the Renascence Editions project at *http://www.uoregon.edu/~rbear/ren.htm*. Greene's fifth and final cony-catching pamphlet, *The Black Bookes Messenger* [1592] is available (in the United States) along with 'The Defence of Conny-Catching' by 'Cuthbert Conny-Catcher' as a digitized book (the 1924 Bodley Head Quarto edited by G. B. Harrison) from Google books: *http://books.google.com*. *The Black Bookes Messenger* is reprinted in Arthur Kinney's collection of cony-catching texts: *Rogues, Vagabonds and Sturdy Beggars* (University of Massachusetts Press, 1990). In reading and discussing these materials it is useful to explore Jonson's relationship with his audi-ence and issues of complicity in confidence tricks. Are these texts some-how parasitic upon the criminal world that Greene and Jonson appear to condemn? Greene arguably makes money from crime, albeit in a different form. Does a comparable operation take place in Jonson's play in which we are voyeuristically situated between condemnation and complicity? This issue can likewise be applied to reading and discussion of *The Alchemist*.

Questions to Consider

Note in particular Greene's allusions to sickness and health in the opening epistle to *A Dispvtation*. What does Jonson have to say about the relationship between health and wrong-doing? What significance do you attach to Volpone beginning to manifest actual symptoms of poor health near the end of the play?

As David W. Maurer observes in his classic study of confidence men, *The Big Con*, 'A confidence man prospers only because of the fundamental dishonesty of his victim.'[15] Are all of Volpone's would-be victims fundamentally dishonest? To what extent does Mosca's attempt to betray Volpone in the final moments of the play constitute a bizarre form of justice? Are the various schemers and over-reachers justly punished in the end?

Re-read the play's first act with its fluid sequence of scenes as characters are introduced and gulled. Examine the slipperiness of language and in particular the oblique ways that Mosca suggests that each successive suitor is Volpone's heir. Even when they directly ask him if they are indeed named Volpone's heir, Mosca avoids answering with a simple 'yes.' Compare this with the language Sir Politic Would-be uses to describe (or avoid describing?) his 'projects' in Act 4, scene 1 (note lines 57–75 in particular) and with Volpone's speech as Scoto of Mantua in Act 2, scene 2, lines 136–74. Just as Greene provides a lexicon for decoding the cony-catchers' argot in his pamphlets, discuss how Jonson explores the tension between inscrutability and conspiracy in the language of his con men.

Essay Suggestions

Many of the questions offered for discussion above could prove the foundation for a subsequent essay that explores the play in more depth with additional research into relevant primary texts and secondary criticism. Below I offer some additional ideas first for essays and laterally for projects whose end-products take on different forms than traditional literary-critical essays. The projects all require writing and, importantly, present a potentially unique opportunity for students to bring their own intelligences and interests to bear on the play. The various projects outlined below draw upon and challenge the same skills that are demonstrated by the production of a literary critical essay – analytical and creative thinking, the clear articulation of an interpretation or argument and the use of compelling evidence to support, explicate and explain that interpretation or argument. Because each project also requires that students write an accompanying essay in which they analyse their own work, the instructor still has a tangible text to assess for the purposes of assigning a grade.

1. In his book *Shakespeare Among the Animals*, Bruce Boehrer frames his reading of several Renaissance plays by Shakespeare, Jonson and Middleton as a series of interrelated questions:

'How did citizens of early modern England understand the differences between people and animals? How did their understanding of this difference affect their understanding of themselves and their relationships with one another? And how did the resulting formulations of biological and social identity operate with one another?'[16] Although Boehrer reads *Volpone* as part of this study he does not address the arguably fundamental issue of the play's blurring of the human/animal binary. Drawing on recent ecocritical work on the function of animals in literature, including work by Erica Fudge (*Perceiving Animals: Humans and Beasts in Early Modern Culture* (University of Illinois Press, 2002); *Brutal Reasoning: Animals, Rationality, And Humanity in Early Modern England* (Cornell University Press, 2006)), extend Boehrer's reading of the animal/human binary in *Volpone*.

2. Much recent scholarship has examined the performative nature of gender, especially as it applies to early modern England's all-male professional theatre. In light of this criticism, examine Jonson's notion of the feminine and masculine as performed in *Volpone*. Peter Parolin offers one interpretation of this in his essay on Italian Actresses and Female Performance (cited above in materials on Jonson's Venice). Drawing on more recent criticism that discusses the constructedness of the male and female body and of masculinity and femininity as functions of that performance, respond to and re-evaluate Parolin's argument.

3. Scholars have shown considerable interest in the significance of Jonson's Venetian setting for *Volpone*. Consider the ways in which public theatre as it existed in early modern England – a fairly bare stage with no curtain, the audience on three sides of the stage and no roof or lights – made for a certain kind of production. Examining recent criticism on place realism, and performance history, offer an argument on how you believe Jonson's Venice was potentially brought to life in seventeenth-century performance. Is a specific location or setting a function more of a text for reading than for dramatic performance?

4. Investigate primary documents (via EEBO or other sources) and secondary criticism of the issue of 'equivocation' in early seventeenth-century England. What forms of equivocation exist in *Volpone*? What is at stake in the early seventeenth-century debate over 'equivocation' and how does this relate to *Volpone*?

Project Suggestions

1. Design a playbill or poster for a production of *Volpone*. The goal here is to capture, in a single image, what you understand to be the essence – or an essential emotion or idea – of the play. Your playbill/poster should be accompanied by an essay that analyses and explains the image, its significance and relevance to *Volpone*. As part of your research and preparation for creating and analysing your poster or playbill, read Carol Chillington Rutter, 'Shakespeare's Popular Face: From the Playbill to the Poster' in Robert Shaughnessy, ed., *The Cambridge Companion to Shakespeare and Popular Culture* (Cambridge: Cambridge University Press, 2007) pp. 248–71 and Tiffany Stern, "On each Wall | And Corner Post': Playbills, Title-pages, and Advertising in Early Modern London' in *English Literary Renaissance* (ELR) 36 (2006) pp. 57–85. Make specific reference to these two essays in your playbill/poster analysis essay.

2. Develop a film treatment for translating *Volpone* to film. Discuss the overall 'style' of the production (perhaps relating it to other films or directors). Where and when would you set your production and how would you indicate this time and place? Would you maintain the play's original text or would you 'translate' | 'update' the language (as, for example, *Ten Things I Hate About You* (1999) updates Shakespeare's *The Taming of the Shrew*; or *The Honey Pot* (1967) adapts *Volpone*). In an accompanying analytical essay, discuss and defend these choices. Finally, take one scene – or a part of one scene – and render it as a film script, indicating casting notes, notes on lighting, camera angle, sound and visual effects, etc. A free on-line script writing program is available at *http://www.scriptbuddy.com*.

3. Take a scene from *Volpone* and present it in graphic novel format. In an accompanying analytical essay, explain how you translated Jonson's language into visual form: what details and descriptions did Jonson provide, what did you have to invent or embellish? Explain the benefits you see of re-imagining the play as a graphic novel; what sort of audience would this appeal to and why would it be a good idea to 'translate' the play into this medium? Be certain to address how – and why – your visuals communicate the animal aspects of Jonson's characters. Useful resources to examine and consider are Neil Gaiman's adaptations of Shakespeare's *A Midsummer Night's Dream* and *The Tempest* in his *Sandman* series. See *The Sandman III:*

Dream Country, pp. 62–86 and *The Sandman X: The Wake,* pp. 146–84 (Vertigo, 1991, 1997) and Scott McCloud's *Making Comics* (Harper, 2006).

4. Compile a soundtrack for *Volpone.* Select music that might be used in a production (theatre or film) or that simply connects with the play in terms of mood, style or theme. Create a CD of your compiled selections, possibly including album art and liner notes. In an accompanying essay, discuss your musical selections and their relationship to the play text; be certain to draw specific language-based connections between the song lyrics (or if an instrumental selection, the mood or emotion of the music) and the language of the play. If you are musically inclined and wish to compose your own songs as a mode of interpretation you may do that either in addition to or instead of compiling songs by other artists. Your essay should also discuss what, specifically, you would do with the four songs Jonson includes in the play (1.2.66–81: Nano and Castrone's song in praise of the fool, Androgyno; 2.2.120–32 and 191–203 Nano then Nano and Mosca as part of the Mountebank marketing scheme; 3.7.165–83 and 236–39: 'Come, my Celia': Volpone's 'wooing' of Celia). Do you maintain Jonson's lyrics? If so, what kind of music would you set them to? Do you replace the songs with alternate songs? If so, why, and what songs? Useful resources to examine and consider are Mary Chan's *Music in the Theatre of Ben Jonson* (Oxford, 1980) and John Beckwith's *Four Songs from Ben Jonson's* Volpone: *for baritone voice and guitar* (BMI Canada, 1967).

5. Design costumes or a set for either a filmed or theatrical production of *Volpone* (be certain to outline with as much detail as possible the type of production for which you imagine you are designing). Develop sketches for the costumes or set and, in an accompanying analytical essay, discuss the ways in which the costumes or set act as visual symbols for the characters, themes, issues and ideas at work in the play. In other words, use the narrative to explain, justify and sell your design choices. Pay close attention to the visual grammar of clothing and architecture and connect that to the language and ideas of the play. You may, if you wish, build a model of your set. With specific reference to Robert Shaughnessy's essay on the play's performance history (cited above in the material on Jonson's sources), discuss how your costume or set design would or would not emphasize the anthropomorphism or animalism of the characters and why.

6. Develop your own materials for teaching *Volpone* at either the high school or university level. Make an argument for why the play should be taught (perhaps as a supplement to a Shakespeare play) and explain how you would teach the play. Provide detailed lesson plans explaining the age/level of students you will be teaching, the assumptions you have made regarding their reading abilities and comprehension levels and a clear sense of how your approach to teaching *Volpone* fits in with the larger curriculum.

7. Choose one of the following topics and build a web page that provides resources for a deeper understanding of that topic and its relevance to *Volpone*: Beast Fables or Animalism, Venice, Gender and Performance, Equivocation, The Gunpowder Plot, Usury and/or early modern economics and labour. In your accompanying analytical essay, evaluate and justify both the content, organization and design of your materials.

Filmography

Frustratingly, there exists neither a direct presentation of Jonson's play as a staged performance nor a film that does not radically cut the text. Even YouTube, a rich if of variable quality resource for clips of scenes from Shakespeare, yields no unadapted results of Jonson's *Volpone* in performance. Those interested in examining the play in comparison with Moliere's *The Imaginary Invalid* may find of use the multiple French-language film versions of *Volpone* that are available. The play has been the source of several adaptations including as an opera and as a Broadway musical (for more considered analysis, see Rebecca Yearling's chapter on the play's performance history in this volume). In what follows I offer a list of potentially relevant films that adapt the play or offer useful analogous material to consider.

Volpone (Canada, 1969. Color 90 min.) Philippa Shepherd lists and describes this 'radically cut version' of the play in her 'A Renaissance Filmography' and notes that 'A very few copies are available to North American university audiovisual libraries as a loan from the Canadian Broadcasting Corp., in Toronto (contact Roy Harris at 416–205–7608).'[17]

The Honey Pot (United States, 1967. Color 150 min.) In this loose adaptation of the play, Rex Harrison plays Cecil Fox who takes inspiration from *Volpone* and constructs an elaborate con of three women, all former lovers. Fox hires an out-of-work actor, played by Cliff Robertson, to 'stage manage' his 'little production' in which his three former lovers are all summoned to Venice where Harrison pretends to be dying in his opulent palazzo. This film is available commercially on DVD in the United Kingdom but difficult to locate on DVD in the United States; it is, however, viewable for free in the United States (with limited commercial interruptions) at *http://www.hulu.com.*

Dangerous Beauty (United States, 1998. Color 111 min.) Released in the United Kingdom as *The Honest Courtesan*. This visually lush film mingles opulent costumes and sets with anachronistic language to tell the story of a real-life, sixteenth-century Venetian courtesan, Veronica Franco, who used her influence over the most powerful men in Europe to change her own life and the course of world events. A useful film for exploring the role, function and significance of Venetian courtesans.

William Shakespeare's The Merchant of Venice (United States, 2004. Color 138 min.) Likewise rich in its visual detail, this film presents a well-researched representation of late sixteenth-century Venice. The costumes and set of Venice are palpable presences here and the overall interpretation of the play is well managed by the director Michael Radford.

Notes

1   Ann Rosalind Jones, 'Italians and Others: Venice and the Irish in *Coryat's Crudities* and *The White Devil*,' *Renaissance Drama* 18 (1987): 101–19, 101.

2   See, for example, Joseph Candido, 'Teaching Texture in Jonson's *The Alchemist*' in *Approaches to Teaching English Renaissance Drama*, eds. Karen Bamford and Alexander Leggatt (New York: Modern Language Association of America, 2002): 51–58; and Matthew Steggle, 'Ben Jonson' in *Teaching Shakespeare and Early Modern Dramatists*, eds. Andrew Hiscock and Lisa Hopkins (Houndmills: Palgrave Macmillan, 2007): 106–17, 112–14; Chris Coles, *How to Study a Renaissance Play* (Houndmills: Macmillan, 1988) 1.

3   For a detailed discussion of using table readings of plays as a teaching and learning strategy see my 'Learning to Read Shakespeare: Using Read-Throughs as a Teaching and Learning Strategy' *Working Papers on the Web* Vol. 4 (2002): 'Teaching Renaissance Texts'. *<http://www.shu.ac.uk/wpw/renaissance/hansen.htm>*

4   David Bevington, in the opening chapter of his *How To Read A Shakespeare Play* (Oxford: Blackwell, 2006) provides a superb primer on reading Shakespeare's plays generally that has potential value for reading more generally about reading early modern drama. Offering in essence a narrative frame for a series of questions illustrating the basics of active, imaginative reading, Bevington's thirteen-page introductory chapter can make for a helpful preliminary seminar or course reading assignment.

5   In addition to a plot overview; detailed, scene-by-scene plot summaries; and brief character analyses, the materials at SparkNotes.com include terse statements on 'Theme, Motif, Imagery and Symbols'. This study guide concludes with study questions and possible essay topics and a very short list of suggested further reading. A 20-question on-line quiz is also available. Similarly, Gradesaver.com offers materials similar in content – and limited depth; Gradesaver offers a more extensive and potentially useful list of essay topics, however, and a short list of links for further exploration. A series of four, detailed 'Test Yourself!' on-line quizzes is available.

6   R.B. Parker, ed., *Volpone, or The Fox* (Manchester: Manchester University Press, 2nd edn, 1999) 10. Parker's discussion of Jonson's sources for *Volpone* spans pages 10–24.

7   M. Lindsay Kaplan, ed. *The Merchant of Venice: Texts and Contexts* (Boston: Bedford/St. Martin's, 2002); Kim F. Hall, ed., *Othello, The Moor of Venice: Texts and Contexts* (Boston: Bedford/St. Martin's, 2007).

8   *http://people.whitman.edu/~dipasqtm/volpone-s01.htm*

9   Peter Womack, *English Renaissance Drama* (Oxford: Blackwell, 2006).

10 Oliver Hennessey, 'Jonson's Joyless Economy: Theorizing Motivation and Pleasure in *Volpone*', *English Literary Renaissance* 38.1 (2008): 83–105, 102.

11 See above. An older, but still useful Marxist reading can be found in L. C. Knights, *Drama and Society in the Age of Jonson* (London: Chatto and Windus, 1957).

12 Mary Clare Randolph, 'The Medical Concept in English Renaissance Satire', *Studies in Philology* 38 (April 1941): 125–57, 135.

13 Gregory Chaplin, '"Divided amongst themselves": Collaboration and Anxiety in Jonson's *Volpone*,' *ELH* 69 (2002): 57–81, 57.

14 Pollard's essay is accessible as part of the book's free preview on Google Books: <*http://books.google.com*>.

15 David W. Maurer, *The Big Con: The Story of the Confidence Man* (Originally published 1940; New York: Anchor Books, 1999) 2.

16 Bruce Boerher, *Shakespeare Among the Animals: Nature and Society in the Drama of Early Modern England* (Houndmills: Palgrave, 2002).

17 Phillipa Sheppard, 'A Renaissance Filmography' in *Approaches to Teaching English Renaissance Drama,* eds., Karen Bamford and Alexander Leggatt (New York: Modern Language Association of America, 2002): 13–19, 18.

Volpone: A Selective Bibliography

Baker, Christopher, and Richard Harp. 'Jonson's *Volpone* and Dante', *Comparative Drama* 39.1 (2005): 55–74.

Barish, Jonas A., ed. *Volpone: A Casebook*. London: Macmillan, 1972.

Barish, Jonas A. *Ben Jonson and the Language of Prose Comedy*. Cambridge, Mass.: Harvard University Press, 1960.

Butler, Martin, ed. *Re-Presenting Ben Jonson*. Houndmills: Macmillan, 1999.

Cave, Richard, Elizabeth Schafer, and Brian Woolland. *Ben Jonson and Theatre: Performance, Practice and Theory*. London: Routledge, 1999.

Chaplin, Gregory. '"Divided amongst Themselves": Collaboration and Anxiety in Jonson's *Volpone*', *English Literary History* 69.1 (2002): 57–81.

Craig, D. H., ed. *Ben Jonson: The Critical Heritage*. London: Routledge, 1990.

Dutton, Richard. *Licensing, Censorship and Authorship in Early Modern England: Buggeswords*. Basingstoke: Palgrave, 2000.

Dutton, Richard. *Ben Jonson, Volpone and the Gunpowder Plot*. Cambridge: Cambridge University Press, 2008.

Evans, Robert C. *Ben Jonson's Major Plays: Summaries of Modern Monographs*. West Cornwall, CT: Locust Hill Press, 2000.

Greenblatt, Stephen J. 'The False Ending in *Volpone*', *Journal of English and Germanic Philology* 75 (1976): 90–104.

Hennessey, Oliver. 'Jonson's Joyless Economy: Theorizing Pleasure and Motivation in *Volpone*', *English Literary Renaissance*, 38.1 (2008): 83–105.

Jensen, Ejner J. *Ben Jonson's Comedies on the Modern Stage*. Ann Arbor, Mich: UMI Research Press, 1985.

Jonson, Ben. *Ben Jonson*, ed. C. H. Herford and Percy and Evelyn Simpson, 11 Vols Oxford: Clarendon Press, 1925–1952.

Jonson, Ben. *Four Comedies*, ed. Helen Ostovich. Harlow: Longman, 1997.

Jonson, Ben. *Volpone, or The Fox*, ed. Brian Parker. Manchester: Manchester University Press, 1999.

Kay, W. David. *Ben Jonson: A Literary Life*. New York: St. Martin's Press, 1995.

Knight, Sarah. 'He is indeed a kind of Scholler-Mountebank', in *Shell Games: Studies in Scams, Frauds, and Deceits (1300–1650)*, ed. Mark Crane et al. (Toronto: CRRS Publications, 2004), 59–80.

Knights, L. C. *Drama and Society in the Age of Jonson*. London: Chatto and Windus, 1937.

Leggatt, Alexander. *Ben Jonson: His Vision and His Art*. London: Methuen, 1981.

Lehrman, Walter D., Dolores J. Sarafinski, and Elizabeth Savage. *The Plays of Ben Jonson: A Reference Guide*. Boston: G. K. Hall, 1980.

Loxley, James. *The Complete Critical Guide to Ben Jonson*. London: Routledge, 2002.

Maus, Katharine Eisaman. 'Idol and Gift in *Volpone*', *English Literary Renaissance* 35.3 (2005): 429–53.

McEvoy, Sean. *Ben Jonson: Renaissance Dramatist*. Edinburgh: Edinburgh University Press, 2008.

Miles, Rosalind. *Ben Jonson: His Craft and Art*. London: Routledge, 1990.

Parker, R. B. 'Jonson's Venice', in *Theatre of the English and Italian Renaissance*, ed. J. R. Mulryne and Margaret Shewring (Basingstoke: Macmillan, 1991), 95–112.

Partridge, Edward B. *The Broken Compass: A Study of the Major Comedies of Ben Jonson*. London: Chatto and Windus, 1958.

Pollard, Tanya. *Drugs and Theatre in Early Modern England*. Oxford: Oxford University Press, 2005.

Riggs, David. *Ben Jonson: A Life*. Cambridge, MA: Harvard University Press, 1989.

Sanders, Julie, Kate Chedgzoy, and Susan Wiseman, eds. *Refashioning Ben Jonson*. Houndmills: Macmillan, 1998.

Sanders, Julie. *Ben Jonson's Theatrical Republics*. Basingstoke: Macmillan, 1998.

Slights, William W. E. *Ben Jonson and the Art of Secrecy*. Toronto: University of Toronto Press, 1994.

Watson, Robert N. *Ben Jonson's Parodic Strategy: Literary Imperialism in the Comedies*. Cambridge, Massachusetts and London: Harvard University Press, 1987.

Womack, Peter. *Ben Jonson*. Oxford: Basil Blackwell, 1986.

Woolland, Brian, ed. *Jonsonians: Living Traditions*. Aldershot: Ashgate, 2003.

Notes on Contributors

Stella Achilleos is a Lecturer in English at the University of Cyprus. Her research interests lie in the field of early modern literature and culture, focusing in particular on the production and transmission of literary texts in relation to social and political contexts. Her publications have mainly concentrated on seventeenth-century poetry, sociability and cultural exchange, and include a number of essays on the dissemination of the Anacreontea within various social and political networks in early modern England, with special focus on the appropriation of the genre by Ben Jonson and his 'sons' and its use as a royalist marker in the mid-seventeenth century. Her current research concentrates primarily on the discourses of friendship in early modern literature and culture.

James P. Bednarz is Professor of English on the C. W. Post Campus of Long Island University, where he has received the Trustees' Award for Excellence in Scholarship and the Newton Award for Excellence in Teaching. He specializes in Shakespeare and English Renaissance culture. His articles on early modern literary relations have appeared in *ELH, Shakespeare Studies, Shakespeare Survey, Renaissance Drama, Medieval and Renaissance Drama in England, Comparative Drama, The Huntington Library Quarterly, Spenser Studies, The Ben Jonson Journal*, and the Cambridge Companions to *Christopher Marlowe* and *Shakespeare's Poetry*. His book *Shakespeare and the Poets' War* (Columbia University Press, 2001) was selected as an "International Book of the Year" by *The Times Literary Supplement*. He is currently completing *Shakespeare and the Truth of Love*, a study of the poet's co-authorship with Marston, Chapman and Jonson of the *Poetical Essays* of *Love's Martyr*.

Rick Bowers is Professor of English at the University of Alberta. He has published widely on topics in early modern English drama, literature and culture, including *Radical Comedy in Early Modern England: Contexts, Cultures, Performances* (Ashgate, 2008). He has a piece titled "Shakespearean Celebrity in America: The Strange Performative Afterlife of George Frederick Cooke" in press at *Theatre History Studies*.

Robert C. Evans has taught at Auburn University Montgomery since 1982, earning his PhD from Princeton University in 1984. He is the author or editor of roughly twenty-five books, four of them on Ben Jonson. An editor of the *Ben Jonson Journal,* he is the recipient of fellowships from the NEH, the ACLS and UCLA and from the Folger, Huntington and Newberry Libraries. His most recent work has focused on Renaissance women writers, on pluralist literary theory and on modern American literature. Recent or forthcoming work on Renaissance literature includes essays on Anne Vaughan Lock, John Donne, Thomas Middleton and Ben Jonson. With Eric J. Sterling, he is editor of the recent *Seventeenth-Century Literature Handbook* and is a contributing editor of the *Donne Variorum Edition*.

Matthew C. Hansen is Associate Professor of English at Boise State University. He has published on Shakespeare, the teaching of Shakespeare and on the Renaissance poet Fulke Greville. From 2005–2007 he was the writer of the General Shakespeare Criticism section of *The Year's Work in English Studies* (Oxford University Press) and he is currently working on a project on the intersection of Memory, Materiality and Revenge in Elizabethan and Jacobean Revenge Tragedies. His interest in performance studies extends into practise in his occasional work as an actor and director.

Matthew Steggle is Reader in English at Sheffield Hallam University. His publications include *Wars of the Theatres* (1998); *Richard Brome: Place and Politics on the Caroline Stage* (2004); and *Laughing and Weeping in Early Modern Theatres* (2007). Together with Eric Rasmussen, he has co-edited *Cynthia's Revels* for the forthcoming *Cambridge Works of Ben Jonson*. He is editor of the e-journal *Early Modern Literary Studies*, and his current project is a text of *Measure for Measure* for the third edition of Stephen Greenblatt's *Norton Shakespeare*.

Frances Teague is the Josiah Meigs Professor of English at the University of Georgia. She has published a number of books and articles about Renaissance drama, including *The Curious History of "Bartholomew Fair," Shakespeare's Speaking Properties, and Shakespeare on the American Popular Stage*. A secondary research interest is work about early modern women writers, including *Bathsua Makin, Woman of Learning* and *Educational and Vocational Books* in the *Early Modern Englishwoman* series. She lives in a townhouse renovation of an old factory's paint room and is active in local theatre.

Sam Thompson is a Lecturer in English Language and Literature at St. Anne's College, Oxford. He has published in *The Year's Work in English Studies,* the *Times Literary Supplement* and the *London Review of Books.*

Rebecca Yearling is a teaching fellow at Bristol University. She completed her D.Phil. on the relationship between playwright and audience in the works of Ben Jonson and John Marston at Oxford University in 2006, and she is currently engaged in turning her D.Phil. thesis into a monograph. She is also working on an edition of James Shirley's *The Doubtful Heir* for the Oxford University Press *Complete Works of James Shirley.* Her previous publications include articles on Jonson's last plays, the 1599–1603 War of the Theatres, and Marston's later comedies.

Index

Page numbers in **bold** denote tables.

LRC
St. Francis Xavier College
Malwood Rd
London SW12 3EN